The State in Contemporary Society

The State in Contemporary Society

An Introduction

John Schwarzmantel

University of Leeds

HARVESTER WHEATSHEAF

New York   London   Toronto   Sydney   Tokyo   Singapore

First published 1994 by
Harvester Wheatsheaf
Campus 400, Maylands Avenue
Hemel Hempstead
Hertfordshire, HP2 7EZ
A division of
Simon & Schuster International Group

© John Schwarzmantel, 1994

Typeset in 10/12pt Times
by Hands Fotoset, Leicester

Printed and bound in Great Britain by
T.J. Press (Padstow) Ltd

British Library Cataloguing in Publication Data

A catalogue record for this book is available from
the British Library

ISBN 0-7450-1537-9

1   2   3   4   5   98   97   96   95   94

For Julie, with thanks

Contents

Preface

The purpose of this book is to provide an introduction to the study of politics by surveying a number of theories which analyse the nature of the modern state, and which offer contrasting views of the distribution of power in liberal-democratic and other forms of state. The book also aims to discuss the main characteristics of liberal-democracy as a type of political system, and to contrast this form of state with fascist and communist systems, those political forms which were powerful rivals to liberal-democracy for much of the twentieth century. In addition, it covers theories of feminism and deals with the role of nationalism, which has remained such an influential force in the politics of our time. These are all large topics, and the hope is that the material treated in this book covers at least some of the central themes and methods of analysis necessary to make sense of the rapidly changing political world of the late twentieth century.

This book is designed to be an updated replacement of, and in some ways is complementary to, my earlier text, *Structures of Power: An introduction to politics* (1987). While the present work covers some of the same topics as that earlier text, this is an entirely new work, which shares the aim of illuminating the workings of the modern state and the key themes of modern politics. After an introductory chapter which explains the nature of the modern state, it offers an analysis of theories of pluralism, elitism, Marxism and feminism, and applies these to the modern liberal-democratic state. The second part of the book then discusses fascism and communism as rival forms of state – rivals to each other and to liberal-democracy. The second part of the book also includes a chapter dealing with nationalism as a force which at least in some of its forms challenges liberal-democracy. A concluding chapter seeks to evaluate the different theories of power and to discuss some of the challenges facing the modern state.

I am very grateful to a number of friends and colleagues who have helped in the preparation of this text. My thanks are due to David Beetham who made some very helpful suggestions at the planning stage, and also to Nina Biehal, Julie Buchheit, Bryan Cheyette, Justin Grossman, Ralph Miliband, Max

Silverman, Gabrielle Syme and Ellis Tinios, among others, who provided advice and encouragement along the way. The reports of two anonymous readers on an earlier version of the manuscript were most valuable in suggesting ways of improving the work, and I am also very grateful to Clare Grist of Harvester Wheatsheaf for her efficient and supportive assistance. I hope the finished product will prove useful to all those who wish to gain some understanding of the complex and challenging political world in which we live.

John Schwarzmantel

Introduction

1 | What is politics? Power and the state

We live in times of rapid and bewildering transition, and this makes the task of understanding politics all the more difficult. This book has as its aim the analysis and discussion of some basic ideas of politics, in the hope that these concepts will provide tools for understanding the complex political world of today. The starting point for this investigation is the analysis of the state. It should be made clear from the outset that the term 'state' is used throughout to signify a particular institution, or set of institutions, within the wider society. The aim of this introductory chapter is to explain what is meant by the idea of the state, and to present in brief outline the different theories which explain how state power is exercised in practice.

The debate on the state

Ralph Miliband wrote in his 1969 study of *The State in Capitalist Society* that 'more than ever men now live in the shadow of the state'.[1] These words, extending them to women as well as to men, are no less true today than they were then. There are two particular features of the present situation, however, which seem worth singling out as preliminaries to an analysis of what the state is. The first is the apparent triumph of one type of state, that of liberal-democracy. In the course of the nineteenth century, in the epoch opened up by the French Revolution, democracy seemed to be moving to victory, at least in the European world. This led to the growing acceptance of the idea of popular sovereignty as the sole legitimate basis of a political system. Of course this was not an easy process, and was marked by bloody struggles, revolutions, and bitter opposition both to the democratic principle as such, and to the extension of the citizen body and citizenship rights to workers, to women and to members of immigrant groups or ethnic minorities. Yet as the end of the nineteenth century approached it seemed that democratic progress was irresistible. Whether one exulted with Engels that 'democracy, nowadays that is communism', or lamented with the Duke of Wellington that democracy would lead to the ruin of property and of civilisation, the victory of democracy seemed certain.[2] Not only that, there were hopes or fears, depending on which side of the barricades one stood, that political democracy or citizen equality would inevitably mean a progression to social equality, indeed to socialism. Hence Engels' prediction that democracy meant communism. Various theorists agreed, despite differences of political perspective, that democracy was the inevitable reality of modern politics. Some observers feared that, unless it was tempered, manipulated or restrained in various ways, the struggle to extend democracy and widen democratic rights would lead to an even more radical outcome, to socialism. How to prevent this happening was the challenge which faced the politicians of the established order. As one contributor to a recent survey of democracy has noted, 'Democracy after the French Revolution meant, if nothing else, that numbers were the major resource of politics. Quantity counted, whether in counting votes or filling the streets.'[3] He further observes that 'Given the power of number, the most effective way to avert social upheaval was not by attempting outright reaction, but by patiently weaving restraints on the possible abuses of pure democracy.'[4] Whether those restraints involved limiting the electorate, or restricting their power, or seeking to channel mass discontent into 'safe' channels – for example, through the use of nationalism (what E. J. Hobsbawm calls 'waving flags')[5] – these ruling-class strategies represented a rather desperate 'King Canute' type of reaction against a seemingly inevitable tide. The nineteenth-century liberal thinker Alexis de Tocqueville spoke of democracy as a current that could not be resisted. There seemed to be no alternative to the democratic state, nor to the accommodation, however reluctant, of liberals and indeed conservatives with democratic pressure and mass politics. The process of history seemed to be moving towards the establishment of the liberal-democratic state. This form of state combined representative government with some degree of popular participation, at least to the extent that the male part of the population gained the right to vote in elections.

This process was keenly contested, and the history of the twentieth century provides ample evidence of regimes that opposed the state form of liberal democracy. Moreover, it seemed quite possible during the second quarter of the twentieth century that these regimes, these alternatives to liberal-democracy, would triumph over corrupt and ineffectual liberal-democratic systems. The chief alternatives in question were, at least in the European context, the fascist state and the communist or Soviet system. Different in fundamental respects though they were from each other, each seemed to be more successful, dynamic and effective than liberal-democracies which often appeared divided, weak and lacking in strong leadership when faced with crisis. Fascist systems mobilised the masses under a single leader, commanding a mass-based party. Communist systems initially claimed to have achieved the goal of a more genuine democracy than liberal-democracy could ever realise, and this ideal was articulated in Lenin's idea of a Commune-type state. Later, when the 'leading role of the party' was formally installed as the guiding principle of these systems, the emphasis of such systems was not so much on the direct democracy they had earlier proclaimed, but on the social equality and economic growth which the centralised command economy seemed able to produce. In their quite different ways, in the course of twentieth-century politics, fascist and communist systems offered a potent alternative to the liberal-democratic state whose legitimacy had seemed so promising during the nineteenth century.

However, the challenges of both types of system have been beaten off, or so it seems. Fascist regimes were defeated at the end of the Second World War, not least because of the alliance of the liberal-democracies and the Soviet Union. From the end of the Second World War until quite recently, the chief rival to the liberal-democratic state was the model of Soviet-type systems. They still seemed to offer a picture of a planned economy capable of economic growth and development, and offering, or so it appeared, more social equality and a form of participation which paid tribute to democratic ideals. C.B. Macpherson in his book *The Real World of Democracy*, published in 1966, suggested that the Soviet system was a 'vanguard state' which represented what he called a 'broader concept of democracy as equality'. Such a view of democracy, he suggested, was 'historically speaking, equally legitimate' and no less authentic than the democratic tradition celebrated by the representative liberal-democracies of the West.[6] He saw the Soviet system as a system in which a vanguard party sincerely acted in the interests of the people, and sought to remove social deprivation and to combat inequality.

However, the collapse of the communist system, at least in its European variants and notwithstanding the continued existence of China, has dealt a severe blow to the main rival or alternative model to the liberal-democratic state, which has been left in command of the field. Liberal-democracy now seems to command universal admiration as the model of the desirable political system. Of course, it is necessary to give a clearer definition of the liberal-democratic state, and this is done in the following chapter, but in terms of a minimal definition, this form of state has the following elements. Liberal-democracies are systems where a number of different political parties compete through elections to gain power. Regular elections are held in which an electorate, unrestricted in its composition except in terms of a minimum age requirement, chooses a government. Finally, such systems possess a representative assembly which supposedly acts as a check on executive power and as a forum for public debate. This political structure is set in the social framework or context of a free market system – even if such systems are subjected to some degree of state intervention, giving what is called a 'mixed economy' which still remains mainly in private hands. This, in our age, is now proclaimed to be the unchallenged model, or desirable structure, for the modern state. The two main rivals to liberal-democracy either no longer exist, as in the case of fascism, or, with regard to communist regimes, occupy a much diminished area of the world, with China remaining as a solitary, though of course significant, exception to the fall of communist state systems.

The implications of this situation need to be thought through. We start here from a distinction between the *normative* and the *explanatory* approaches to political science, the former presenting a picture of what is desirable, what ought to be the case, and the latter concerned to explain what the structures of power actually are, who holds power and with what consequences. The first aim of what follows is to offer a survey of explanatory theories, which in different ways try to explain who holds power in liberal-democratic systems and what the nature of such systems of power really is, and in that way to investigate the functioning of the state in such systems. The first object of investigation, therefore, is the nature of the state in liberal-democracy. This also leads to discussion of alternative models, as exemplified by fascism and the communist state, which show contrasting pictures of the role of the state and in that sense illuminate the liberal-democratic model. We are concerned to explain the main features of the liberal-democratic state, and to review a number of central theories which in their contrasting ways focus on and seek to reveal the workings of that form of state system. This is set against the background of the apparently unchallenged victory of liberal-democracy as a form of state in the contemporary world, even though this supposed triumph of the liberal-democratic state seems to have been exaggerated in the present period.

The role of the state

There is, however, a further feature of the present time which again is central to understanding modern politics. While recent years have seemed to seal the triumph of liberal-democracy as a form of state, within that political system there has been intense debate over the role of the state. There is a distinction to be made between types of political system, such as liberal-democracy, communism and fascism, and a different question, which concerns the role of the state within a particular type of state system. The politics of contemporary liberal-democratic systems have been marked by a concern to reduce the role of the state, to change the relationship of state and society by limiting the sphere of state action at least in certain areas, and to proclaim the superiority of the market over the state as part of this attempt to restructure the role of the state in liberal-democratic society. This was in part the result of the political success of movements of what has been called 'the New Right'. Such movements had as their aim the freeing of society, and notably the market, from the grip of the state.[7]

The nature of the state and its role in different types of political system are questions of crucial importance. This moves the topic away from the explanatory mode and more to the normative dimension of state action. What should the state do? What are the limits of justifiable state action? How far, in other words, should the role of the state extend? Before one can understand this debate and its significance, it is necessary to understand what exactly the state is, how its power is exercised, and what functions states undertake.

The contemporary debate on the state has been much influenced by the 'New Right' attempt to shift the boundary between state and civil society. Against a view which holds that the task of the state is a 'positive' one, of enabling people to develop their capacities and to that end providing them with certain basic conditions or requirements necessary for that purpose, there has come a challenge asserting a much more limited or 'negative' view of the state. This view rests on a classical liberal perspective with regard to the state, and its recent most powerful advocate has been Hayek.[8] Such a perspective holds that the role of the state should be much more modest with respect to civil society, that its task should be restricted to providing minimal conditions for a market economy to develop freely and independently, and that it should not provide individuals with resources which they should attain and can acquire by their own efforts. Thus one of the central problems of politics, and one which has certainly played a central role in contemporary political debate, is the normative question of how far the role of the state should extend. However, the aim here is to discuss a range of theories explaining what the role of the state is, because understanding and assessing such theories is a necessary prerequisite for discussing the normative theories about what the role of the state ought to be.

What is the state?

The idea of sovereignty

Before we can explain the main features of the liberal-democratic or indeed any other state, we need to be clear about what we mean by the term 'the state'. Of course, 'the state' is an abstraction, there is no such thing as the state as such. However, there are certain features common to all states which define what a state is. It is argued here that the state is the central political association, and that any study of politics has to be concerned with the analysis of this institution or set of institutions. The sociologist Michael Mann has noted that 'the state is undeniably a messy concept'.[9] This 'messiness' should not, however, prevent us from attempting to grasp some of its central features.

The state, whether modern or ancient, is an apparatus of domination and coercion. A recent analysis by G. Poggi, *The State: Its nature, development and prospects*, makes this coercive aspect of the state its central feature: 'the control a state exercises over a population typically involves coercion', as Poggi notes.[10] What is typical of the modern state is its increasing distinctiveness as a separate, specialised and increasingly complex apparatus of power. This has been well brought out by Quentin Skinner, who wrote of the emergence in modern politics of a

> distinct form of 'civil' or 'political' authority which is wholly autonomous, which exists to regulate the public affairs of an independent community and which brooks no rivals as a source of coercive power within its own *civitas* or *respublica*.[11]

The modern state emerged as a specialised apparatus of power, a set of institutions of domination distinguishable and separate from the particular person (or group) who happens to control the state at any one time. Skinner traces out the development of the idea of the modern state as something essentially impersonal, a separate apparatus of government, not dependent on or existing to support the power of a particular prince or sovereign.

There is another feature of the modern state well brought out in Skinner's account, which he notes derived from those thinkers opposed to republican ideas and theories of popular sovereignty. The state is the sovereign body, in the sense of an institution superior to and different from the mass of the citizens. It is a separate apparatus of domination which exercises sovereign power. In Skinner's words, 'the state came to be accepted as the master noun of political argument', and this involved acceptance of the state as both a supreme and an impersonal authority.

The idea of the modern state was expressed by a succession of theorists such as Machiavelli and Hobbes. Hobbes spoke of the state as the great Leviathan or whale, a sovereign body artificially created by human reason, as a means of keeping order, of settling the conflicts which arose in society and which, if there were no state, would lead to the ruinous conflict and chaotic situation of a 'war of all against all'. Historically, there developed the idea of a central political association, the state, free of any religious controls: in other words a secular state with concentrated and centralised power, owing allegiance to no other body. The idea of the modern state is thus the idea of an association which, unlike the feudal state, is in principle unlimited in its power. The modern state aspired to set the terms on which it dealt with other associations or subordinate groupings: this was the meaning of the idea of sovereignty. Whereas in feudalism political power was associated with the ownership of land, we see in the modern state the growth of a specialised apparatus of coercion, not constrained by other associations. The idea is thus of a public power regulating a particular national territory and settling the disputes or conflicts which arise in that territory.

State and society
The state can therefore be described as a set of institutions constituting a specialised apparatus of domination. Not only is the modern state in this sense distinct from the society over which it rules, but it is also a centralised apparatus of power, which rules over a territorially demarcated area and which possesses a monopoly of authoritative rule making. In Mann's words, the state involves

four elements: it is *differentiated*, it is *centralised*, it exercises its power over a *territorially demarcated area*, and finally it has or claims a monopoly of *authoritative binding rule making* over that particular area.[12]

All these features can be summed up in the term *sovereignty*. The exercise of this sovereignty involves laying down the rules which regulate life within a particular territory. The state can be seen as 'the supreme law-making and law-enforcing agency for society'.[13] Those who staff the institutions of sovereign power form the state elite: they are vested with the impersonal authority of the state and execute its functions.

There are a number of points here which deserve more emphasis. First, we note the idea of the state as a differentiated set of institutions. It is differentiated from society, or from what some theorists call 'civil society'. We are dealing here with a set of institutions or structures which have a separate and defined existence, over and above civil society. These institutions have the specialised function of laying down the rules for the wider society, and claim a monopoly of that function.

From this antithesis of, or separation between, the 'state' and 'civil society' comes one of the central questions of political analysis: what exactly is the relationship between state and civil society? The French historian and social scientist Pierre Rosanvallon puts the question clearly when he writes:

> Writing the history of the state involves the analysis of the conditions which shape the relationship between state and society. For there is no history of the state separate from the understanding of a relationship: the state exists only in its relationship to society.[14]

However, if the state exists only through its relationship with society, we need to know exactly what that relationship is. Here the different theories of politics studied in this book give conflicting answers. Is the state in a relationship of neutrality towards the different groups which make up civil society, as the pluralist view asserts? Or is the relationship of state and society one which exists to maintain a particular power relationship in civil society, that of the ruling class, as the Marxist view maintains? The state is certainly differentiated from civil society as an apparatus of domination, but the terms of the state/civil society relationship need to be investigated, so that the power of the state can be assessed.

Pierre Rosanvallon defines four aspects of this state–civil society relationship:

1. A democratic idea, according to which it is society as a whole (the people) which constitutes and forms the state. The state is the emanation of the popular will.
2. The state as a nation-state, functioning as an instrument of cohesion. The state creates and reinforces the social bond, constituting the nation, through, for example, a common educational system, instilling national awareness.

3. The state as a welfare state, as the means of providing people with basic
    and perhaps more than basic needs. In this way the liberal 'nightwatchman'
    state becomes the welfare state – a role, as we noted above, challenged by
    theories of the New Right.
4. Finally, the state as economic regulator, as steering the economy. This is
    a role which the 'Keynesian revolution' made possible, intervening in the
    economy to secure such goods as full employment, monetary stability and
    economic growth. Again, this is something challenged by theories of the
    New Right.

Divisions in the state apparatus

The state is thus separate from society but exists in a relationship with society,
a relationship which can be considered under these four headings and which
different theories of politics view in contrasting ways. However, when
reference is made to the differentiated nature of the state, the meaning is not
merely that the state is separate from society, but also that it is, so to speak,
internally differentiated. The state is an apparatus of domination, but it is
important to realise that this apparatus has different branches or sections. The
representative assembly, the government in the sense of the political executive,
the bureaucracy, the military, the police, the judiciary, sub-central government: these all form the state apparatus as a differentiated totality, and the
relationships between these different elements vary in different types of state
system. It is claimed as a characteristic of the liberal-democratic state that the
different elements of the state apparatus check and control each other, so that
the power of the state is internally neutralised. This is the venerable idea of
the separation of powers, often cited with reference to Montesquieu, as a way
in which the awesome and dangerous power of the modern state, this
centralised and territorial power, is kept in check.[15]

Here too the analysis of the state raises questions concerning the relationship
between different branches of the state apparatus. For example, if the elected
branch of the state (the government) comes up against obstruction or active
hostility from other elements in the state apparatus, such as the civil service
or bureaucracy or the military, then this may cast doubt on the democratic
nature of the state in a supposedly liberal-democratic society. Cases such as
the fate of the Allende government in Chile, overthrown by military coup in
September 1973, show the possible constraints on the reformist power of a
radical government, constraints stemming from within the state apparatus
itself.

We have thus seen that the state is best understood as a differentiated set of
institutions, differentiated both internally and externally: divided internally
into distinct sections, and separated from society, though the exact nature of
the state/society relationship needs investigation in particular instances.
However, we need to probe further the idea of the state as carrying out certain
functions: above all, the function of setting the rules or terms for the working

of civil society. The state is the supreme or sovereign power deciding the rules of social life, the terms on which groups in civil society can compete and exercise their own power. Yet the state itself is a 'site' of power struggle. Because the state is the crucial institution which sets the rules of social interaction, it is of the utmost importance which person or group has the power to make the rules, and the extent of that rule-making power. Mann notes that 'The central question for us here, then, is what is the nature of the power possessed by states and state elites?'[16] The different theories of politics give contrasting answers to this question, but there can be no doubt of the significance of the power possessed by the state elite, by those who control the modern state.

Following on from this, precisely because of the significance of the coercive power of the modern state, the question of the limits to that power is of equal importance. To quote Poggi again, 'Exactly because coercion can be put to so many uses . . . it is critical that it should be exercised in as restrained and controlled a manner as is compatible with its effectiveness.'[17] The concern to limit state power has led to the aim of having a state system provided with checks and balances, internal to the state system and external to it, stemming from the wider society. Clearly some of the classical representatives of this concern for power limitation are those in the tradition of liberalism, concerned above all to make sure that state power is restricted: to prevent it doing damage, as they see it, to the spontaneous order of the market in the economic sphere and of individual rights in the political sphere. Thus the study of politics is centrally concerned with two questions. First, who has control of the state apparatus, in its different branches, and with what consequences? And second, how can this vast power of the modern Leviathan, theorised so clearly by Hobbes, be limited and contained? Hobbes for his part thought that the significance of this sovereign power lay precisely in the fact that it was supreme and uncontrolled, since nothing less would suffice to maintain order and prevent the 'war of all against all'. Liberal thinkers, by contrast, have sought to check and control the power of the state, believing that an uncontrolled state is an arbitrary power source, capable of annihilating sources of progress and diversity and hence of destroying the variety of civil society. From this comes the importance of the state as a site of power struggle, and the fact that politics is centrally concerned with both the contest for state power and the attempt to regulate this struggle, at least by controlling or restricting state power and establishing rules for the conduct of political competition.

This question of what ought to be the limits on state power should be distinguished from the question of the factual limits or constraints on state action. The state has been described here as the sovereign or supreme political association, unlimited at least in theory by any other grouping, and setting the rules for the interaction between the various groups in society. This does not mean, however, that this theoretically unlimited power might not be constrained in practice, for example by an international (or interstate) context of economic power. As Beetham puts it, 'sovereignty as the exclusive right to law-making and law-enforcement within a given territory is not to be equated with power *tout court*, or the state's ability to achieve its various purposes'.[18] There may well be constraints on the state's ability to get its own way and actually exercise its sovereignty. Such constraints may stem from the weak economic situation of a particular state, or its insertion in a particular structure of military and political alliances, and these affect the practice of sovereignty. Thus, in explaining the power of the state and the nature of the state elite, we need to pay attention to the weight of the state, the power it wields and the theoretical expression of that power in the idea of sovereignty. However, in the real world this power may be, and of course is, constrained by factors stemming from the national or international context in which the state is situated.

The nation-state

We should note one important feature of the modern state, which is that it is, or claims to be in most cases, a nation-state. This is expressed in the modern idea of nationalism, which holds that state and nation should coincide. Each nation, however that is defined, should have its own state, and, by the same token, the state should rule over and express the common interests of the members of a relatively united nation. We have seen that the modern state is a differentiated, centralised, rule-making body whose power is exercised over a particular territory, which in this perspective is a national territory, inhabited by members of a nation. The question of what defines a nation is a problem in its own right, but we can suggest that the idea of the modern nation-state involves the idea of a link between an apparatus of coercion (the state) and a group of people having certain historical and cultural features in common (a nation). In many cases the state has sought to bolster its power by spreading ideas of nationalism and national identity. In the words of a recent study of *Citizenship and Nationhood in France and Germany*:

> In one uncontested sense almost all modern states are (or claim to be) nation-states. Almost all subscribe to the legitimating doctrine of national or popular sovereignty. Almost all claim to derive state power from and exercise it for (and not simply over) a nation, a people.[19]

The nature of the modern state is thus fundamentally affected by the nationalist idea, which holds that state and nation should coincide. The modern state is not merely a territorial association which rules over a certain territory. It is also a *membership* organisation, bringing together as members of the nation *citizens* who are entitled to its protection and benefits: 'Political sociology has treated the state as a territorial organisation, neglecting the fact that it is also a membership organisation, an association of citizens.'[20] By the same token, the modern nation-state not only brings together citizens, but also involves citizenship as a means of 'social closure': 'non-members' are excluded from citizenship, sometimes with significant results. According to the study just cited, which compares the two modern states of France and Germany, in Germany it is much more difficult for immigrants, even of the second generation, to become citizens. This issue is highly significant in the light of recent events in that country, and racially motivated attacks on immigrants who are not citizens.

The modern state therefore bases itself on the idea of a national group, a nation ruling itself, and the state is the institution or set of institutions appropriate to the task of national security and national defence. In contrast to previous states, therefore, the modern state rules over a territory which is, or is claimed to be, nationally homogeneous, and the state has often sought to heighten that feeling of national identity.

The state elite and its power

It was pointed out above that state power is exercised by human beings, a group of people who constitute the *state elite*. In this context, one feature of the modern state is the growth in its staff or personnel, a growth signalled by the social theorist Max Weber, among many others.[21] The modern state as an apparatus of power requires a body of people, trained administrators, whose sole task is the exercise of state power, carried out according to certain impersonal rules. The idea here is of a trained bureaucracy, exercising the power of rational administration.

The modern state has assumed an ever wider range of tasks and functions. There was a historical transition away from the idea of the liberal state as a 'nightwatchman' state, concerned minimally with maintaining 'order', securing the free working of the market by enforcing contracts and providing security from external attack. It is important to point to the subsequent expansion in the range of tasks carried out by the centralised apparatus of the state, including the task of securing welfare for its citizens through social legislation, based on the idea of the welfare state. In the words of a recent study,

> the *welfare state under capitalism* is generally understood . . . as defining a society in which the state intervenes within the processes of economic reproduction and distribution to reallocate life chances between individuals and/or classes.[22]

The result of this expansion of the role of the state was the growth in the administrative apparatus necessary to achieve those ends. Already in the middle of the nineteenth century, Marx described the growth of the French state and its bureaucratic machinery when analysing the stifling weight of the Bonapartist state, the regime of Napoleon III who was Emperor of France from the time of his coup d'état in December 1851 until military defeat at Sedan in 1870. Marx wrote of this state, in often-quoted words, that 'the executive power possesses an immense bureaucratic and military organisation, an ingenious and broadly based state machinery, and an army of half a million officials alongside the actual army, which numbers a further half million'.[23]

He further described the Bonapartist state in the same passage as 'a frightful parasitic body which surrounds the body of French society like a caul and stops up all its pores'.

The modern state in all systems has expanded its functions and increased the number and also the powers of the state elite, and thus the modern state has to be understood in terms of a vast and separate (differentiated) administrative apparatus. This has important theoretical implications for the idea of the relationship between state and society. One useful term is *the autonomy of the state*. The problem again is the relationship between state and society. The question is whether this vast machinery of domination, realised in the modern state as an impersonal apparatus of power, has interests of its own. To what extent, if any, is the state a body which is over and above society and independent of social pressures? Alternative theories of power in the shape of pluralism suggest that the state merely reflects the diverse interests of society, while Marxist theories suggest that it is one particular social interest (the economically dominant ruling class) which is dominant and reflected in state action.

The term 'the relative autonomy of the state' has been used, as A. H. Birch notes, by writers in the Marxist tradition, as 'a fairly elastic concept that covers several distinguishable views about the precise relationship between the capitalist class and the institutions of government'.[24] Birch points out that in the Marxist tradition the state and its apparatus, the state elite who operate that apparatus, are seen as only *relatively* autonomous from the capitalist class, since the state is seen as constrained in various ways by the economic power of that class and not able to escape from the structure of economic power. It should be noted that, within the Marxist tradition, writers from Marx onwards have suggested that in certain conditions the autonomy of the state is extended, that the interests of the state apparatus achieve an independence from social pressures and constraints. Indeed, in his early writings on the state Marx emphasised considerably the role of the bureaucracy as having interests of its own, rather than being the channel for any particular social interests. These issues are discussed further in Chapter 5. For the moment we note that any understanding of the modern state has to recognise the expansion of its tasks and apparatus, and the problem of whether the state elite has interests of its own, or whether it exists to further the interests of a particular social class or group. In other words, is the state elite autonomous of social interests, and to what extent is it so?

We can thus sum up the nature of the state in terms of the five sub-sections above. The state is a sovereign association, setting the rules for the whole society. The state is differentiated from society, and the relationship between state and society is itself a problematic one. The state is a complex set of institutions, exercising coercive power, and divided or differentiated internally – a division which liberal theorists see as necessary to limit its coercive power. In the modern world the state is a nation-state, and the aim is a link of the political unit of the state with the cultural unit of the nation. Finally, state power is exercised by a state elite, a group whose numbers and power have been greatly increased in the modern state, and whose relationship with social groups and interests is also a key problem in the analysis of modern politics.

The analysis of power: force and consent

The state has so far been described as an apparatus of coercion, a specialised set of institutions which carry out the functions of rule making and rule enforcement for a particular territory. All of this is encapsulated in the idea of state sovereignty. However, this is not adequate because there is a crucial dimension of power which is distinct from coercion and yet is equally essential to understanding the nature of the state and the power it wields. This dimension of power involves the idea of *legitimation*.

Analysing state power purely in terms of coercion suggests that those who control the state apparatus, the state elite, can get their commands accepted because of their ability to use the coercive power of the state to quell dissent. This involves imprisoning, fining or executing people, if they do not accept the commands of the state elite. To this extent Proudhon's famous diatribe against the state, or against what he called government, is indeed justified: to be governed, he declaimed, was to be 'noted, registered, enrolled, taxed, stamped, measured, numbered, assessed, licensed, authorized, admonished, forbidden, reformed, corrected, punished'. Anyone protesting against the state or complaining at its authority would be 'repressed, fined, despised, harassed, tracked, abused, clubbed, disarmed, choked, imprisoned, judged, condemned, shot, deported, sacrificed, sold, betrayed; and, to crown all, mocked, ridiculed, outraged, dishonoured'.[25] However, while Proudhon was right to see the coercive side of the state, not all power is to be understood in terms of coercion, or what has been called the 'gunman model' of power.[26] State power is not purely coercive, and the state elite seek to secure their power through a process of legitimation of power which it is essential to understand, for the liberal-democratic state as for all other forms of state.

Power is in most, if not all, systems obeyed because at least some of those subject to the power-holders feel that it is right for them to obey. For this reason all power-holders will seek to secure the legitimation of their power, if only for the reason that this enables them to dispense with the apparatus of physical coercion. If power-holders can rely on their power being accepted as legitimate, then there is no need for physical coercion, at least not against the bulk of the population, and so an 'economy of force' is made possible, securing the power of the state elite all the more effectively. For example one could say that for the most part people in a liberal-democratic state obey the law not primarily because they will be put in prison if they refuse obedience, but because they take the view that the power-holders have a right to command.

In turn this stems from the idea that those who form the government have a right to command because they have achieved these positions of power through certain agreed procedures, notably through competitive and open elections. Their power is seen as deriving from certain rules, electoral rules for example, which are seen as giving them a title to command which would not be earned if power had been attained through the processes of a military coup. Thus the stability of a liberal-democratic system is derived from the acknowledgement or the belief that the holders of power in some sense derive their power from the people: they have been freely chosen in competitive elections and their power derives from certain rules which specify how the power-holders are chosen.

Thus state power in a liberal-democratic or any other system does not depend purely or exclusively on coercion, but also on a process of legitimation. In his recent study *The Legitimation of Power*, David Beetham seeks to break with the way of dealing with this process which goes back to Max Weber. Weber's famous typology dealt with belief in the legitimacy of power, depending on whether people believed that the power-holder's power was legitimate because of *tradition*, or because it was held on the basis of certain rules (*legal–rational*), or because of belief in the special personal qualities (*charisma*) of the power-holder. For Beetham legitimacy is not to be reduced to a report about what people believe. He suggests that 'the key to understanding the concept of legitimacy lies in the recognition that it is multi-dimensional in character', and that:

> Power can be said to be legitimate to the extent that:
>   (i) it conforms to established rules,
> (ii) the rules can be justified by reference to beliefs shared by both dominant and subordinate, and
> (iii) there is evidence of consent by the subordinate to the particular power relation.[27]

With respect to the liberal-democratic form of state, it could be said that the power of the state elite in such a system rests on the belief that their power is exercised with respect to certain rules, legal and conventional, and that it is not exercised in an arbitrary way but is subject to the rule of law, for example. Furthermore, the shared belief held by dominant and subordinate groups would be that power can only be acquired legitimately through an open competitive contest (elections) for majority support, so that power acquired in any other way could not be considered legitimate. As for examples of consent, participation in elections by the majority of the population would count as evidence of consent to these rules of gaining power, and the rules would therefore be considered as the criteria of legitimate power. Anyone gaining power through following such rules would be considered as exercising legitimate power, and those subject to their commands would obey without the threat of coercion. At least this would apply to the majority of the population, and impart a considerable degree of stability to the system in question.

To the extent that power is seen to be acquired through the following of such rules, and that such rules are followed by those holding power, the system is stable. The case of corruption in Italy, and the discrediting of the political elite there,[28] would be a case where the power of the elite, or their right to remain in their positions of power, is no longer considered legitimate because their conduct of power does not follow the rules shared by those supposedly subject to the commands of the power-holders. The Italian crisis seems to be an example of the wholesale discrediting of a 'political class' or elite, though not as yet of the whole political system. Other political leaders (such as the leaders of the 'Network', La Rete or the Lombard League, later the Northern League) have come forward within the system to oust and replace the discredited ruling elite. However, in certain cases the discrediting of a political elite or a political class can lead to the total delegitimation of the political system.

State power therefore does not depend on coercion alone. There is a process at work in all systems which can be called the legitimation of power, and this process aims at the justification of power. State elites in all systems seek to achieve the consent of the governed to their rule. We note here that different political systems have, historically, had different legitimations or justifications of power. Absolutist systems sought to instil beliefs in the divine right of kings, or other versions of a religious justification for authority. However, in the modern world all political systems have come to seek legitimation in terms of the idea of popular sovereignty. Increasingly, and perhaps exclusively in the modern world, no political system is considered legitimate unless it can claim, with some degree of conviction and plausibility, that it derives its power from 'the will of the people'.

Of course, there are various ways in which this can be done. Who 'the people' are is a question that can be given various answers. Fascist systems, at least in their Nazi form, claimed that 'the people' meant only those of a particular race and that the leader (Führer or Duce) 'truly' exemplified the will of *das Volk* or the people, and did not need any *electoral* legitimation to do so. The fascist system was a regime of dictatorship, but one which through the device of the mass party paid a perverted homage to ideas of mass legitimation. Hence such systems were very different from traditional conservative-style regimes which sought to exclude the masses from power.

Communist systems, dominated by 'the leading role of the party', also sought legitimation on the basis of ideas of popular sovereignty. The people were the workers, the toiling masses, and the party was composed of workers, at least of a selected elite of (ex-)workers, who were supposed to be truly representative of the interests of the working masses in a supposedly classless society. This vanguard was to keep in touch with 'the people' through a variety of forms of participation, which were indeed controlled and structured from above, through the process of the *nomenklatura* or appointments ratified and proposed in a top-down manner. Nevertheless, the point remains that the party claimed its power was derived from the people, the people were the workers, and the party was merely a vanguard of the toiling masses.

In the modern world, then, all regimes, including the unsuccessful rivals to liberal-democracy, have accepted that fundamental principle of the politics of modernity: that power is to be justified with reference to the wishes and interests of the people, however 'the people' are defined, and by whatever structures, institutions or even mystical processes they are given a voice – even where, as with fascism, the claim is quite bogus. Some version, however perverted, of the idea of popular sovereignty is the sole acceptable form or way in which modern regimes and power-holders try to legitimate their power. We have seen this to be true of non-liberal-democratic regimes, such as fascism and communism, where the rule of the party was legitimated through ideas of the 'leader principle', in fascism, or 'the leading role of the party', in communist regimes. The process of the legitimation of power is equally significant in democratic or liberal-democratic forms of state.

If this is true, then two important conclusions can be drawn for the study of politics and the state. First, the implication is that liberal-democratic states claim their superiority because it is asserted that in such regimes the people, unrestricted by exclusions of gender, class and ethnicity, have the decisive say in the choice of their leaders, who remain accountable to the electorate. This is the core legitimating principle of liberal-democratic regimes. They are political systems supposedly based on acceptance by the people and by the power-holders of certain rules for the attainment and exercise of power. The question then becomes, in terms of explanatory theories of power, whether this legitimation is just a façade or a sham, a device for masking the realities of power, or whether it to some degree corresponds to reality, and if so through what institutions and devices this is realised. If the principle of popular sovereignty is held up throughout the world as the only legitimate basis of political power, then to what extent is it realised in practice in liberal-democratic and other regimes in the modern world? And why has it been given so much importance, replacing other (religious or traditional) sources of legitimacy?

The second conclusion to be drawn is that the earlier emphasis on the state as essentially coercive has to be revised and made more subtle by realising the non-coercive basis of state power in the modern world, and its importance. It was C. Wright Mills who wrote that 'the idea of legitimation is one of the central conceptions of political science', and this should make us aware of the importance of the means by which consciousness is manipulated or affected in modern politics. Different theories of politics seek to grapple with this problem in different ways. Marxist theories, and especially Marxist theories after Marx, such as those of Gramsci, the Italian Marxist, analysed the concept of 'hegemony', the way in which certain conceptions of life became dominant, established and pervasive throughout the society, with crucial consequences for the stability of a particular form of state, or system of power.

Thus the study of politics has to be open to the different dimensions of power, and to the way in which people's consciousness is affected by the state elite, by the holders of state power, and indeed in other ways as well, by the workings of social institutions. This should not be taken to mean, however, that it is a one-way process, that in a conspiratorial way the holders of power 'brainwash' or indoctrinate the mass of the population. The holders of power themselves are not immune from an ideology, a set of ideas which affects their conception of the purposes for which they exercise power. In short, we need to study the way in which state power is legitimised and, if possible, the 'gap' between myth and reality: for example, between the ideas or aspirations to popular power which are proclaimed in contemporary liberal-democratic systems, and the reality of the power structure of that type of system, and indeed of other systems too. Force and consent are the two bases of power in the modern state and both need to be kept constantly in mind.

Key questions of the book

The final section of this introductory chapter seeks to explain the structure of the following chapters and the nature of the argument which is to be put forward. The concern here is with two issues: the first is the nature of the modern state in its different forms; and the second is the analysis of different theories which seek to explain the power structure of some of the different forms which the modern state has taken.

Our first task is to analyse what distinguishes the liberal-democratic state from other forms of state, and to delineate its key features. What is special about the liberal-democratic state, and what features does it have which other forms of state in the modern world do not have? One reason for asking this question is to try to solve the problem of why this form of state seems to have 'won out' over its main rivals in twentieth-century politics, namely fascism and communist regimes. The question also needs to be addressed of whether liberal-democratic systems live up to the claims they make – claims of being states where power is checked and limited (the liberal claim) as well as states in which 'people power' is secured (the democratic claim).

However, in order to carry out this programme of investigating the specific characteristics of the liberal-democratic state and comparing it with other, apparently less successful, types of state system in the modern world, we need theoretical concepts or intellectual tools of the trade. Since no task of intellectual investigation can be carried out without categories, without theories, the aim of this book is to review the available theories to see what help they afford in the task of understanding the world in which we live. This, after all, is the task of social science: to gain understanding of the social world, as a product of human activity and practice, and to investigate the limits of possible change. Without falling into what Kolakowski would describe as the

Promethean myth, which he ascribes to Marxism – a myth holding that human action can create a perfect society free from antagonism – one can more modestly suggest that the political world is capable of transformation in a conscious way, and that the idea (stemming from the Enlightenment) of conscious control of the political and social world is not a Utopian aspiration. But to understand what can and what cannot be achieved through political action, to grasp the structure of power and how it could be transformed, we need theories, concepts and categories.

The first task, then, is to present the key features of liberal-democracy as a type of state, situated in a particular social and economic context (a free market system, so called). This type of state is marked by certain features briefly noted above: competitive elections, competing political parties, a representative assembly, a system of checks and balances within and outside the state system, and a range and network of groups and associations which together form a 'civil society' independent of the state. These features of competition and diversity are held to distinguish a liberal-democratic state from systems of 'monolithic' or even totalitarian power, exemplified by the fascist state and by communist regimes, allowing for distinctions between each of the latter two.[29] Thus the conventional distinction between the liberal-democratic state and its 'competitors' is that the former is a *pluralistic democracy*, where power is shared, controlled and in some genuine sense held by the people, whereas the latter (fascism, communism) are or were 'totalitarian' or monolithic systems dominated by a single party. In these latter systems there may be lip-service paid to democracy and the will of the people, because popular sovereignty is the common coin of modern regimes and all modern regimes claim to emanate from the will of the people. However, so-called totalitarian regimes are ones in which there is no choice of rulers, because of the existence of a monopolistic state party. Furthermore, the line between state and society in such systems is unclear, since the inflated power of the state annihilates the boundaries between state and society. In the words of F. Neumann, 'society ceases to be distinguished from the state; it is totally permeated by political power'.[30]

Thus the first theme of what follows is the contrast between liberal-democratic and other forms of state. On this conventional distinction, each type differs because of the contrast between a pluralistic system (liberal-democracy) in which state power is limited and confined, and monolithic systems in which there is no competition for power and where the role of the state is inflated to the point of 'total power'. These so-called totalitarian states would thus show both the dangers of unrestricted state power, and also the special virtues of liberal-democracy, in which state power is kept within the limits which liberal theory approves.

It will be argued later that this antithesis of the liberal-democratic state and the totalitarian one is misleading or at least inadequate for a number of reasons: it overlooks significant distinctions between fascist and communist regimes, and it may lead to an oversimplified and excessively 'rosy' view of the

WHAT IS POLITICS? POWER AND THE STATE   21

power structure of liberal-democracy. However, more to the point here, in order to investigate both liberal-democracy and its rivals, to see whether this antithesis of pluralism versus totalitarianism (or monolithic systems) is acceptable, one needs to discuss a range of theories which provide the basic tools of analysis. These theories also need to be compared with each other, in terms of their structure and key concepts. The theories to be examined here are those of pluralism, elitism, Marxism and feminism, as applied in the first instance and most extensively to the liberal-democratic state, and then to fascist and Soviet-type systems.

The basic concepts and topics which each theory puts forward are outlined in the relevant chapter, but at this stage we can provide thumbnail sketches to explain what these theories are, why they have been chosen, and the relation between each theory. The debate between these theories provides a good way of grasping the power structure of the liberal-democratic state and the state forms which contrast with it.

Pluralist theories in their general form are based on the antithesis already presented: between liberal-democratic systems which are seen as pluralist, and rival 'totalitarian' systems which are seen as monolithic and undemocratic. Despite a legion of criticisms levelled at pluralism, it still remains highly influential as a mode of explanation which focuses on competing parties and pressure groups as key features of liberal-democratic systems, leading to a diffusion of power that is seen as essential to such a form of state. It thus furnishes a good introduction to the study of forms of state, since it makes such a sharp contrast between the liberal-democratic state and its non-pluralist rivals.

The *elitist* view of politics can be seen as both a challenge to pluralism and also complementary to it. It is a challenge to it, in that classical elitism maintains that the diffusion of power held by pluralism to characterise liberal-democratic systems is a myth. Elitists maintain that in all systems effective power is held by a single elite group, and that this is true of liberal-democratic systems no less than of fascist and communist systems. Elitism is thus a form of 'debunking' of pluralism and its claims for liberal-democracy. Nevertheless, at another level and in some of its forms, elitism is complementary to pluralism. As a theory, it holds that the internal structure of the groups and parties characteristic of liberal-democracy is oligarchical or elitist: they are each dominated by a minority which runs the affairs of the organisation, so that democracy in terms of popular power is not and cannot be realised. However, elitism and pluralism can come together as an explanatory theory of liberal-democracy. This theory holds that liberal-democratic systems are marked by a plurality of elites, and this does not prevent democracy being realised as long as democracy is redefined to mean a competition for power (and to influence power) between different elites. This competition is 'settled' through a choice at certain intervals by the electorate, the mass. Particularly in the form developed by Joseph Schumpeter in his influential book *Capitalism, Socialism and Democracy*, this 'theory of competitive democracy' remains a combination of elitism and pluralism and forms a widely accepted theory of the working of modern democracy. Its strengths and weaknesses will be examined in Chapter 4.

Both pluralism and elitism as theories of the working of liberal-democracy seek to look at the way power is distributed in liberal-democratic societies. They do so by studying (in the case of pluralism) overt conflict, or (elitism) the power structure or hierarchy of the groups whose conflict constitutes the politics of liberal-democratic systems. As theories of power, they are challenged by two sets of theories, which in a fundamental way are similar, though they differ in other respects. *Marxism* and *feminism* each shift the emphasis away from the overt appearance or surface manifestations of politics in liberal-democratic systems to 'deep structures' of power: class for Marxism, gender for feminism. These structures are seen as providing the setting for the pluralistic conflict between groups or elites which characterises liberal-democracy. There is therefore a contrast between these theories of 'deep structure' and the pluralist or elitist theories which highlight the surface appearance of liberal-democracy, comparing the rivalry of parties, groups and elites with the uniformity enforced by a single state party (communist or fascist). Theories of Marxism and feminism seek to situate the pluralist or elitist competition within a wider, hidden, dimension of power, and in this respect they seek to show that there is a conflict or a tension between the universalist claims for citizenship and democracy or 'people power' made by liberal-democratic systems and the inequalities of class and gender which stem from a structure of economic or gender power. These structures affect the nature and composition of the state elite and the purposes for which state power is wielded. The chief concern of each of these views of power (Marxism, feminism) therefore shifts to an emphasis on revealing a covert context of power, and seeking to show the relationship between that context of class or gender power and the overt conflict of parties and groups. In that sense, these perspectives also act as criticisms of the other forms of state examined in this book, since they show that class power and gender power are not specific to liberal-democracy, but also underlie other forms of state. However, it should not be implied here that Marxism and feminism have the same agenda. They may share in certain respects a common concern with what is here called 'deep structure', but they each highlight a quite different dimension of power and envisage distinct modes of action to overthrow or overcome those dimensions of power. It should be added that 'Marxism' is taken here as a theory, as a critical tool or set of tools in the social sciences, not to be identified with a particular regime or form of state system.

Finally, the other theme of this book is the comparison of different types of state and the way in which the various theories of power treated here seek to understand the differences between them. The starting point is the simplified antithesis between pluralist systems on the one hand (liberal-democracies) and systems of one-party rule (communism, fascism) on the other. To this can be added the question of *nationalism*, whose place in this book requires some justification and explanation at this early stage. Clearly, nationalism has proved and remains an extremely important force in modern politics. Hence, any book which seeks to explain the modern state and politics in it would be defective if the topic of nationalism and its appeal made no appearance. We noted above that the modern state claims to be a nation-state, and that the state in the modern world has often, if not always, sought to harness and develop sentiments of national cohesion and loyalty as a way of bolstering the state's power, making nationalism an important tool of legitimation. Thus nationalism seen in this light is a powerful force assisting the process of legitimation of power.

Why then does nationalism appear in Part Two of this book, which is concerned with *rivals to the liberal-democratic state*, rather than in Part One, which is concerned with different theories of that state form? The reason is what is described in Chapter 9 as the protean or malleable character of nationalism. Nationalism certainly functions as a reinforcement or cohesive factor in the modern liberal-democratic state. However, it does not require much knowledge of modern politics to see nationalism as a force seeking to remodel states that do not fit the nationalist prescription of a (tight) nation-state in which 'nation' and 'state' coincide. Nationalism with its harnessing of ethnic loyalties and conflicts seeks to break up multinational states, and nationalist movements seek to subordinate the state to the nation. Thus nationalism, at least in many of its guises, works in politics to undermine or attack the pluralism which characterises the liberal-democratic state. Any introduction to modern politics has to show how the state in the modern world is, or aspires to be, a nation-state. Nationalist movements seek in conditions of modern politics to mobilise and arouse support from all those who are perceived to be in the same nation, and in many cases this is a powerful factor in movements seeking to mount an ethnic challenge to liberal-democracy. Thus nationalism has to be examined as both a prop to the modern liberal-democratic state and also as a battering ram against the state in its liberal-democratic and other forms.

It only remains to describe the rationale for the choice of topics in Part II: rivals to the liberal-democratic state. The aim is to show the main features of those states which in the twentieth century were the chief rivals to the liberal-democratic state, to explain why those states collapsed, and to show the nature of the alleged 'superiority' of the liberal-democratic system. It is also the purpose to examine nationalism as a powerful force in modern politics, both reinforcing and undermining states of all kinds. The aim is to see not just how these different forms of state compare in their structure and in the ideas underlying them, but also how the different theories, of pluralism, elitism, Marxism and feminism, apply to forms of state other than the liberal-democratic one, since applying them to a wider framework serves as a test of their validity.

Thus the aim is to present the main features of the state today, in its liberal-democratic form, and in the form of those systems which have challenged it. This can only be done by reviewing and analysing a range of theories which offer conceptual tools for the understanding of politics, by comparing those theories and seeing which ones are helpful, and why. The purpose remains the same: to seek to build up a body of theory and ideas which helps to make sense of the bewildering and rapidly changing world of late twentieth-century politics, and to examine the structures of power which confront humanity in this time. Only then can the possibilities for change be assessed.

Notes

1. Miliband, R., *The State in Capitalist Society*, Weidenfeld & Nicolson, London, 1969, p. 1.
2. Engels' remark is contained in an article on 'Das Fest der Nationen in London' written in 1845. F. Engels, 'Das Fest der Nationen in London', Marx, K., and Engels, F., *Werke*, Vol. 2, Dietz Verlag, Berlin, 1970, p. 613. For Wellington's remark, see White, R.J. (ed.), *The Conservative Tradition*, A. & C. Black, London, 1964, p. 155.
3. Maier, C.S., 'Democracy since the French Revolution', in Dunn, J. (ed.), *Democracy: The unfinished journey 508 BC to AD 1993*, Oxford University Press, Oxford, 1992, p. 130.
4. Maier, 'Democracy since the French Revolution', p. 132.
5. Hobsbawm, E.J., *The Age of Empire*, Weidenfeld & Nicolson, London, 1987, p. 142.
6. Macpherson, C.B., *The Real World of Democracy*, Clarendon Press, Oxford, 1966, p. 22.
7. For a discussion of the New Right, see King, D.S., *The New Right: Politics, markets, citizenship*, Macmillan, London, 1987.
8. On whom see Kukuthas, C., *Hayek and Modern Liberalism*, Clarendon Press, Oxford, 1990.
9. Mann, M., *States, War and Capitalism: Studies in political sociology*, Blackwell, Oxford, 1988, p. 4.
10. Poggi, G., *The State: Its nature, development and prospects*, Polity, Cambridge, 1990, p. 21.
11. Skinner, Q., 'The state', in Ball, T., Farr, J., and Hanson, R.L. (eds), *Political Innovation and Conceptual Change*, Cambridge University Press, Cambridge, 1989, p. 107.
12. Mann, M., 'The autonomous power of the state', in Mann, *States, War and Capitalism*, p. 4.
13. Beetham, D., *The Legitimation of Power*, Macmillan, London, 1991, p. 121.
14. Rosanvallon, P., *L'État en France de 1789 à nos jours*, Seuil, Paris, 1990, p. 15.
15. See Vile, M.J.C., *Constitutionalism and the Separation of Powers*, Clarendon Press, Oxford, 1967.
16. Mann, 'The autonomous power of the state', p. 4.
17. Poggi, *The State*, p. 15.

18. Beetham, *The Legitimation of Power*, p. 122.
19. Brubaker, R., *Citizenship and Nationhood in France and Germany*, Harvard University Press, Cambridge, MA, and London, 1992, p. 28.
20. Brubaker, *Citizenship and Nationhood in France and Germany*, p. xi.
21. Weber, M., 'Politics as a vocation', in Gerth, H.H. and Mills, C.W. (eds), *From Max Weber: Essays in sociology*, Routledge & Kegan Paul, London, 1948, p. 82.
22. Pierson, C., *Beyond the Welfare State?*, Polity, Cambridge, 1991, p. 7.
23. Marx, K., *The Eighteenth Brumaire of Louis Bonaparte*, in Marx, K., *Surveys from Exile: Political writings, Vol. 2*, ed. D. Fernbach, Penguin, Harmondsworth, 1973, p. 237.
24. Birch, A.H., *The Concepts and Theories of Modern Democracy*, Routledge, London, 1992, p. 191.
25. Proudhon, P.-J., *General Idea of the Revolution in the Nineteenth Century*, trans. J.B. Robinson, Pluto, London, 1989, p. 294.
26. Hart, H.L.A., *The Concept of Law*, Clarendon Press, Oxford, 1961, p. 19.
27. Beetham, D., *The Legitimation of Power*, p. 16.
28. On which see T. Abse, 'The triumph of the leopard', *New Left Review*, vol. 199, 1993, pp. 3–28.
29. On totalitarianism, see Rupnik, J., 'Totalitarianism revisited', in Keane, J. (ed.), *Civil Society and the State: New European perspectives*, Verso, London, 1988; Friedrich, C.J., Curtis, M., and Barber, B.R., *Totalitarianism in perspective: three views*, Pall Mall Press, London, 1969; Schapiro, L., *Totalitarianism*, Macmillan, London, 1972.
30. Neumann, F., *The Democratic and the Authoritarian State: Essays in political and legal theory*, The Free Press, New York and London, 1957, p. 244.

Part I

The liberal-democratic state and critical perspectives

2 | The liberal-democratic state: democracy and liberalism, theory and practice

Introduction

The purpose of this chapter is to examine the nature of the liberal-democratic state. The aim is to make clear what are the core ideas which that form of state seeks to realise, and to present its characteristic institutions. The liberal-democratic state claims to realise the goals of both liberalism and democracy, but before assessing the degree to which it succeeds in this aim it is necessary to have some conception of what those goals or values are. This will make possible a general answer to the question of the extent to which liberal-democracy in practice achieves the theoretical goals it is supposed to realise. Subsequent chapters will examine the liberal-democratic state from the perspectives of, respectively, pluralist, elitist, Marxist and feminist theory. The concern of this chapter is with the ideas underlying this state form, and the problems involved in realising them in practice. There are thus three questions which form the subject matter of what follows:

- What is democracy, and the meaning of the democratic idea?
- What is meant by liberal-democracy, as a particular type of democratic system?
- What are the institutions and processes characteristic of liberal-democratic systems, and how do they seek to achieve the realisation of the democratic idea?

Democracy and the democratic idea

What is democracy? What is a democratic political system? One answer to this question might be simply to maintain that democratic systems are those societies like the USA, Britain and France which call themselves 'democracies' and have certain institutions such as open and free elections fought between competing parties, a parliament or representative assembly, rights of meeting and opposition. The theoretical task of definition would thus be unnecessary: the term 'democracy' would refer to any political system that calls itself democratic, and there would be no need to specify any particular normative values or goals that are essential to democracy.

This seems unsatisfactory, for various reasons. First, in the modern world many different kinds of regime have called themselves democratic, and have sought to claim that they realise 'the will of the people'. This is true of the former Soviet systems, the so-called 'People's Democracies' of Eastern Europe, and even fascist systems claimed a democratic basis. This line of argument leads to the conclusion that 'democracy' can mean anything, that any regime which invokes the title of a democratic regime can legitimately do so. Democracy would thus be nothing more than a 'pro-word', a word used to evoke approval of a particular regime, and there would be no core meaning, or way in which one could deny the title of democracy to any regime that claimed to be democratic.

If this approach is rejected, and 'democracy' is used to refer to those regimes that have certain institutional characteristics, like free elections, a choice of candidates, a free press and ways of making the rulers accountable to the ruled, this still begs the following question: what is it about those institutions, processes or structures that justifies giving the label of 'democracy' to a political system in which they have a place? Why do those institutions and processes give regimes possessing them a claim to be considered 'democratic'? The answer has to be that those institutions and practices are democratic to the extent that they realise the core values and goals of democracy, and those goals and values have to be independently specified. Thus the perspective taken here is to suggest that 'democracy' must be used as a normative criterion, a standard by which to judge particular political systems. Democracy is capable of some independent definition in terms of certain basic values or goals, and cannot be defined purely by reference to certain institutions. A democratic system of government is one which possesses institutions and practices capable of achieving those goals and realising those values.

Before going on to specify what exactly those values and goals are, one should also note the historical transformation which democracy has undergone. Whereas democracy was generally once regarded as dangerous, revolutionary and threatening, we now live in an age where democracy and democratic values are universally invoked as desirable and as the only acceptable basis for a political system. As David Held notes, with reference to the fall of communism in Central and Eastern Europe, 'Liberal democracy was championed as the agent of progress and capitalism as the only viable economic system: ideological conflict, it was said, is steadily being displaced by universal democratic reason and market-orientated thinking'.[1] Our task here is to examine why liberal-democracy has been elevated to the position of being the only desirable political system. As many writers have pointed out,[2] for many centuries democracy, whether in its liberal form or any other shape, was not considered desirable at all, but rather was feared as leading to the rule of the mob and hastening the end of 'civilisation'. Democracy, at least in its liberal-democratic form, is now celebrated throughout the world, even by conservative politicians, whereas conservative and liberal politicians in the last century feared its revolutionary potential. Liberal-democracy is considered to be the truly desirable form of a modern political system.

The most widely discussed celebration of liberal-democracy recently has been the argument of Francis Fukuyama in *The End of History and the Last Man*. The implication of Fukuyama's argument is that the liberal-democratic state is now held up to be the universal model for societies everywhere. By contrast, as was noted in the previous chapter, not only have communism and fascism, which were the main rivals to that system, lost any power of attraction they once had, but also, Fukuyama suggests, no other alternatives to the liberal-democratic state are now envisaged as possibilities. In his words,

> The apparent number of choices that countries face in determining how they will organise themselves politically and economically has been *diminishing* over time. Of the different types of regimes that have emerged in the course of human history, from monarchies and aristocracies, to religious theocracies, to the fascist and communist dictatorships of this century, the only form of government that has survived intact to the end of the twentieth century has been liberal democracy.[3]

He draws the conclusion that 'for a very large part of the world, there is now no ideology with pretensions to universality that is in a position to challenge liberal democracy, and no universal principle of legitimacy other than the sovereignty of the people . . . Even non-democrats will have to speak the language of democracy in order to justify their deviation from the single universal standard.'[4]

This apparently almost universal praise for liberal-democracy is something relatively recent. Traditionally, democracy was viewed as threatening freedom, defined in liberal terms, rather than celebrated as guaranteeing it. This points to a deep tension within the liberal-democratic state between its *liberal* and its *democratic* elements, which will be explained below. Certainly, until relatively recently democracy was seen as giving power to the masses, the people, and this was far from being considered desirable. It was seen as giving power to a dangerous and uneducated mob. Political democracy was held to give rise to demands for social equality, as well as political equality, and both were thought to be dangerous. Giving power to the people would lead to the overthrow of the social hierarchy, to the power of numbers over the influence of wisdom, property and stability. Even a liberal like John Stuart Mill who finally welcomed the coming of democracy expressed the fear that it would lead to an uneducated mass taking over power from wise and educated leaders.[5] Before explaining the reasons for this recent change, the way in which democracy has become 'respectable', we need to elaborate on what the idea of democracy involves, and what institutions and processes are required to realise it.

glob. opinion

Liberal's classical view of democracy

Popular sovereignty

If a particular political system is democratic to the extent that it realises certain values, then the chief value of democracy must be the idea of 'people power', of the people ruling themselves, and being governed by laws that they themselves have made. The core democratic idea is that of popular sovereignty, of a society governed by rules or laws that each person as a citizen has contributed to forming, either directly, as in ancient Athens, or indirectly, as in modern systems, through the choice of representatives who rule or take decisions on behalf of the citizens. The central aspiration is one of popular power and, in terms of the ways of realising or implementing this goal, there is an important distinction between direct democracy and indirect or representative democracy.

A particular society is therefore democratic to the extent that it achieves the goal of people power, of rule by the people. A society is democratic not just because it possesses certain institutions (e.g. free elections); it is democratic because those institutions or procedures go some way towards making a reality of the aspiration towards self-rule or autonomy. The goal is to achieve a situation in which people are ruled by decisions that they themselves as citizens have taken, whether directly or through the mediation of their representatives.

The basic democratic values of autonomy or self-direction mean, if they are realised, that the citizens of a democratic society will be ruled by their own will and not by the will of someone else (autonomy, not heteronomy). This involves an idea of what it is to be free, which is different from the liberal idea of freedom. The democratic idea of freedom is one of self-determination: people are free if they are governed by laws which reflect their own will, which are not imposed on those subject to them without their own involvement. A clear statement of this idea comes from the classical theorist of democracy, Jean-Jacques Rousseau, who wrote in the *Social Contract* (1767) that 'obedience to a law which we prescribe to ourselves is liberty'.[6] Democracy therefore does not mean absence of law; it is a form of state, a political order in which people are free to the extent that the decisions taken in the society are ones which in some sense could be said to emanate from the people themselves. The idea of freedom as self-government involves as a corollary some idea of participation, of being involved, directly or indirectly, in making those key decisions in the society. The democratic aspiration is to create a society in which the laws are made by the people, and in which the distinction between state and society is narrowed, if not done away with altogether. The government, in some sense, should reflect the will of the people, and this can only be achieved if supreme or sovereign power is held by the people.

There have been many political theorists through the ages who have argued that this democratic aspiration is impossible to realise. A number of arguments have been deployed against democracy. Among them is the claim that such a society would impose too great demands on its citizens. They might not have

the knowledge or capacities for informed political judgement, or indeed the
wish or interest to exercise them. Joseph Schumpeter, in his critique of what
he calls the classical doctrine of democracy,[7] argued that there is no such thing
as the will of the people. This is an abstraction because the people are not a
uniform block, there are different interests represented by various groups, and
in any case leadership is required to articulate these varied interests.

There is also the problem of scale, the size of the unit within which a
democratic polity can function, and the question of whether the goal of self-
rule or autonomy is at all feasible in large-scale societies which go beyond the
size of the Greek polis or city-state. Does it make sense to talk about a society
of millions of people ruling themselves? And how can this democratic
aspiration be achieved? The contemporary Italian political theorist Norberto
Bobbio notes that the gap between the promises of democratic theory and the
reality of democratic politics stem from the fact that 'the project of political
democracy was conceived for a society much less complex than the one that
exists today'.[8] Problems of size or scale may not make democracy impossible,
but they certainly pose challenges to the democratic perspective. They raise
the question of how to achieve the democratic aspiration of popular
sovereignty or people power in a large and socially diverse or complex society.

From a different line critical of democratic theory has come the argument
that, even if the people could to some extent participate in political life, this
would be highly undesirable because politics is a science where a wise minority,
an elite, knows best what the right decisions are. The interference of the public,
uneducated as they are, is not for their own good. What has been called the
'guardianship' model of politics implies that there are 'right' decisions in
politics and that political leadership requires specialised skills and knowledge
which only an elite possesses.[9] The elite criticism of democracy is treated more
fully in Chapter 4, but it should be noted here as a line of criticism directed
against the desirability of a democratic society. It formed part of the battery
of arguments of those who sought to oppose the realisation of a democratic
society.

Core democratic values

Returning to the definition of democracy as 'power to the people', or the
aspiration to popular sovereignty, the realisation of this democratic ideal is
bound up with three important ideas. A democratic society seeks to realise the
following three values:

- An idea of participation.
- An idea of accountability of leaders to led, of popular control.
- An idea of equality.

First, participation: the democratic idea that people should rule themselves involves a commitment to participation. Political participation is necessary to freedom, so that the people themselves affect and control their political fate. To be free, people have to be in some way involved in making the law, they must share in the formation of what Rousseau called the 'general will'. The extent of that participation, and the conditions required to make it feasible, especially in a large and complex society, raise a key question of democratic theory. Should participation be constant, which seems a highly unrealistic demand, or need it be only intermittent? Does it involve direct involvement in taking the decisions, or merely choosing and controlling those who do take the decisions? And if the latter, how is this to be achieved? A stringent requirement for democracy was laid down by Rousseau. In his view there had to be direct democracy, or no democracy at all. He was a stern critic of representative democracy, since he asserted that sovereignty could not be delegated or represented. Following this line of argument, he argued that the English people were free only at election time, because once they had elected representatives their freedom was lost. This leads on to the key problem of representation and its implications for democracy, in terms of the problems or challenges it presents for the defender of the democratic view.

Democracy also involves an idea of popular control or accountability. If democracy means the rule of the people – in other words, the aspiration to popular power – then a democratic political system has to have devices for making sure that governmental decisions do conform to the will of the people. Therefore, there have to be structures of popular control or accountability, ways of testing whether those entrusted with political power do have the approval of the people. Hence, as a minimal requirement to achieve this end, a democratic society requires an electoral process for governmental office, with a choice of different candidates and a process for imposing loss of public power on those office-holders whose actions deviate from or do not reflect the public will. There should also be mechanisms of interest representation, for channelling wishes to the government, the power-holders, and of imposing costs or sanctions if they do not respond to such popular wishes. The possibility of popular control is a key feature of a democratic system, and without such popular control there can be no democracy. Thus there is here an 'anti-paternalist' principle, to the effect that democracy is not compatible with a situation where a leadership group acts in the best interests of the people, because that could legitimise a system of benevolent despotism. The people themselves must be able to decide what their interests are and have the ability to remove officials or governments which do not respond to their interests as the people define them. The challenge for a democratic system is to work out or decide on mechanisms or strategies for implementing these goals.

The democratic idea further involves a commitment to equality. A democratic society would be one realising the goal of citizen equality. Those who are members of such a society are held to be all equal as citizens. As members of the citizen body, they have the capacity and intelligence to decide on what their interests are and how the society should be regulated. The democratic idea is one which suggests that people should be equal in the contribution they are entitled to make to the decision-making process. Distinctions of wealth or economic resources, intelligence, gender and age should not count in the say a person has in contributing to making the law. As with the concept of freedom, there is a distinction between the liberal concept of equality and the democratic one. The liberal perspective emphasises equality before the law, and the claim that everyone has an equal right not to be interfered with by the state or society ('the tyranny of the majority'). The democratic idea, on the other hand, is that everyone has an equal right to contribute to making the law, to be involved in politics, so there should be equal rights of citizen participation. Political institutions should be arranged to achieve this idea of equality. This democratic concept does not assume that people are in fact equal in intelligence or capacity, but that such differences of individual capacity and fate should not count in the contribution each makes to the political process.

In this sense the democratic view rests on an idea of *political equality*. In his survey of *Democracy and Its Critics*, the American political scientist Robert Dahl has recently formulated what he calls a 'strong principle of equality' to serve as a justification for democracy, in the following terms:

> All members are sufficiently well qualified, taken all around, to participate in making the collective decisions binding on the association that significantly affect their good or interests. In any case, none are so definitely better qualified than the others that they should be entrusted with making the collective and binding decisions.[10]

Dahl adds that 'The set of persons to whom such a principle may be applied could be called the demos, the *populus*, or the citizen-body. Its members are *full citizens*.' Clearly, equality is one of the core values of democracy, not in the sense that people are necessarily equal in terms of property, nor in terms of personal characteristics such as intelligence, ability in their job, or whatever, but in the sense that whatever differences there are between citizens *should not count* with respect to their participation in the democratic process.

In turn this raises the large question of whether economic and social divisions and inequalities can undermine the idea of citizenship equality which is basic to the democratic view. The realisation of democracy cannot be separated from the social and economic context, the structure of economic power within which democracy in the modern world is situated. The aspiration towards political or citizen equality is negated or limited by the existence of substantial economic and social inequalities in the society of contemporary liberal-democracy. This question is basic to the Marxist view of liberal-democracy (see Chapter 5). As the American economist Charles Lindblom notes, 'we must still turn back to Marx to understand, for example, the adverse effects on democratic government of property rights and of their grossly unequal distribution'.[11] This tension in liberal-democratic systems between economic and social inequalities

Equality

and the ideal of citizen equality was noted by R.H. Tawney, who referred to a 'type of society which combines the forms of political democracy with sharp economic and social divisions'.[12] In certain circumstances these 'sharp social divisions' can threaten or erode the system of citizen equality and effective popular rule. Social inequalities are an obstacle to the democratic aim of equality of input into the political process.

The central idea of democracy is therefore popular sovereignty, a situation in which people are autonomous in the sense of ruling themselves. The essential democratic values associated with this are those of participation, accountability and equality. Following on from this analysis, it should be noted that democracy is a matter of degree, rather than an all-or-nothing situation in which societies are either fully democratic or not democratic at all. A particular political system is more or less democratic depending on the range of positions in that society open to popular choice and control. The idea of 'democratic deepening' refers to the process of opening up more areas of life to democratic involvement. This is a point well made by Bobbio, who suggests that democracy is a process which is not completed with the attainment of universal suffrage. As he puts it, talking about the space in which democracy operates,

> In other words, when people want to know if a development towards greater democracy has taken place in a certain country, what should be looked for is an increase, not in the number of those who have the right to participate in making the decisions which concern them, but in the number of contexts or spaces in which they can exercise this right.[13]

This suggests that democracy refers to a process, an 'unfinished journey' which is not finished in those countries which call themselves liberal-democratic.

The idea of democracy as a *process* also suggests that democracy historically has been a process of struggle, of seeking to extend to broader sections of the people those democratic rights of participation and control. Democracy is not something created overnight in a once-and-for-all movement; rather the aspiration to form a democratic society is something which has involved, over a long historical period, a series of conflicts to open up areas of public life to sections of the people hitherto excluded. This suggests that complacent rhetoric about the British or American, or indeed any other, system being 'the oldest democracy in the world' misses the point. Democracy is something still to be achieved, rather than a state of affairs accomplished and finalised for all time. Even the full achievement of that most basic of democratic rights, the right to vote, involved a series of bitter and protracted struggles to extend that right to the full adult population.[14] Women in France did not get the vote until 1944; in Switzerland it was not until much later, in 1971.[15] Black Americans in the southern states of the USA did not achieve the effective use of the suffrage until the 1960s, after the impact of the civil rights movement. The struggles to extend democracy are thus by no means of purely historical

those — a
these — te

concern. They concern events and processes of democratisation going on at the present time.

Democracy should also be understood in terms of a set of procedures, meaning here a set of rules designed to guarantee the involvement of the people in political decision making. It has been noted above that as a minimum this involves the idea of elections as a way of exercising what the English Utilitarian philosopher Jeremy Bentham called the 'dislocatory' power, the power to get rid of rulers who do not follow the wishes of the people. A political system can genuinely be called democratic only if it is endowed with institutions through which the popular will can be expressed and turned into practical policies. Moreover, for a system to qualify as democratic, there must be procedures to ensure that those who exercise power are bound by the popular will, and that there are sanctions for defying it, including the loss of office and power.

There are thus a number of basic procedural criteria which decide whether a system is democratic or not, since they are ways of ensuring that the values of democracy are realised in a large and diverse society. In other words, they function as the means to achieve the fundamental democratic goals of popular sovereignty. They represent procedures for the achievement of liberal-democracy, rather than the direct democracy envisaged by Rousseau. Following on from Bobbio's idea of democracy as 'characterized by a set of rules (primary or basic) which establish *who* is authorised to take collective decisions and which *procedures* are to be applied',[16] these procedural conditions can be seen as comprising the following minimal criteria:

1. Equal and universal adult suffrage, irrespective of distinctions of race, religion, economic conditions and gender: in other words, the possession of the equal and basic right of the suffrage. Each citizen's vote must count for one: in the words of Jeremy Bentham, 'everyone to count for one, no-one for more than one'. This expresses the equality inherent in the democratic idea.

2. Civic rights which assure the free expression of opinions, and rights of citizens to organise, to have a 'space' in civil society free from the hold of political power. These rights would include the ideas stemming from the liberal tradition: freedom of belief and conscience, assembly, exchange of information, private meeting and so on.

3. The operation of the majority principle, according to which decisions must be taken by a numerical majority. This may be seen as a necessary condition of democracy in a complex modern society, where unanimity is impossible to achieve. However, the problem is to prevent democracy deteriorating into what liberals feared would be a 'tyranny of the majority', in which minority rights could be infringed through majority action. Hence there follows the next condition.

4. Guarantees of the rights of minorities against abuses on the part of majorities. As Bobbio puts it, 'No majority decision can restrict the rights of the minority, in particular the right to become a majority, subject to the same

conditions.'[17] This idea is one of *reciprocity*, the idea that 'today's majority may become tomorrow's minority', and vice versa. If a majority fails to respect the rights of the minority, then this undermines the consensus necessary for a democratic society to work. Democracy as a procedure thus requires agreement, as Bobbio insists, on certain 'rules of the game'.

Democracy must thus be understood as a set of rules seeking to facilitate and involve the mass of the citizens, seeking to achieve full political participation 'of the majority of citizens, whether directly or indirectly, in the decisions which affect the whole of society'.[18] In any society apart from a small-scale one such as the Greek polis, or indeed the Geneva city-state which Rousseau idealised, it is highly unlikely that there will be agreement of all the citizens. Different sections of the people will think different things, and have conflicting opinions and interests. The majority principle is one device reflecting the inevitable differentiation of opinion among the people, but there must also be protection for the minority in order to prevent majority opinion becoming dominant and despotic.

We have so far come to understand democracy as a system involving the aspiration to popular power and autonomy, and the key values of participation, accountability of power-holders, and equality. However, there are two further central issues in the democratic state which need to be probed. The first of these is the question: who are the people? Who forms the citizen body?

Who are the people?

The process of democratic politics has been one of seeking to overcome certain exclusions. The establishment of democracy involved the destruction of the barriers preventing participation and inclusion in the citizen body. Historically, these barriers or criteria of exclusion were ones of property, gender and age, as well as those of race and colonial subjection. To this list could be added education, although it has conventionally gone along with the property distinction, as in the phrase *Bildung und Besitz*, culture and property, used by German liberals to suggest the cultivated property-owning classes who alone could be trusted with political rights, as distinct from the uneducated masses, the dangerous crowd.

Thus starting from the idea of democracy as popular power, the first problem is that of who forms the people, of what are the scope and limits of the body that governs itself. A society might be highly democratic in the sense that those who are citizens practise a high level of participation, yet at the same time this society could be highly undemocratic because it placed strict limits on who was entitled to participate. Such indeed was the society of classical Athens, as a recent account observes:

> The Athenian democracy was one of the most participatory of all time – if one
> focuses on the powers and privileges of those who were included in its operations.

But the total of those *excluded* was large . . . slaves, women, subject-allies in the two periods of naval hegemony, metics.[19]

There are thus two dimensions of democracy: the number, or rather the degree of *inclusiveness*, of the citizen body, as a percentage of the total population; and the *degree or intensity* of their participation.

Participation and representation

Defining democracy in terms of popular sovereignty thus leads to the first problem: who are the people? The second question is an equally central one: in what sense can they be said to rule? What is the meaning of rule? A democratic system is one in which the people rule themselves, in which every person who is a citizen is entitled to make an equal contribution to the laws under which he or she lives. But how is this equal contribution to be made? How can the whole people rule themselves?

There is a clear distinction between a system in which decisions are taken by the people, themselves, with no representatives, and a system of representative democracy. An example of the former would be the Athenian democracy of the classical epoch, in which, although participation was not absolutely direct, the number of those attending the sovereign assembly 'as a percentage of the enfranchised population [was] awesomely large by modern standards'. Some 6,000 citizens could and did attend the assembly, out of the total Athenian citizen population of a notional 30,000.[20] This can be contrasted with a system of democracy in which indirect rather than direct participation is practised. It seems hard to deny that, if democracy is to be practised in a unit of greater size than the Greek city-state, on grounds of practicality it has to take the form of representative democracy.

This raises the obvious problem of representation. If one person, or group of persons, represents the citizen body, or a section of citizens, how can the representative in fact speak for or represent the will of others? The clear danger is that those who do the representing become distanced from, or independent of, those whom they represent. If one adds here certain assumptions about human nature, namely that people who have power want to keep it, and possibly increase it, then the problem is deepened. The fear of representation as leading to the loss of liberty was classically expressed by Rousseau in the *Social Contract*. For Rousseau, as we have seen, sovereignty could not be represented or delegated, and representation meant only the alienation of one's liberty. As he put it,

> Every law the people has not ratified in person is null and void – is, in fact, not a law. The people of England regards itself as free; but it is grossly mistaken; it is free only during the election of members of parliament. As soon as they are elected, slavery overtakes it, and it is nothing. The use it makes of the short moments of liberty shows indeed that it deserves to lose them.[21]

If one assumes, however, that Rousseau's prescription of direct democracy is unrealisable in a complex and large-scale society, one is left with the difficulty of representing and articulating the views of others in a coherent fashion. Both elitist theorists and anarchist theorists of politics agreed about the existence of this difficulty, although of course they offered different solutions to it. Elite theorists, as discussed further in Chapter 4, suggested that a skilled minority in ruling positions would do what they could to elude popular control, or at least minimise it. The elite theorist Michels in his study *Political Parties* suggests that the mass, the rank-and-file of the political party (German Social-Democratic Party, in this case) would not in fact wish to place much pressure on the ruling group, and would be happy for them to continue in their exercise of power.

From their very different point of view, anarchist theorists insisted that any state structure by definition involved representation. Therefore even a socialist 'transitional state', in which workers assumed positions of responsibility in the state apparatus, would suffer the same fate. As Bakunin classically expressed it,

> The universal right of each individual among all the people to elect so-called representatives and members of the government, that is the final word of the Marxists and of the democratic school.

However, he concluded, this would just result in the rule of a privileged minority. This minority might consist of workers, or rather of *former* workers, who would

> come to regard the whole blue-collared world from governmental heights, and would not represent the people but themselves and their pretensions in the government of the people. Anyone who does not see this does not know anything of human nature.[22]

It was not just elitist theorists or anarchists who were aware of the problem of political representation. The Utilitarians, from James Mill on, were concerned with the danger that officials of the state apparatus, whose activity was necessary to secure order and stability, might usurp or accumulate power and themselves become dangerous enemies of stability and liberty. James Mill in his essay 'On Government', written in 1823, explicitly mentioned this possibility and offered his remedy. As he put it, in order to prevent the abuse of governmental power, representatives of the people had to check the actions of government officials. But the danger was that these representatives themselves would abuse their power, so their duration of office had to be limited: 'As it thus appears, that limiting the duration of their power is a security against the sinister interest of the people's Representatives, so it appears that it is the only security of which the nature of the case admits.'[23] This view was shared by Jeremy Bentham, whose solution was to vest in the body of the electors the power to replace rulers or officials who showed signs of exceeding their power, or accumulating too much of it. The power to remove the representatives, to limit or restrain their powers, was essential to control them and their tendency to seek to distance themselves from those whom they represented.

Representation in a pluralist society – that is to say, a complex society with varied interests and perspectives – is made possible through organisations such as parties and pressure groups. Political parties form programmes which appeal to certain interests in the society. In the language of political science, they 'aggregate' interests, putting together in a relatively coherent framework some wants which people have in common. They articulate some wishes which people share with others, and the same is true of pressure groups. The shared interests on which these associations are based are of two kinds: first, interests or beliefs in a type of society, in common conceptions of the social good; and second, interests which are shared because of a particular role or function in society, arising out of one's place in the productive process. Organisations like trade unions and business groups represent people in the sense that they put together the interests shared among people who have a common function in society, as workers, business entrepreneurs, farmers, and so on. Parties and pressure groups are thus crucial institutions through which people are represented in politics, and they provide structures which, at least in theory, are supposed to provide means of checking and controlling the representatives. These matters are dealt with further in Chapter 3, which deals with the pluralist perspective on power.

The solution to the problem of representatives escaping popular control clearly involves some idea of accountability, seeking to maximise the control which the represented, the people, have over the delegates or representatives. These latter terms are not the same: the idea of a *delegate* implies someone who is bound or controlled by those whom that delegate represents, and who therefore has limited autonomy; a *representative*, on the other hand, is someone who speaks for those who are represented, but who is not closely tied by restrictions imposed by the constituents. The distinction between the two and the defence of the idea of the representative was classically given by Burke in his speech to the electorate of Bristol. Burke declared that 'Your representative owes you, not his industry only, but his judgement; and he betrays, instead of serving you, if he sacrifices it to your opinion'.[24] Clearly, if the represented are supposed to exercise control over those who, for primarily practical reasons, are to represent them, then this presupposes the capacity of the people to exercise this control over their representatives. Such control assumes the *will* on their part to do so; it presupposes the *knowledge and interest* which will make such popular control effective. In other words, it assumes a knowledgeable participatory citizen body, who have the powers to make their control felt. This may in practice impose considerable burdens on the citizens of a democracy.

The liberal-democratic state

Democracy in the modern world predominantly takes the form of liberal-democracy. Indeed, to take an argument from Bobbio, if we are talking about 'real existing democracy', the democracy which exists in the contemporary world, there is no other: liberal-democracy is the only one.[25] What is the liberal-democratic state? What are its characteristic ideas and institutions?

The liberal-democratic state can take a variety of forms, but it is possible to point to a number of basic elements in this type of system. It combines the very distinct elements of liberalism and democracy, and the tensions between the two are of crucial importance to understanding the nature of the liberal-democratic state today. As C.B. Macpherson has pointed out, the liberal-democratic state was liberal before it was democratic.[26] The striving to develop democracy, and to extend popular participation in the democratic process, took place within the context of the liberal state and the particular economic framework within which it was situated.

The core doctrine of liberalism is the protection of the individual, and the rights of the individual. The state is seen as a limited state, whose purpose is to protect those rights. In the liberal perspective, individuals exist within a private sphere, within which people can do as they wish. They think their own thoughts, form their own projects, buy and sell their own property, and meet with other people to exchange thoughts, ideas and property through contract. The task of the state, of those who hold political power, is seen in the liberal view as the defence of these basic rights of the individual.

The liberal view of freedom is well expressed by the twentieth-century philosopher Friedrich von Hayek, who wrote that

> The liberal conception of freedom has often been described as a merely negative freedom, and rightly so . . . The liberal demand for freedom is thus a demand for the removal of all man-made obstacles to individual efforts, not a claim that the community or the state should supply particular goods.

Hayek also claims that what he calls 'the decline of liberal doctrine, beginning in the 1870s, is closely connected with a re-interpretation of freedom as the command over, and usually the provision by the state of, the means of achieving a great variety of particular ends'.[27]

The liberal state is supposed to be the guarantor of the rights of the individual. The state therefore has to protect individuals against arbitrary interference, whether the source of that interference is other individuals, society at large (what liberals from de Tocqueville onwards called 'the tyranny of the majority') or indeed the state itself. In the liberal view the state is always a necessary evil, a potential threat to the liberty which it exists to secure. Bentham wrote of 'those evil-doers, whose means of evil-doing are derived from the share they respectively possess, in the aggregate of the powers of government. Among these, those of the highest grade, and in so far as supported by those of the highest, those of every inferior grade, are everywhere irresistible'.[28] State power, in the liberal view, is necessary – but dangerous too.

Liberalism and democracy are quite different principles, resting on a different view of freedom. The democratic idea rests on a view of freedom as autonomy or self-direction. The democratic citizen is someone who achieves freedom through participation, through involvement in making the laws or rules under which the community lives. This contrasts with the liberal view of freedom, which is freedom to be left alone to 'do one's own thing', a freedom guaranteed by legal rules. The democratic conception of freedom envisages people participating in a collective body to determine the laws under which they live. Liberals fear the possibly unbounded power of that democratic collective body. The liberal concept of freedom sees it as stemming from a situation in which people are protected *by* and *against* the state in their basic rights: rights of privacy and conscience, rights to follow out their own projects, think their own thoughts and exchange their own property.

From this basic distinction between the liberal and the democratic views of freedom comes a basic distinction between their respective views of the state. The liberal view of the state is that it is a device or set of institutions created to secure and guarantee the basic rights of the individual. However, there is in the liberal view always a danger that the state will become too powerful, so that the remedy would be worse than the disease. To prevent this, the state and its institutions should be strictly controlled, to keep those vested with state power from overstepping the mark. The state must be limited in its functions, it must not infringe the basic liberties of the person, and these liberties include the right of private property and accumulation.

In this sense, the liberal view of the state is not egalitarian or democratic. For classical liberalism there was no need for those holding state power to be selected by the people as a whole. It was sufficient for the state to be checked and controlled by a representative institution or parliament, selected by those property owners who had 'a stake in the country'. They would form the 'active citizens', while for the mass of the population was reserved the role of 'passive citizens', protected from arbitrary interference by the state, but not entitled to any say in making the laws or choosing the representatives. Historically, it was the case that liberals were fearful and suspicious of the democratic push to extend participation to 'the masses'. The 'masses', the people, it was felt, were liable to be uneducated and poor, and hence would want the state to intervene in the market for the purposes of securing social equality, going well beyond political equality. This could lead to a strong state, to the tyranny of the majority, and to the extension of equality from the political to the social sphere.

The democratic view of the state does not share this fearful attitude to the state as a necessary evil. In contrast to the liberal view of the state as at least the potential enemy of freedom, the democratic state is seen as the organ or instrument of the collective will, as the means for realising the will of the

people. The state in democratic thinking is legitimate to the extent to which
all citizens participate in its activities. In the democratic perspective, if the state
is a democratic state – that is, if it reflects the 'will of the people', however that
is ascertained or whatever that may be – then there are no necessary limits on
that state power.

Historically speaking, the democratic challenge took the form of a
movement to democratise the already-existing liberal state. Liberals were not
slow to point out that a democratic state was highly likely to be a state that was
not limited. Political equality would most likely lead to demands for social
equality, as liberals like de Tocqueville noted, and the state would be the
instrument of this social equality. 'Once the people is sovereign it is rarely
miserable', was de Tocqueville's surmise. If state power came under the
control of the masses, they would most likely use it to satisfy the demand for
social equality. A state that aimed to achieve some degree of social equality
was, liberals feared, a state that would override property rights and hence no
longer be the minimal state which they desired. Thus the democratic view of
the state is that all must participate in it, and that it could be the vehicle or
instrument for achieving social equality. From the time of the French
Revolution onwards, this antithesis between liberalism and democracy has
remained a central feature of political struggle.

The liberal state was conceived in terms of ideas of *constitutionalism* and the
rule of law. Since the liberal state had to be a limited state, there had to be
devices and institutions for checking and controlling the holders of state power.
The hallowed device was the separation of powers: the power of one part of
the state apparatus to check another. The arbitrary and unrestricted use of
power was to be prevented by a system of checks and balances. The separation
of powers has traditionally involved the division of government into the three
branches or departments of legislature, executive and judiciary. In the words
of a study of the separation of powers, 'the persons who compose these three
agencies of government must be kept separate and distinct, no individual being
allowed to be at the same time a member of more than one branch'.[29]
More generally, the liberal state is one in which there is a competition
between political parties, and the right of opposition parties to scrutinise
and debate the policies of the governing party. These were originally not the
mass parties of a modern democracy, but limited coteries of parliamentary
representatives.

In so far as the liberal aim of restricting state power is quite different from
the democratic purpose of ensuring political participation and popular power,
there is thus an inherent conflict within the liberal-democratic state between
its liberal origins and its democratic claims. The whole history of this type of
state can be seen and interpreted as a process of democratisation. The struggle
to extend democratic rights, above all to widen the right to vote, released
popular pressures. The demand was for 'the people', the masses, to take their
place within the liberal state's existing institutions of parliament and political

parties. The other side of the coin was the attempt by those in power to adopt a policy of 'containment' and to resist the pressures for democratisation.[30]

The liberal-democratic state thus combines institutions characteristic of both liberal and democratic ideas. It is a state form in which there are checks and balances to prevent the state from exceeding certain limits, and at the same time there are institutions and processes which are meant to make possible popular participation in politics as part of the democratic ideal. In the words of one theorist, speaking of liberal-democracy and the relationship between its two fundamental elements, 'we find a relationship that is both one of mutual necessity and a source of tension or antagonism'.[31] Democracy requires the existence and guarantee of the rights of the individual, which liberalism enshrines. Without freedom of speech, assembly and other rights of the individual, democracy could not work – the popular control over government would not be possible. Criticism and opposition to government need the protection which the liberal concept of individual rights and 'private space' involves. Similarly, the essentially liberal ideas of separation of powers and a representative assembly to control governments, the existence of a private sphere separate from the state, and the rejection of the idea of one single truth which all have to accept (the notion imposed in a totalitarian system) are all essential conditions for democracy to exist: 'Attempts to abolish these liberal features in the name of a more perfect democracy have only succeeded in undermining the democracy in whose name they were attacked'.[32]

Yet at the same time, liberals historically resisted democratisation, as we have seen, because they thought that extending the suffrage and developing participation might challenge the right of private property. As C.S. Maier notes: 'The history of democracy in the nineteenth and twentieth centuries involves the story not so much of making the world safe for democracy, as Woodrow Wilson wanted it, but of making democracy safe for the world.'[33] He points out that many nineteenth-century observers feared that democracy would have revolutionary consequences. Because of social developments the property-less masses formed or would come to constitute the majority of the population. Democracy would empower them politically, and then, as Maier puts it, 'the advance of democracy must appear an alarming trend'.[34] The point is not of purely historical interest, since in more recent times there has been a resort to authoritarian rule under conditions where democratic politics have appeared likely to challenge seriously a structure of social and economic inequality. The case of fascism in the twentieth century is the most extreme, but by no means the only example of this process. The history of liberal-democracy contains several other examples in which democracy, or rather liberal-democracy, has been abandoned by groups and classes who resorted to authoritarian rule because of their fear that the pressures of democracy would erode or oppose their economic and social privilege.

In this sense, liberal-democracy is open to the risk that, if social demands are expressed which are too 'dangerous' from the point of view of the dominant classes, then the democratic system itself becomes expendable. In certain circumstances such a reaction goes beyond the framework of liberal-democracy, leading to the installation of a form of 'strong state'. The present situation of politics, at least in the European context, may make a radical challenge to the existing property system unlikely, but the tension between social inequality and the idea of citizen equality and democracy remains a fundamental feature of this type of system.

We can conclude this chapter with the following summary. The liberal-democratic state seeks to realise the twin goals of liberalism and democracy. We have seen, first, what the goals of democracy are, and that in this system they are reached through representation, with the problems that it brings. Second, the liberal-democratic state involves tensions between the liberal aim of limiting and containing state power, and the democratic goal of popular sovereignty. We now turn to different theories which seek to explain, from different perspectives, the power structure of the liberal-democratic state and the society in which it is situated.

Notes

1. Held, D., 'Democracy: from city-states to a cosmopolitan order', in Held, D. (ed.), *Prospects for Democracy: North, South, East, West*, Polity, Cambridge, 1993, p. 13.
2. For example Macpherson, C.B., *The Real World of Democracy*, Clarendon Press, Oxford, 1966, p. 1.
3. Fukuyama, F., *The End of History and the Last Man*, Hamish Hamilton, London, 1992, p. 45.
4. *Ibid.*
5. See Mill, J.S., 'Representative Government', in Mill, J.S., *Three Essays*, Oxford University Press, Oxford, 1975, especially Chapter VIII, 'Of the Extension of the Suffrage'.
6. Rousseau, J.-J., *The Social Contract*, in Rousseau, J.-J., *The Social Contract and Discourses*, ed. G.D.H. Cole, Dent, London, 1968, p. 16.
7. Schumpeter, J.A., *Capitalism, Socialism and Democracy*, Unwin University Books, London, 1965, Chapter XXI.
8. Bobbio, N., *The Future of Democracy*, Polity, Cambridge, 1987, p. 37.
9. The term 'guardianship' model of democracy is taken from Dahl, R.A., *Democracy and Its Critics*, Yale University Press, New Haven, CT, and London, 1989, p. 52.
10. Dahl, R.A., *Democracy and its Critics*, p. 98.
11. Lindblom, C.E., *Politics and Markets: The world's political-economic systems*, Basic Books, New York, 1977, p. 8.
12. Tawney, R.H., *Equality*, Allen & Unwin, London, 1964, p. 78.
13. Bobbio, *The Future of Democracy*, p. 32.
14. Therborn, G., 'The rule of capital and the rise of democracy', *New Left Review*, vol. 103, 1977, pp. 3–41.
15. Lovenduski, J., *Women and European Politics: Contemporary feminism and public policy*, Wheatsheaf, Brighton, 1986, p. 44 (France) and p. 233 (Switzerland).

16. Bobbio, N., *The Future of Democracy*, p. 24. For a discussion of Bobbio's views on democracy, see Anderson, P., *A Zone of Engagement*, Verso, London, 1992, p. 109.
17. Bobbio, N., 'Alternatives to representative democracy', in Bobbio, N., *Which Socialism? Marxism, socialism and democracy*, Polity, Cambridge, 1986, p. 66.
18. Bobbio, *Which Socialism?*, p. 66.
19. Hornblower, S., 'Democratic institutions in Ancient Greece', in Dunn, J., (ed.), *Democracy, The unfinished journey, 508 BC to AD 1993*, Oxford University Press, Oxford, 1992, p. 12.
20. Hornblower, 'Democratic institutions in Ancient Greece', p. 13.
21. Rousseau, *Social Contract*, ed. G.D.H. Cole, p. 78.
22. Bakunin, M., *Selected Writings*, ed. A. Lehning, Jonathan Cape, London, 1973, pp. 268–9.
23. Mill, J., 'Government', in Mill, J., *Political Writings*, ed. T. Ball, Cambridge University Press, Cambridge, 1992, p. 25.
24. Burke, 'Speech to the electors of Bristol', in Hill, B.W. (ed.), *Edmund Burke on Government, Politics and Society*, Fontana/Harvester Press, Glasgow, 1975, p. 157.
25. Bobbio, *The Future of Democracy*.
26. Macpherson, C.B., *The Real World of Democracy*, p. 6.
27. Hayek, F.A., *New Studies in Philosophy, Politics, Economics and the History of Ideas*, Routledge & Kegan Paul, London, 1978, p. 134.
28. Bentham, J., 'Leading principles of a constitutional code, for any state', in Parekh, B. (ed.), *Bentham's Political Thought*, Croom Helm, London, 1973, p. 199.
29. Vile, M.J.C., *Constitutionalism and the Separation of Powers*, Oxford University Press, Oxford, 1967, p. 13.
30. See Miliband, R., *Capitalist Democracy in Britain*, Oxford University Press, Oxford, 1982, for an analysis of the British political system in terms of containment of popular pressure.
31. Beetham, D., 'The limits of democratization', in Held (ed.), *Prospects for Democracy*, p. 56.
32. Beetham, 'The limits of democratisation', p. 57.
33. Maier, C.S., 'Democracy since the French Revolution', in Dunn, J. (ed.), *Democracy*, p. 126.
34. Maier, 'Democracy since the French Revolution', p. 127.

3 | The pluralist view of politics

Introduction

The aim of this chapter is to explain the theory of pluralism. In its broadest terms, pluralism is a view of the political structure of liberal-democracy which emphasises the diffusion of power in such systems. The key problem which the pluralist view addresses is the question of how democracy can be realised in large and complex societies. In Chapter 2 it was argued that democracy is to be understood as a system in which 'the people' rule. The liberal-democratic state is one claiming to realise the twin, yet in some ways conflicting, values of democracy ('people power') and liberalism (the limited state). Pluralism suggests a solution to the problem of how to achieve popular power and at the same time limit the power of the state. This solution lies through participation in a network of groups and associations, which form multiple and competing centres of power. In the words of Robert Dahl, one of the most important contemporary writers on pluralism, 'Independent organisations are highly desirable in a democracy, at least in a large-scale democracy'.[1] The pluralist view thus offers a general theory of politics, the state and society. According to H.S. Kariel,

> In the context of public affairs and political thought, pluralism refers to specific institutional arrangements for distributing and sharing governmental power, to the doctrinal defence of those arrangements, and to an approach for gaining understanding of political behaviour. Political pluralism is therefore an historical phenomenon, a normative doctrine, and a mode of analysis. As the exclusively proper way of ordering and explaining public life, it remains the heart of the liberal ideology of the Western world.[2]

This is a useful beginning, which reminds us of the many dimensions and characteristics of pluralism both as a normative theory and as a way of explaining and analysing the power structure of the liberal-democratic system. Pluralism refers to a theory which has been also called 'the group theory of politics', which offers an explanation and analysis of the nature of contemporary liberal-democracy. This explanation sees the political process in

THE PLURALIST VIEW OF POLITICS

such systems as one of ongoing competition between different parties and pressure groups. A recent account of pluralism by Paul Hirst summarises this perspective, deriving from what he calls 'a body of modern American political theory', as follows:

> In this competitive process a plurality of organized interests strive to control government through taking part in electoral contests and/or strive to influence the policies a government adopts, and in either case each of the competing interests has some reasonable chance of success in the contest for office or influence.[3]

Hirst contrasts this with what he labels the 'English' variety of pluralist theory, which in his words 'is less a doctrine of political competition than a critique of state structure and of the basis of the authority of the state'.[4] Pluralism in this latter sense is seen as a normative view which holds that the state should share its power with a variety of groups and associations. As Harold Laski, a central contributor to the 'English' brand of pluralism, put it, such a theory

> does not deny the need in society either for rules or for organisations to maintain those rules; but it does deny that such a need involves the concept of a sovereign state, or the attribution to that state of an inherent supremacy which enables it to dominate all other associations in the community.[5]

The purpose of the following section is to present some of the characteristics of pluralism as a social and political theory, and then to investigate the ways in which, it is claimed, contemporary liberal-democratic states and societies realise the goals or aims of pluralism. The fundamental distinction is between pluralism as a *normative* theory, suggesting the features of a desirable social and political order, and pluralism as an *explanatory* theory, which argues that contemporary liberal-democracies do indeed meet the normative criteria of pluralist theory. In that vein, pluralists attach great importance to *interest groups*, and to *political parties*, both of which are seen as central to a pluralist system. Finally, the *pluralist theory of the state* is examined, since in pluralist theory the state is seen as an institution sharing power with the groups of civil society, responsive to them, yet also maintaining a certain consensus which prevents society from dissolving or fragmenting into a pathological form of pluralism.

Pluralism: characteristics of the theory

Pluralism is to be understood as a general theory, explaining how democracy can be realised in complex modern societies. In such societies, it is argued, it is unrealistic to continue with the classical democratic assumption that 'the people' form a single block, sharing common interests and acting collectively to decide on issues of common concern. Pluralist theory is closely related to liberal theory. Both start from an assumption of diversity and variety. In the pluralist perspective in its broadest sense, 'the people' as a whole, as a single unit, do not exist. Because pluralism takes its starting point to be a modern society in which there are different interests, popular power is realised through group activity, the working of political parties and pressure groups or interest groups, each of which represents one of the many interests into which a developed society is split. Pluralist perspectives salute and emphasise this diversity of interest, and like liberal theorists they see this variety as a necessary and positive dimension of social life.

This raises the question of how unity can be reconciled with this diversity, how pluralism can be prevented from ending in fragmentation and disaggregation. The problem is raised of how this variety can be contained within a consensus, an agreed framework of common rules. This is seen as in large part the role of the state.

Furthermore, there is what Dahl calls 'the problem of pluralist democracy'. Pluralism depends on organised groups having a certain autonomy and independence. However, these independent organisations can also distort democracy. If they have too much independence, the possibility of 'deformed civic consciousness' may arise: 'Because associations help to fragment the concerns of citizens, interests that many citizens might share – latent ones perhaps – may be slighted.'[6] *some group might shape the power*

In order to understand the core characteristics of pluralism as a theory of politics, it is helpful to present pluralism in summary form in terms of a number of antitheses or apparent contradictions which are present in the theory. Pluralism is characterised by the following paradoxes:

- It is both *normative* and *explanatory*.
- Pluralism involves the values of both *liberalism* and *democracy*.
- It is a *modern* theory, yet with strong *historical* antecedents linking up with key themes of liberal theory.
- It is a theory of *the state*, and also one of *society*, and of the links between them.
- Finally, pluralism celebrates *diversity*, as opposed to *monism*; it involves the opposition of 'the many', a view of different sources of truth and interest, to the idea of a single source of value. In that respect pluralism welcomes ideas of compromise, of reconciliation between a diversity of views and interests, and opposes what is seen as a dangerously totalitarian or monolithic view that there is one truth, one valid source of judgement.

These paradoxical statements need further explanation. With regard to the first of them, pluralist theory both asserts what ought to be the case, how society and the state *should* be structured, and also offers an analysis of the reality of contemporary liberal-democracy. In the former sense, it is a view of political philosophy, deriving from the liberal perspective. Yet pluralism is also a view of *what is*: in other words, a perspective of political science, seeking to analyse existing society and show the reality of the power structure.

Pluralist perspectives in their normative aspect have at the heart of their concern the liberal fear of the concentration and hence possible abuse of power. Pluralist perspectives seek to apply this to the conditions of advanced modern society. It is held that there should be multiple and competing centres of power, within the state and outside it, so that power is fragmented and diffused. This is held to be desirable because it prevents the concentration of power in the hands of a single person or group. Such concentration could lead to tyranny, despotism or totalitarianism, to the monolithic and all-pervasive state as opposed to the limited one. Thus pluralism views the desirable society as one in which power is dispersed and diffused, in which the values of diversity are realised and celebrated.

However, to pursue this antithesis further, pluralist theorists also hold that pluralism is an explanatory theory, that in modern liberal-democratic societies there is in fact a diffusion of power, and these systems are ones where the normative goals of pluralism are realised. Thus pluralist analysis focuses on institutions such as political parties and interest groups, whose presence and activity realise the normative goals of the theory. Pluralism is not just a theory of what ought to be; it claims to offer a scientific analysis of those institutions and processes which in liberal-democratic systems achieve the goal of power diffusion. Pluralism is thus a mode of analysis, a way of explaining political behaviour. It gives the label of 'pluralist' to those systems where institutions exist to diffuse and disperse power.

Second, while pluralism as a theory is closely related to liberalism and its view of the limited state, pluralist analysis is also a theory of democracy. A pluralist society is one where a range of groups and associations, inside and outside the state, realise the liberal aim of checking and controlling state power, making sure it is not concentrated in any one group or person. Yet such a society is also claimed to realise democracy. Representative democracy is achieved through citizen participation in the variety of organisations and political parties that are held to characterise a pluralist system. Thus pluralism is a theory of both liberalism and democracy. It shares the democratic aim of citizen participation and involvement, if only indirectly, in the key decisions of society.

Third, pluralist theory is both 'old' and 'new'. The term 'pluralism' is often used to describe modern theories of liberal-democracy, developed from what was called 'the group theory of politics' in the USA, with such people as A. Bentley and D.B. Truman the forerunners of latter-day pluralists like Robert Dahl. However, pluralism stems from a much older perspective, which is linked with liberalism and arose historically as a reaction to the seemingly all-powerful modern sovereign state. Chapter 1 presented the enormous power of the modern state, as that body which exercises sovereign and unchallenged power. Pluralism can be said to be an attempt, in theory and practice, to cut the state down to size, to force this modern Leviathan to share its power with other groups in the modern polity and economy, and to maintain a separation of power within the state apparatus itself. In that sense, pluralism has its origins in an older tradition of liberal thought. It aims at ensuring that the state is one power centre among others, and that it does not swallow up other centres of power. These other centres of power include notably the producer groups which represent the main economic interests of the modern economy. Here again, pluralism is a brand of theory which seeks to combine new and old: it tries to achieve the realisation of the liberal view by prescribing and analysing a situation in which power is distributed from a single centralised state to the producer groups and other organisations of a diversified modern political and social system.

The pluralist aim, in its normative aspects, is to achieve a situation in which there is power diffusion within the sphere of the state, but it is not limited to the state sphere. Pluralism is a theory of the state, but also a view of the wider society. It is not enough for there to be a separation of powers within the state; there has to be power dispersion in society at large through the mechanisms of group politics. Furthermore, the state in a pluralist society is seen as being responsive to the wide range of interests expressed in 'civil society'. Thus pluralism as a theory of the state in its relationship with the wider society can be summarily represented as suggesting the following points:

- The state apparatus should have several divisions, to check and control the holders of state power. This is the venerable liberal idea of the separation of powers.
- In society, there should be a range of groups and associations to represent the variety of interests in civil society.
- The state should not only be fragmented, but also be responsive to the variety of interests emanating from civil society, so that the state should be in a way the servant of society and not its master.

Finally, in terms of the various antitheses or oppositions which are characteristic of pluralist theory, we can add that of diversity versus monism. A pluralistic society is opposed to one which is monistic or unitary. Clearly pluralism, as the term suggests, values diversity. In explanatory mode, pluralist perspectives insist that modern liberal-democratic societies are ones where no single dominant ideology or world view prevails. There are conflicting ideas and interests which are articulated and hence have an impact on the holders of state power. Pluralist theory contrasts the opposition and conflict of a pluralistic society to what is seen as the false or imposed unity of a monolithic one, where only one view and set of interests are articulated. The latter model of a non-pluralist system is said to be exemplified by the former communist systems dominated by the will of the single Communist Party (or the party leadership), or fascist systems dominated by the will of the single leader (Duce, Führer or whoever) and his 'Caesaristic' party. These systems are seen in their different ways as representing a totalitarian political system, which is the polar opposite of the pluralist model. In such totalitarian systems the aspiration is not to diversity, but to total control, and the imposition of one view (ideology) on to all aspects of life and society. This is achieved through the device of the single party, the vehicle articulating what is perceived as a single truth which all in the society must accept.

By contrast, politics in the pluralistic view is seen as a process of conflict and compromise between different and in a sense equally valid interests. No interest is privileged above any other one. In this sense, pluralism echoes John Stuart Mill's praise of diversity, of the importance of different views being held and given free and open expression. Pluralism as a normative theory asserts the importance of an active, informed and educated citizen body. As an explanatory theory it asserts that in contemporary liberal-democracy a multiplicity of views do in fact make themselves felt – there is no one dominant mould of public opinion. Politics emerges from the clash or conflict between different interests and various groups, a clash and conflict openly expressed and peacefully resolved within a framework of rules maintained by the state.

There is here a fundamental problem, encapsulated in the antithesis of diversity and consensus. Pluralism, whether as normative philosophy or explanatory political science, insists on the key value of diversity and difference. Yet the differences between citizens, acting within groups, in a pluralistic society, are seen as being resolved peacefully, through acceptance of a consensus or agreement on a framework for dealing with conflict. There is here a problem of reconciling difference and agreement. There has to be some degree of consensus, some agreement on values and procedures (Bobbio's 'rules of the game'), otherwise pluralism might go too far and society split up under the pressure of diverse views. In other words, there is a need to reconcile diversity and unity, to maintain a system in which different groups can express their aims freely. In pluralist theory this consensus is achieved through three main means:

- The state as the arbiter or neutral force to regulate the competition between different groups in society.
- The idea of 'cross-cutting cleavages'. This means that there is no single and unbridgeable source of cleavage in society because people are members of many different groups, some of which overlap. The pluralist idea offers the suggestion of a multiplicity of conflicts and divisions which are not mutually exclusive. People can be members of more than one group, and the fact of multiple membership both diffuses and defuses conflict.
- An agreement on values of tolerance and compromise. The legitimate expression of different interests is seen as part of the necessary conditions for a pluralistic society to flourish.

Pluralism, then, asserts in normative mode the idea that no one group should hold a monopoly of power, so that there can be no single source of power which would lead to dictatorship. In this sense, pluralism is a version of liberalism. It seeks to realise the goal of limiting and containing the power of the state: power checks power. In the wider sphere of society, beyond the state, the term of 'countervailing power', coined by the American economist J.K. Galbraith, can be used as a way of showing how in the pluralist view one set of interests or one group will arise to challenge the power of another. The sum total of these groups can be said to constitute *civil society*, a sphere of life free from the control of the state. Pluralist theory insists on a separation of civil society from the state; this is seen as a necessary condition of a free society.

However, the pluralist view also asserts that, through the various groups, parties and associations which constitute both state and civil society, there arises the possibility of citizen participation, that chief element of democratic society. Pluralism is a theory which asserts normatively that a society should have a network of associations through which citizen participation can take place. This participation is not the direct democracy envisaged by Rousseau in his *Social Contract*. It is a form of democracy achieved through representative institutions and through groups which express the diverse interests of the population. In a complex society, it is argued, direct participation by the mass of the population is impossible. There have to be professional representatives, whether these are professional politicians or union leaders or business leaders. These all influence the exercise of power, but such representatives are held to be accountable to their followers, whether because of the competition of electoral politics, or through popular participation in the pressure groups or interest groups which form a pluralist society. In the pluralist view there should be opportunities for citizen participation in the various groups and political parties, so that the democratic aim of popular participation and involvement is realised.

Pluralism as explanatory theory: parties and pressure groups

The theoretical basis of pluralism thus involves as a central value the diffusion of power and by the same token the fear of power concentration. Power should not be held by a single group or person, since this would lead to the danger of the abuse of power, to dictatorship or despotism, and at the limit to the possible politicisation of all aspects of social life by an all-powerful state, which is precisely what is meant by the idea of totalitarianism. The dispersion of power which the pluralist view commends is seen as valuable because it realises two objectives: first, the liberal one of controlling state power; and second, the democratic one of political participation, through the groups and associations which make up civil society, and through the political parties which compete for political power.

Within the system of contemporary liberal-democracy, it is argued, there is no concentration of power either at the level of the state or at the societal level. There are a number of centres of power, and this results in a situation in which there is peaceful and relatively stable competition and conflict for power. Representative democracy is achieved through the network of political parties and interest groups which are seen as legitimate contenders for political power (parties), or for influence (pressure groups).

While pluralism in its normative form arises from the liberal perspective, with its fear of the top-heavy or all-powerful state, in its explanatory mode it originated in 'the group theory of politics' developed in American political science. The broad thrust of this analysis was to focus on the groups and parties whose competition constituted 'the governmental process', to take the title of a classic work of pluralist analysis. Pluralism focuses on groups and parties, and it offers a theory of the role of the state. The state is seen as *neutral* between the various groups, as *responsive* to the pressures emerging from society, and as maintaining a *framework* on which there is consensus, and within which the different groups can pursue their various interests.

The pluralist analysis starts from the diversity and complexity of interests in a modern society. A range of groups is seen as a sign of this complexity, the various interests finding open expression in pressure group activity. Thus the hallmarks of a pluralist society include the open activity of a variety of associations, separate from the state, and competing with each other. These groups represent different interests, such as those of employers or of workers as represented by trade unions, or various causes which attract people and which those supporters wish to see reflected in government legislation and policy. If Aristotle thought that man was a political animal, in this pluralist perspective human beings are group-forming animals, at least those who want a taste of power and influence. The individual is nothing, the group is everything: as David Truman says in one of the seminal texts of pluralism, *The Governmental Process*, 'We do not, in fact, find individuals otherwise than in groups; complete isolation in space and time is so rare as to be an almost hypothetical situation.'[7] The representation of interests in a diversified society involves group formation, the organisation of people in groups to pursue different interests, what Madison in *The Federalist Papers* called *factions*.[8] Pluralist theory obviously takes a positive view of open group activity and conflict, which is seen as a necessary part of the politics of a pluralist society.

If pressure groups are one central element in pluralism, then political parties are equally important. Gordon Smith has called political parties 'the summation of pluralist traditions'.[9] In the pluralist perspective, state power is captured through peaceful political competition. Parties are the vehicles of this competition. Just as the consumer is sovereign in the market place, so is the voter, the citizen, sovereign in the political sphere. Governments are chosen by the citizens, in free and open elections, and political parties are the instruments of this voter choice. Thus, whatever other characteristics constitute a pluralist system, it has to have two or more political parties competing for votes in free and open elections, which decide on who will be invested with governmental power. This governmental power commands, at least in theory, the state apparatus, although there is a substantial difference between taking governmental office and exercising full state power.

In the pluralist perspective, political parties are central institutions in a liberal-democratic system. Political parties put together and offer to the voters a political programme, based on a set of principles which form the ideology of the party. The voters choose between the competing parties, and that party (or parties, if a coalition is envisaged) which obtains the support of the majority of the voters is invested with governmental office and, in theory, state power. This expresses in simplified form the core importance of political parties to a pluralistic political system. In such a system, political parties have many functions. They are vehicles of public choice, since they provide the means whereby the citizens can choose between alternative political programmes. Furthermore, parties are seen as channels for the emergence of political leaders. Political parties, like pressure groups, express the different social interests of a diversified and complex society. But the obvious difference between parties and pressure groups is that parties aim to capture state power, and use that state power in the service of a broad programme of government. Pressure or interest groups, on the other hand, aim to influence the holders of state power, but do not seek to capture state power themselves.

What, then, is a political party, and why is it important for the politics of a pluralist system? The conservative philosopher Edmund Burke, writing in 1770, defined a political party in often-quoted words as 'a body of men united, for promoting by their joint endeavours the national interest, upon some particular principle in which they are all agreed'.[10] This classic view sees as necessary to a political party some broad principles of politics which the party seeks to implement when in office. Indeed Burke in this same text spoke clearly of the task of politicians as being to capture state power in order to put those ideas into practice:

> Therefore every honourable connexion will avow it as their first purpose, to pursue every just method to put the men who hold their opinions into such a condition as may enable them to carry their common plans into execution, with all the power and authority of the State. As this power is attached to certain situations, it is their duty to contend for these situations.[11]

Writing in 1957, the political philosopher Otto Kirchheimer suggested that parties in twentieth-century politics had become less concerned with such broad principles of politics, or what could be called *ideologies*. Parties in liberal-democratic societies had become more like vehicles of interest representation. As Kirchheimer wrote,

> The rise of the consumption-oriented individual of mass society thus sets the stage for the shrinking of the ideologically oriented nineteenth-century party. After the unlimited extension of the party concept, first in the traditional *Weltanschauungs* party and more recently in the totalitarian movement, its recent reduction to a rationally conceived vehicle of interest representation becomes noticeable.[12]

Kirchheimer claimed that there was a tendency 'for the party to exercise a brokerage function for specific interest groups'. The role of opposition parties related less to 'the sum total of style, philosophy, and conduct of government, but concentrates on some concrete measure where the government decision may reflect a balance of forces disadvantageous to the interests the party represents'.[13] The danger was that parties in liberal-democracy had been transformed into what were termed 'catch-all' parties, led by politicians or party leaders who appealed to as wide a range of social interests as possible in order to gain power. Such, Kirchheimer suggested, was the nature of parties in a modern and complex democratic system. They were not so much vehicles for articulating broad philosophies of politics, but rather machines for capturing political power (the brokerage function). In the pursuit of power, they had to appeal to different groups in the society. In that sense, the party competition of a democratic society could lead to a 'deradicalisation' of politics, as a contemporary social scientist, Adam Przeworski, points out with respect to parties of the Left. In order to gain power, they have to appeal for as broad support as possible:

> In order to be successful in electoral competition, social democratic parties must present themselves to different groups as an instrument for the realisation of their immediate economic interest, immediate in the sense that these interests can be realised when the party is victorious in the forthcoming election. Supra-class alliances must be based on a convergence of immediate economic interests of the working class and of other groups.[14]

If this is true, then the political party as a vehicle for offering different views of 'the good society' is less important than the party as a power-seeking apparatus or machine, linked to certain social interests and seeking to attach as many social interests to its bandwagon as possible in order to gain power. We might draw a distinction between an 'American' conception of the political party and a more 'European' one. The 'American' conception would be that the party is not so much the vehicle of broad philosophies of life, but rather that it aggregates interests, putting together a potentially winning coalition ('rainbow coalition') of groups. In this sense, the party is not so different from a pressure group: it takes interest representation one stage further by capturing, rather than merely influencing, the levers or machinery of state power. In contrast a more 'European' concept of the party would start from Burke's view of the party as a body of people united on some broad principles of government, and aiming at power in order to put those principles into effect. The pursuit of power in the conditions of electoral democracy does indeed of necessity involve responding to social interests, and taking them into account. But the task of the political party, in particular of its leaders, is to some degree to distance itself from purely sectional demands, or at least to offer a broad programme of policy that offers some idea of a common good, distinct from a mere aggregate of particular interests.

The conclusion remains that the political party is a vital element in pluralist politics. It is seen as essential to a pluralist political system because it satisfies the liberal and democratic aims which that system is supposed to achieve. Through a pluralistic political system, the rights of legitimate opposition are maintained: in other words, the party or parties which have not gained control of the state are the agents, among others, of checks and balances, of criticism and control of the holders of state power. They articulate alternative views, opposing the policies of the government in terms of an alternative philosophy of social and political life. This is an important means of realising the liberal aim of controlling the holders of state power.

Moreover, the political party is seen, along with the interest group, as centrally important in achieving democracy within a liberal-democratic society. Through the structure of parties, citizens, in particular the 'active' ones, can participate in political struggle, help shape party policy and contribute to the formation of the general will. Political parties in modern democracies are mass parties. We have to signal here the historical transformation of political parties from elite groupings in the representative assembly to mass parties with an extra-parliamentary apparatus. This development was classically sketched by Max Weber, and also by Maurice Duverger in his study *Political Parties*.[15] They both showed how political parties in democratic systems developed from rival coteries of leaders within the parliamentary assembly to large bureaucratised machines which existed outside the parliamentary context. The development of British political parties in the nineteenth century shows this path particularly clearly. With the extension of the suffrage and the need to mobilise the newly enfranchised masses, there needed to be institutions to 'get out the vote' at election times. There developed a party machine, existing outside parliament, an apparatus which was there for the purpose of mobilising the voters, and which soon extended its functions between elections, to include political education, fund-raising and discussion of political issues. Political parties provide the perfect example of the democratisation of the liberal state that was outlined above.

The social democratic parties of Europe represent perhaps the fullest flowering of this idea of the political party as an apparatus, almost a community within a broader community, fulfilling the functions of education, mobilisation and, indeed, community. Here the classic example of such a 'cradle to the grave' party was the German Social Democratic Party, the SPD.[16] This was a party which in the only partially democratic system of Imperial Germany developed a vast apparatus which functioned almost as a 'state within a state', a 'counter community', educating its members and providing for many of them a network of jobs, a career structure and an apparatus within which they could exercise power.

Many observers of this party structure drew from it the conclusion that, while the extension of the party apparatus to the extra-parliamentary sphere was an aspect of the democratisation of society, this democratisation was more apparent than real. In the eyes of Max Weber, and most notably in the theory of Robert Michels, the party apparatus gave rise to a new elite, the party bureaucracy or oligarchy. Weber drew attention to the fact that this new party elite was presided over by a leader who became 'the dictator of the electoral battlefield'.[17] Democratisation thus gave rise to a new elite, rather than changing the fact of minority domination. Here again the implications for parties of the Left were especially striking. They were staffed by people who owed their careers to the party apparatus or bureaucracy. They would thus be unlikely to risk the structure of the party in radical politics. They had, as Michels memorably observed, achieved 'their own social revolution' by rising to commanding positions in the party apparatus, and hence would not wish to engage in the politics of revolution.[18]

Thus the political party occupies a pivotal place in the pluralist perspective on liberal-democracy. The political party is meant to educate its members, mobilise them for political activity, and provide a channel and training ground for the emergence of new elites or new leadership teams. In other words, political parties are vehicles of democratic participation. They are also meant to aggregate social interests, to be the link between state and society, by connecting social interests with the state, by providing channels through which social interests can influence state power. Parties provide a connection between society and the state. Finally, they are meant not just to be agents of participation, but in addition fulfil the liberal aim of control, by checking the holders of governmental power and by offering alternative programmes and an alternative team or teams of leaders. Parties are thus essential in a democracy, they are crucial for the liberal goal of power checking, they are institutions which carry out the pluralist idea of competition through peaceful means, in accordance with the 'rules of the game', for the control of state power.

Linked with the importance of parties in the pluralist perspective is the institution of the representative assembly, or parliament. It is in that arena that parties in a pluralist liberal-democratic system do their public work, or part of it. The representative assembly is the forum in which opposition and critique of the ruling party is expressed and alternative policies are exposed. In this sense, parties carry on what has been called a 'permanent election campaign', although of course not just within the representative assembly.[19]

Liberal-democratic systems are marked by a division of labour between representatives and the people at large, those who are represented. There is a group of professional politicians, which could be called the 'political class', devoted full time to the activity of deliberation and scrutiny. As for the rest, the majority of the population, their task is the one 'that is compatible with their more limited time span: deciding between the broadest principles for policy and legislation that are embodied in competing electoral programmes, and assessing the calibre of those responsible for implementing them'.[20] It is the parties which are responsible for presenting and elaborating the competing electoral programmes, and the claim is that without a party system, a set of distinct organisations (i.e. political parties), this essential task would not get done.

However, in the conditions of modern politics, there have been doubts expressed as to whether political parties do in fact carry out the tasks attributed to them in the pluralist view sketched out here. The question is whether parties are being bypassed by other channels of representation, and whether they do in fact attract the participatory activity of more than a small minority of citizens. The danger is that political parties in the modern world have become nothing more than vehicles for the emergence of a political elite. If this were so, it would cast doubt on the democratic potential or capacity of political parties. Similarly, the problem arises of whether the competition between different parties is merely a discussion which takes place within a quite narrow confine of what is considered 'legitimate'. The spectrum of party competition in contemporary liberal-democratic systems would then not really reflect different philosophies, but be concerned only with marginally different ways of managing a system agreed on by all parties. Parties in the modern world might remain crucial institutions for a democratic system, but could decline into institutions of decreasing effectiveness as a channel for democratic activity by citizens, since citizens in modern liberal-democracy systems might not want direct involvement in party activity. Parties then would have little significance as channels for debate except for an increasingly minority force of party activists.

The pluralist theory of the state

Historically, pluralism as a normative theory arose from a protest against what was seen as monolithic and overbearing state sovereignty. The pluralist demand was for a state that shared powers with other groups in the society at large. A pluralist society would be one in which important decisions were taken by associations of citizens, acting independently of the state. The pluralist fear was of a society in which the state was the sole centre of power, and in modern times this has been seen as culminating in the nightmare of the totalitarian state. The desired goal is one of a decentralised and associative society.

Even in those forms of pluralism which take a less hostile view of the state, and recognise the state as the supreme decision maker, the pluralist view sees it as necessarily responsive to the groups and associations which constitute civil society. In normative terms, the pluralist perspective holds that within the state itself there should be a separation or division of powers, so that the state does not constitute a monolithic bloc, which can weigh down on civil society. State power must be divided.

Furthermore, state power must be responsive to pressures from the various interest groups of the wider society. The state is seen as a kind of 'pincushion', which answers to the pressures that are expressed by social groups of various kinds. In the picture presented in pluralist theory, the state is that body which takes key decisions, but its agenda is set by the demands emerging from the wider society, from the group activity which is such a central part of the pluralist perspective. Citizens mobilise and organise through parties and pressure groups. They seek a response from the state, they seek allocation of resources through policy decisions and actions to satisfy their demands. State power-holders respond, according to the strength and intensity of demands emerging from the society.

This view presents the state in a relatively passive light. The pluralist view of the state offers a normative picture of what the role of the state should be. The state is held to be at least relatively neutral, an impartial arbiter, which allocates resources and responds to pressures from social groups. This fits in well with the pluralist ambition to cut the state down to size, to prevent the emergence of a monstrous Leviathan which erodes the autonomy of civil society. Thus the pluralist perspective wishes the state to be a limited state – limited in the sense that its functions are restricted to leave civil society a 'space' of its own. The state is also seen as an internally divided state, the apparatus of which provides a structure of checks and balances to prevent power concentration, and a responsive state, in the sense that it is responsive to the variety of pressures emanating from society.

The antithesis to the pluralist state is a state that is all-powerful or unlimited, monolithic and thus lacking in any internal checks and balances or separation of powers. As a result this non-pluralist state is not responsive to its social environment, but dominates it: it moulds society, instead of reflecting its pressures, and this model of power is seen as captured by the concept of totalitarianism. Pluralists would see examples of the totalitarian state in the Stalinist system, in which the state sought and imposed the restructuring of society, seeing society and human beings as clay to be remodelled according to the wishes of those in power. Similarly, the fascist state with its wish to create a new person, the 'Fascist Man', would be seen as an antithesis to the pluralist state. The aim is for 'total control'; the means are to annihilate pluralism and diversity.

Of course, this contrast between the pluralist model of the state and the totalitarian model uses ideal types, broad antitheses to delineate two models of the state. The pluralist model of the state, which it is held is satisfied in a liberal-democratic system, is that the state is responsive to social pressures, internally divided through a separation of powers, and limited in its functions, so that civil society is autonomous of state power. The pluralist state is contrasted with its opposite ideal type, that of the totalitarian state, in which the state is non-responsive, moulding society instead of being responsive to it. Such a state is seen as monolithic and all-pervasive, presiding over a society in which everything is politicised. These are also ideal types in the sense that they could be said to be extremes of a spectrum, rather than representing two all-or-nothing alternatives. To the extent that a particular state shared the three features of being responsive to social pressures, internally divided, and limited in its functions it would move towards the 'pluralist' end of the spectrum.

There is a further element in the pluralist perspective on the state, again looking at the matter in both its normative and explanatory dimensions. One of the key problems of pluralism is the combination in society of social diversity with a degree of unity. Pluralist perspectives emphasise the dispersion of power, yet this raises the question of how, in any society, the unity of society is to be preserved. How is this diversity to be prevented from degenerating into a pathological form, into fragmentation, into a situation in which there is no representative of a common interest?

Within pluralism there is contained, at least in some of its versions, a view of the state more positive than the pincushion view sketched out above. The state is not just a passive recipient of pressures emerging from civil society. The state is invested with the function of maintaining a consensus, of keeping unity and enforcing certain rules of the game on the contenders for power and on those who wish to influence power. In a pluralist society the only interests which can be considered or responded to are those which are legitimate, which operate through recognised channels, and express what are considered as justified grievances or demands. Yet the state is responsible for the task of deciding which interests are legitimate and should be responded to, and which ignored or even suppressed. In this sense, the state is seen as a supreme judge, a neutral arbiter of the validity of the different interests which clamour for its recognition. According to this view, the state is not a pincushion; it is more proactive or judgemental, and not as passive as was suggested above.

Yet the state is not an abstraction. State power is held, in a liberal-democratic as well as in any other system, by human beings. We need to recall also that the state system has different branches or elements of its state apparatus. In a liberal-democratic system, the government is formed by one or more political parties, who have particular programmes, particular policies, in line with their ideology or theories. Of course, it is possible to suggest that political parties and those who lead them are just stimulated by the search for power on any terms whatsoever, but even to gain power a party needs to aggregate interests in some particular way, to present them in the context of a particular programme. In other words, if a particular party controls the state, or at least forms the government, then the state apparatus is not necessarily a neutral one. Some interests will be responded to more positively than others; others will be ignored. In the British case, if there were a Labour government in power, this might respond to some interests, say union interests, more favourably and positively than a Conservative government. This suggests the need to modify the view of the strict neutrality of the state.

The pluralist perspective for explaining the role of the state in contemporary liberal-democracy can offer an answer to this challenge. The fundamental problem is that the state is at one and the same time the supreme decision-making body in the society and also a site for struggle, or rather the prize in the struggle. Pluralist theory sees the state as a neutral agency, yet it is an apparatus contended for by different parties, representing different social interests and ideologies or views of politics. In this way, the state, once captured, is anything but neutral; it is a machine for enforcing particular interests. The state is supreme, functioning as the institution for judging the worthiness of particular interests and responding to them, yet at the same time state power is fought for by particular groups who want to use it for their own purposes. There is a tension here between the idea of state power as sovereign and impartial, and the concept of state power as fought for and captured by particular groups and parties. Both views seem to grasp part of the truth of the role of the state in liberal-democracy.

A pluralist response to this problem would suggest that, while the neutrality of the state is compromised to the extent that a particular group, or party, forms the government and steers state power in particular directions, this partiality of the state is contained in the contemporary liberal-democratic system by various mechanisms. First, the neutrality of the state is preserved by the fact that the state is not a single institution, a monolithic bloc. There is, in liberal-democratic states, a variety of elements within the state apparatus. These are held to check and control the powers of the ruling party. The pluralist state is a divided state.

Second, a pluralist system involves competition of parties. Ruling parties are challenged by opposition parties, and they have to justify their policies in representative assemblies. The liberal-democratic state allows the elements of opposition to challenge and up to a point to obstruct the policies of a government.

Finally, while in a liberal-democratic system the government may favour some groups more than others, and hence the pluralist state is not a totally neutral state, the pluralist argument is that, because this state is a *limited* state and not a totalitarian one, it allows 'space' in civil society for groups to press their interests, even against an unsympathetic state.

Thus the pluralist perspective sees the state in a liberal-democratic system in two ways. In one key role, the state responds to the pressures from civil society and acts as a neutral arbiter to maintain the unity and cohesion of the political system. The state is seen as representing a certain general interest or common good, which group pressure and the play of conflicting interests cannot on their own represent. However, at the same time the impartiality of the state is limited, since state power is slanted in certain directions, given the purposes of the political party (or parties) which has (or have) gained control of state power through the process of democratic elections. In other words, the state in pluralist theory is an agency of social cohesion, representing a common interest, but at the same time the state is 'steering society' in a certain direction, the direction given by the aims of the governing group (the ruling political party).

This raises a number of crucial problems about the role of the state in modern liberal-democratic systems. The pluralist view attempts to reconcile the tension between the above two roles of the state by holding that in a pluralist society the capacity of the holders of state power to 'steer' society in a particular

direction is limited both by divisions within the sphere of the state itself and
by the ability of groups within civil society to voice their interests and maintain
autonomy from state power. The state does not challenge or seek to undermine
the independence of diverse groups and centres of power outside the state
system. This is seen as the great difference between a 'totalitarian' society, or
a state form which is nearer the totalitarian end of the spectrum, and one which
approximates the pluralist aspiration to a limited state. The latter is seen as
subject to controls, which mitigate the danger of the state's partiality.

It should be clear that pluralism is a theory both of society (divided into a
range of groups and associations) and of the state. The state is seen as internally
divided and responsive; neutral yet pushing society in a certain direction.
However, the extent to which the state can undertake this regulation of social
life is limited by divisions within the state and in the sphere of civil society.
State power is contained both in the state and in the wider society by a
separation of powers in the state, and by the plurality or diffusion of powers
in society at large.

The pluralist view sees the state apparatus as a complex of different
branches, which are staffed by diverse people in different groups. Such
divisions within the state prevent its excessive power. State power is directed
by a ruling party, a group of people who have received democratic legitimation.
This is acquired through election, since power in a liberal-democratic society
is acquired through electoral competition for the people's vote. The holders of
state power thus in some sense represent the majority of the population. Their
'driving' of the state machine is supported in general terms by a popular
majority. Moreover, their hold on state power is supposedly limited by checks
and controls in the state apparatus and outside it.

Pluralism as a theory of society holds that a pluralist system is one where a
range of groups and associations represent the diverse interests of citizens, and
exert pressure on the holders of state power. Power is seen as 'non-cumulative',
which means that everyone in the system has some power base which can be
turned into a political power resource to give people influence on the state.
Unlike the Marxist view, pluralism does not see the power stemming from
ownership and control of the productive resources of society as either the sole
or necessarily the most important power base in society. There are a number
of bases of power, of which wealth and economic power are only one, and
therefore the state is not the preserve of, or at the service of, one set of social
interests.

Critical evaluation of the pluralist perspective

The problem that remains is to assess how valid the pluralist view is as a view
of the power structure of contemporary liberal-democracy. Here the best way
of proceeding is to contrast the pluralist theory of power distribution with the

three rival perspectives which will be examined at greater length in the following chapters.

The first challenge comes from the side of elite theory. Elite theory suggests that the crucial dimension of power is the division between a cohesive elite, controlling the apparatus of the state, and the apathetic mass. In this sense, then, elitism challenges pluralism in two ways. The state elite is seen as being cohesive, a relatively united 'Establishment' bloc. The divisions of power within the state are seen as secondary and inessential, since power is held by a unified political elite.

Moreover, while the pluralist view sees liberal-democracy as a system in which the people have the opportunity to participate through the network of groups and associations which proliferate in a pluralist system, the elitist challenge suggests that the structure of these groups and associations is 'oligarchic', or dominated by a minority who can set the agenda and determine policy. The elitist challenge is to question the degree of democracy, by seeking to establish that the internal structure of groups and parties of the pluralist system is oligarchic. If a pluralist system is supposed to offer opportunities for voluntary participation and citizen involvement, then surely this is limited if not totally negated by the elitist structure of the groups which are the supposed vehicles for this participation.

Second, from the side of Marxist theory comes a further set of challenges to pluralism. The first argument is that the group competition saluted by pluralist theory takes place within a 'deep structure' of economic and social power – in other words, of class power – which is not taken into account in the pluralist view. The next criticism is that the state is not a neutral body, nor is it as limited as pluralist theory suggests, since it is a set of institutions that exist to bolster the power of the ruling class and defend a system of private property.

Finally, from the side of feminist theory comes the argument that there is another 'deep structure' which is neglected by pluralism, and that is the structure of gender power. This not only affects the composition of the state elite, making it more difficult for women to gain positions of power, but also conditions the attitudes and expectations of the participants in the power struggle, and excludes certain elements from the political agenda.

The point of these various criticisms, which are evaluated in the chapters which follow, is that they suggest that the pluralist view is inadequate as a full theory of the power structure of liberal-democracy. However, pluralist perspectives do point out the surface variety of interests and organisations which characterise liberal-democratic systems, and pluralists like Dahl are certainly alive to the problem of combining the need for diversity and group autonomy with the danger that particular organisations may become too independently powerful for the health of the democracy. Some groups may use their power to maintain an inegalitarian structure of social power, and to distort the agenda of democratic politics. It may even be possible for groups to prevent certain issues coming up on the agenda of democratic politics for open debate and recognition. At the limit this power could be such that subordinate groups of people would not even realise that certain demands and interests were being excluded from the political process. This type of power has been called 'the mobilisation of bias', a hidden face of power that is not realised by at least some theorists of pluralism.[21] This points to the need to examine other theories of power which attempt to place the pluralist competition of liberal-democratic systems within a wider context of power. While a wider assessment of pluralism, and a comparison with other theories of power, is left until the concluding chapter, Chapter 4 deals with the elitist challenge to the pluralist view.

Notes

1. Dahl, R.A., *Dilemmas of Pluralist Democracy: Autonomy vs control*, Yale University Press, New Haven, CT, and London, 1982, p. 1.
2. H.S. Kariel, 'Pluralism', in *International Encyclopedia of the Social Sciences*, ed. David L. Shils, Macmillan, New York, 1968, vol. 12, p. 164.
3. Hirst, P.Q. (ed.), *The Pluralist Theory of the State: Selected writings of G.D.H. Cole, J.N. Figgis and H.J. Laski*, Routledge, London and New York, 1989, p. 3.
4. Hirst (ed.), *The Pluralist Theory of the State*, p. 3.
5. Laski, H.J., 'Law and the state', in Hirst (ed.), *The Pluralist Theory of the State*, p. 214.
6. Dahl, *Dilemmas of Pluralist Democracy*, p. 44.
7. Truman, D.B., *The Governmental Process*, Alfred A. Knopf, New York, 1958, p. 48.
8. Madison, J., Hamilton, A., and Jay, J., *The Federalist Papers*, ed. I. Kramnick, Penguin, Harmondsworth, 1987, p. 126.
9. Smith, G., *Politics in Western Europe*, Heinemann, London, 1972, p. 48.
10. Burke, E., 'Thoughts on the cause of the present discontents', in Burke, E., *Pre-Revolutionary Writings*, ed. I. Harris, Cambridge University Press, Cambridge, 1993, p. 187.
11. *Ibid.*
12. Kirchheimer, O., 'The waning of opposition in parliamentary regimes', in Dogan, M. and Rose, R. (eds), *European Politics: A reader*, Macmillan, London, 1971, p. 294.
13. Kirchheimer, 'The waning of opposition', p. 294.
14. Przeworski, A., *Capitalism and Social Democracy*, Cambridge University Press, Cambridge, 1985, p. 27. For a recent survey of social democratic parties in Europe, see *West European Politics*, vol. 16, no. 1, Jan. 1993, special issue on 'Rethinking Social Democracy in W. Europe'.
15. Weber, M., 'Politics as a vocation', in Gerth, H.H., and Mills, C.W. (eds), *From Max Weber: Essays in sociology*, Routledge & Kegan Paul, London, 1970; and Duverger, M., *Political Parties*, Methuen, London, 1954.
16. On German social democracy, see Schorske, C.E., *German Social Democracy 1905–1917: The development of the great schism*, Harvard University Press, Cambridge, MA, 1955. For a recent survey of political parties see Panebianco, A.,

Political Parties, Organization and Power, Cambridge University Press, Cambridge, 1988; and Graham, B.D., *Representation and Party Politics: A comparative perspective*, Blackwell, Oxford, 1993.
17. Weber, 'Politics as a vocation', p. 106.
18. Michels, R., *Political Parties: A sociological study of the oligarchical tendencies of modern democracy*, trans. E. and C. Paul, Dover Publications, New York, 1959, p. 305.
19. Crick, B., *The Reform of Parliament*, Weidenfeld & Nicolson, London, 1970, p. 26.
20. Beetham, D., 'The limits of democratization', in Held, D., (ed.), *Prospects for Democracy: North, South, East, West*, Polity, Cambridge, 1993, p. 63.
21. For a classic analysis of this, see Bachrach, P., and Baratz, M.S., 'Two faces of power', *American Political Science Review*, vol. 56, 1962, pp. 947–52; and discussion in Lukes, S., *Power: A radical view*, Macmillan, London, 1974.

4 | The elitist theory of politics

Introduction: the nature of elite theory

The previous chapter presented a theory, pluralism, which sought to give both an explanatory and a normative view of the power structure of the liberal-democratic state and the society in which that state form is situated. This chapter deals with a different theory of power, namely elitism. The aim is to present some aspects of the historical development of elitist thought, to analyse the main features of elitism as a theory of power, and to assess its contemporary relevance. First, however, we wish to introduce the theory by explaining in general terms what elitism is, what kind of theory it claims to be, and what kind of analysis it offers of power in the liberal-democratic and other forms of state.

Elite theory as an explicit theory of politics arose towards the end of the nineteenth century, as a challenge to the progress and claims of both democracy and socialism. The chief names associated with this attempt to debunk or unmask classical democratic theory are the Italians Vilfredo Pareto and Gaetano Mosca, and the Swiss Roberto Michels. In its broadest sense, the elitist view can be put very simply: it asserts that in all societies, past, present and future, the few will always rule the many. Elitism maintains the inevitability of minority rule, and hence its stance is to deny the possibility of popular sovereignty. Democracy can never be achieved, according to elitists. Elitism as a theory thus confronts the claims or *theory* of democracy with what, according to elitist theorists, is the *reality* of democracy, and maintains that scientific examination of the latter reveals the impracticability of the former.

Elite theory developed as an explicit challenge to the apparently irresistible progress of, and widespread belief in, democracy. Nevertheless, it should be pointed out that deep scepticism and fear of democracy have marked a wide range of the traditional classics of political theory, from Plato onwards. Indeed the modern elite theorists are sometimes referred to as the 'Machiavellians' to suggest their similarity with Machiavelli, since they are held to share a common approach to politics.

The stance of elite theory is one of realism. Elitists claim to offer a scientific and explanatory approach to problems of power, which sees through the masks or mystifications used to veil the realities of the power structure. Thus, to revert to the distinction between *explanatory* and *normative* theories used in Chapter 3, elitists claim to be exemplifying a purely scientific and explanatory approach to politics: they are concerned with what is, not with what ought to be. In the elitist perspective, the approach is one of hard-nosed realism. The social scientist is concerned to reveal the universal laws, the inevitable structure which prevails at all times and in all places. The discovery or revelation of such laws of social science, the most explicit of which is the 'iron law of oligarchy' (Michels), is held to reveal the impossibility of democracy or popular power, and the inevitable distinction between a creative elite or minority and a relatively passive mass or majority.

Elite theory thus claims to be realistic and explanatory, rather than normative. The classic elite theorists wished to prove that democracy was a sham or façade masking minority power. In their different ways, Mosca, Pareto and Michels all insisted that they were revealing certain constant features of social and above all political life which rendered democracy impossible. It might be claimed by those who exercised power in a democracy, and sincerely believed by its citizens, that power rested in the hands of the people and that the rulers were the mere servants or agents of the popular will or general will. Elite theorists were keen to show that such claims were fraudulent, whether they were sincerely held or not. The aspiration to popular power could not, they said, be realised. Examination of the unchanging realities of political life would reveal the aspiration to popular power and the wish to create a truly democratic society as what Michels called 'an undiscoverable treasure'. People might think they lived in a democracy, but they were fooling themselves.

Elite theory differs radically from pluralism, at least at first view, in the obvious sense that the elitist perspective initially and originally emphasised a single elite group, a minority (whether a minority of one person or a single quite cohesive group) which monopolises the effective exercise of power. Elite theory emphasises the single versus the many: the co-ordinated and integrated elite versus the passive, fragmented and disorganised mass. Pluralism, by contrast, is a theory of diversity and the role of the many, who organise in groups and associations to influence the power-holders and to compete for power. In contrast to the pluralist picture of dispersion and diffusion of power, and the related concept of multiple sources of power, the elitist hypothesis is one of power concentration, of a single power elite that dominates a mass which is grateful to be led. Elitism later moved into a different relationship with pluralism, and it is true that pluralism and elitism can indeed be reconciled, but we wish to start our exposition here by emphasising the opposition between elitism as a 'monist' theory, and pluralism as a theory of dispersion and diversity. Elitist theory asserts that beneath the surface appearance of democratic diversity there is a single power elite. What that

power elite is, how its power arises, and how it is exercised are the questions
that the next section seeks to answer.

The development of the elitist argument

Elite theory offers a view of all political systems as marked by one fundamental
division: that between a ruling minority and the vast majority of people, who
form the mass. The basic division in all societies is that between *elite* and *mass*.
A democratic society is not and cannot be an exception to this law, which
commands all political systems. This bold statement therefore requires
analysis. What is the nature of the ruling group? Why do elite theorists hold
that the domination of the few over the many is inevitable and irresistible?
Who forms the elite, what is their power base, and what, by contrast, is the
nature of the passive mass?

The classic statement of elite theory offered by Gaetano Mosca in his book
known in English translation as *The Ruling Class*, offers boldly the following
propositions:

> In all societies – from societies that are very meagrely developed and have barely
> attained the dawnings of civilisation, down to the most advanced or powerful
> societies – two classes of people appear – a class that rules and a class that is ruled.
> The first class, always the less numerous, performs all political functions and enjoys
> the advantages that power brings, whereas the second, always the more numerous
> class, is directed and controlled by the first, in a manner that is now more or less
> legal, now more or less arbitrary and violent, and supplies the first, in appearance
> at least, with material means of subsistence and with the instrumentalities that are
> essential to the vitality of the political organism.[1]

Elite theory thus sees the power structure of a liberal-democratic society as a
dichotomous one. At the top is a ruling group, diversely called by the various
elite theorists a governing elite (Pareto), a ruling class (Mosca) or an oligarchy
(Michels), to mention only the most common terms, which are all labels for
the same phenomenon. Underneath, ruled by this elite group in various ways,
are the mass, the non-elite, the people, directed and controlled by the creative
few. In general terms, then, we can list the features of the elite as follows:

- They are a minority: the ruling group is always 'less numerous' than the
  governed, the mass.
- They are more cohesive and organised than the non-elite, if only because
  they are a minority.
- They, the elite, possess some quality or characteristic which the mass or
  non-elite does not have, and which is relevant to and useful in the exercise
  of power. Such a quality may vary from society to society, but whatever is
  valued in the particular society, and helps in the gaining of power, the elite
  will have more of it than the non-elite. It may be military skills, intellectual

ability, organisational cohesion, skills in political manipulation and leadership, but whatever it is, the minority is more richly endowed than the majority.

The ruling elite has some feature or combination of features which form its 'power base'. There is an important point of contrast here between elite theory and Marxist theories of a 'ruling class'. While matters are made somewhat confusing by the English translation of the title of Mosca's *Elementi di Scienza Politica* as *The Ruling Class*, it should be kept in mind that the elite concept of ruling class or dominating elite is quite different from the Marxist concept of ruling class, for various reasons. The chief reason is that, in the Marxist concept, the main power base of the ruling class is its ownership and control of the means of production, stemming from the economic structure of society. Elitists see things differently: the power base of the ruling minority is seen not as its economic power, its control over the economic resources of society, but as stemming from a variety of non-economic factors, some of which have already been enumerated. We can list here the kind of factors which elitists give as the ones enabling elites to exercise their domination:

- Organisational cohesion.
- Intellectual superiority.
- Psychological characteristics: for example, a greater 'hunger' for power than members of the non-elite.
- Rhetorical skill or ability to manipulate 'the crowd'.
- In general, possession of the skills and capacities necessary for political success: for example, organisational ability and the capacity to influence and manipulate people.

In this context, two related ideas can be put forward as characteristic of the elitist stance. One is the stress on what Bottomore in his survey of elitist thought calls 'the inequality of human endowment'.[2] We saw in Chapter 1 that one of the core values of democratic thought was the insistence on equality, the idea that whatever differences there might be between individuals, these did not invalidate their equal entitlement to participate in politics and control their lives. The elitist position stresses the different capacities of individuals, and insists that in every field of human activity, including politics, some will be more skilled than others. The classic exemplification of this is Pareto's argument that in each kind of human pursuit there will be a minority of individuals who are particularly successful and competent. Pareto claimed this to be a neutral and scientific judgement, and argued that people could be given marks on a scale depending on their capacity in the relevant activity. Those who excel in that activity get the maximum mark of 10, and form the elite. Those who are thoroughly incompetent in that aspect of human affairs get a correspondingly low grade.[3]

In politics, as in any other activity, there will be an elite, who show particular ability in the skills and capacities needed to gain and hold on to political power, the ones listed above. This group of people forms the *governing elite*, the class of people whose capacities and inclinations make them particularly fitted for the exercise of political power. In any political system, whatever may be the justification for their position, the political class will have a grip on power. This elite group is to be distinguished from the *non-governing elite*, the minority or minorities of those who excel in other 'non-political' dimensions of life. The overall argument remains the same: human beings are not equal, some will have greater capacities than others, and in the political field this results in the separation between the political or governing elite, who want to exercise power and have the capacities which equip them for that task, and the mass, who lack both the will and the capacity for political leadership. Two questions follow from this assertion of the inequality of human endowment and the separation of mass and elite:

- The formation of the elite: how is the elite formed and how is its composition determined? The crucial idea here is Pareto's *circulation of elites*, which is examined below.
- The way in which the elite rules the mass, the different blend of force and consent which marks the relationship between elite and mass: how exactly does this creative minority, the governing elite, maintain its rule over the reactive and relatively passive mass? Elite theorists give widely different answers to this question.

The political skill of an elite group, its possession of a quality valued in the society of which it is part, its cohesion, its ability to manipulate the mass, its control of organisational factors: these are the kinds of quality which in elite theory give the minority group its dominating force. The elite hypothesis is that all societies contain a group – the ruling elite – that is small (a minority); possesses some distinctive qualities which the majority do not have; is powerful; and is able to keep its control over the non-elite or mass. Elitist arguments maintain that this elite–mass distinction prevails in all societies, and that this universal law admits of no exceptions. So where does this leave a democratic society which, as we have seen in Chapter 2, proclaims the ideal of 'people power' or popular sovereignty and aspires to realise that goal in its power structure?

For elite theorists, there can be only one answer to this question: democracy is a façade or a sham. It is a means by which the elite group seek to hide from the masses, and maybe from themselves as well, the reality of minority rule. Democracy is something unattainable, and functions as what Mosca called a 'political formula': a justification or rationalisation that serves to mask the true facts of the situation, namely the rule of the elite.

Elitism and democracy

Before explaining in more detail the analysis given by the classic elitist thinkers, Pareto, Mosca and Michels, we can present in broad outline the essence of the elitist critique of democracy. In the elite perspective, the emergence of a political leadership group is inevitable. It is inevitable because of the inescapable differences in human capacities: an elite group will emerge with the capacity and skills to exercise leadership and hold on to power. The obvious corollary of this view is that democracy is impossible, if democracy is held to be a system in which the mass of the people rule or share in ruling, a system in which popular sovereignty is to a large degree realised. For elitist thinkers, social reality as discovered by a realistic social science disproves such aspirations. The gap between elite and mass is a constant fact of all social and political formations. Elite theory claims to be realistic and scientific, describing the inescapable realities of power which prevail everywhere, inevitably. Popular sovereignty is seen as a myth, a fiction which serves only to mask the realities of power. As Pareto put it, 'we need not linger on the fiction of popular representation – fine words butter no parsnips', implying that the elite did not in any meaningful sense represent the people, nor could they ever do so.[4]

What, then, is the elitist stance with respect to democracy, and also to socialism, which the elitists saw in certain respects as the natural offspring of democracy? Democracy can never be realised, because of the inevitable emergence of a ruling elite. Instead of the flow of power going up from bottom to top, from people to rulers, the realistic social scientist observes it going from top to bottom, as the controlling elite are able to control the agenda of politics and take the initiative in decisions. In any large-scale society, democracy will be a practical impossibility: there has to be some controlling group, however this might be disguised by affirmations of popular power and the rule of the people.

By the same token, elitism at least in its classical manifestations can be seen as a critique of pluralism and the 'group theory' of politics. If pluralism with its emphasis on associations points out the group structure of politics and the opportunities that this affords for citizen participation and involvement, elitist theorists are keen to identify the barriers to participation within these organisations. This is most clearly shown in Michels' 'iron law of oligarchy', in which he sought to establish the elitist structure of the organisations such as parties and trade unions which are the hallmark of a pluralist society. Elite theory suggests that within each of these organisations an elite emerges, and thus the group structure of society does not and cannot lead to the participatory democracy which pluralist theory claims.

In sum, the elite theory suggests the following picture of the power structure of society, and this is held to apply to all societies, whether liberal-democratic, socialist or avowedly autocratic. We can use here Pareto's idea of the social

pyramid, a triangle with a narrow peak, the elite, broadening out to a wide
base, the mass. This is the shape of the power structure of any society. At the
top of this pyramid is the elite, or political class, or oligarchy. We can say that
in contemporary liberal-democratic societies this minority or political class
would include the top parliamentarians, the leading civil servants, high sections
of the military and the senior judiciary. These all form what could be called
the state elite or, more popularly, the Establishment of 'the great and the
good'.

To what extent this elite group acts as a unified bloc is an issue which needs
more discussion. It raises the question: 'one elite or several?' Some versions
of elite theory are compatible with pluralism, emphasising the competition
between different parts of the elite in the state sector, or indeed between
different elite groups throughout society. However, for the moment we can
remain with the idea of what the American sociologist C. Wright Mills called
the *power elite*, a minority of people occupying top positions in the state
apparatus and outside it, linked by a common consciousness of their shared
interests and power positions.[5] Some sections of this power elite may be
elected; others, like top civil servants and military leaders, elude popular
control and election, gaining their positions through appointment and co-
optation. Even when members of the power elite are elected, however, they
can still creatively influence and manipulate the popular will. Wright Mills, it
should be noted, broadened his concept of the power elite beyond the political
class narrowly defined, to include business leaders and top military com-
manders. His concept involves a trinity of political leaders, top military
personnel and leaders of large corporations: in other words, a minority group
of exceedingly powerful people whom Mills saw as united by a common
consciousness of their shared interests and power.[6] Mills pointed to the
interchange of personnel between the different branches of the power elite,
and to the common interest between those who controlled the large
organisations of society, political, economic and military.

Thus the myth of democracy, democracy as a political formula, is seen as
undermined by the realities of the power structure of the pyramid, with a
cohesive and powerful elite secure in its position over the passive majority.
This is a picture of liberal-democracy obviously at odds both with the
normative aspiration to popular power (the democratic view) and the pluralist
picture of democracy as achieved through group competition and pressure
group activity. Democracy is seen as an impossibility.

Elite and mass: the classical perspective

The picture thus emerges of the inevitability of a powerful controlling group,
the political elite, which holds effective power. How did the three classical
elitist theorists, Pareto, Mosca, and Michels, argue for the inevitability of such

a group? And how applicable are their arguments to contemporary reality?
Three issues are raised here:

- The core concepts of classical elite theory.
- Their acceptability on theoretical and empirical grounds.
- Later developments of elite theory, and the relationship of elitism and
  pluralism.

Pareto has been seen as one of the founders of classical elite theory, on the
basis of his vast *Trattato di Sociologia Generale* and his other studies, notably
his criticism of socialism in *Les Systèmes Socialistes*. We can take from his
voluminous writings the key concept of 'the circulation of elites' as crucial to
understanding the concepts of elite and mass, and the relationship between the
two. For Pareto, the shape of society's power structure was inevitably a social
pyramid, with the small elite at the top and the mass at the bottom. The crucial
point in his analysis is the relationship between elite and non-elite. We have
seen that he distinguished between a governing elite and a non-governing elite,
the former being those who possessed the characteristics necessary for success
in political leadership. However, what of the relationship between governing
elite and the mass? This is what the concept of the circulation of elites was
designed to explain.

For Pareto, the ideal relationship between elite and mass was that the elite
was open and receptive to new talent from below. An open elite maximised
its chances of survival by casting out incompetent members and absorbing
skilled members of the non-elite. An added advantage was that in this way
discontent from the non-elite would be averted: the chances of a revolution
were reduced by creaming off the talented potential leaders of the rank and file.

However, Pareto's analysis, drawn from somewhat sweeping generalisations
across all of history, revealed that elites did not usually behave like this. They
rather tended to seal themselves off from the non-elite, preferring to favour
their own descendants and relatives. Thus the inevitable course of history was
for elites to decay, to lose the qualities which enabled them to stay in power,
and hence in the long run to be overthrown by a new and vigorous counter-elite,
hitherto excluded from power. In *Les Systèmes Socialistes*, Pareto explained
this in terms of elite 'A' being opposed and finally overthrown by elite 'B'.

For elite theory in general, the power base of the elite is seen in non-
economic terms, with a variety of factors deployed to explain the predomi-
nance of the elite. For Pareto, the governing elite was distinguished from the
mass by its possession of certain psychological qualities. A stable elite group
would possess what he termed the right balance of 'lions' and 'foxes'. The
'lions' were those willing to use force to defend their power, and the 'foxes'
were those who were skilled in guile and the manipulation of the people: in
short in those qualities needed for success in a democratic system.

However, for Pareto, the likelihood was of the elites degenerating or
decaying, and losing their vigour. The consequence would be revolution, but

in the elitist concept revolution cannot do away with the distinction between elite and mass. Pareto insisted that the consequence of past revolutions in history would apply to any possible future socialist or communist revolution. Revolution would only result in a change in the composition and nature of the elite, but would not do away with the basic distinction between a creative elite and the passive mass. The masses might rally to the standard or banner of the counter-elite under the false impression that their lot would improve when the new elite came to power. The counter-elite would encourage them in this illusion in order to get mass support, but once the revolution had been achieved a new elite would be in power, and the masses would remain as they always were, passive and controlled.

Thus Pareto's concept of history is a cyclical one – also, one could add, a cynical one. As he put it, 'history is a graveyard of aristocracies' and reveals nothing but the eternal circulation of elite decay and renewal.[7] This renewal could be accomplished through an 'open elite' replenishing its ranks from the non-elite, or the eventual wholesale replacement of a feeble elite by a new counter-elite. Thus, on this analysis, the Bolshevik Revolution of October 1917 was a manifestation of the circulation of elites. The slogans might be ones of socialism and workers' power, but the reality was one of minority rule. Similarly, the democratic language and claims of the French Revolution of 1789 were for Pareto purely rhetorical means by which a dynamic new elite mobilised the people against the old order, only to fasten the yoke of the new elite on to the passive masses.

Thus elite theory insists on the inevitable passivity and incompetence of the mass. Talented members of the non-elite may rise into the elite, either through peaceful means or through the total replacement of the old elite through social upheaval and revolution, but the fundamental line or division remains between elite and mass. A controlling minority group remains in power.

We can illustrate this basic feature of the elite–mass division by taking similar arguments from Mosca and Michels. For Mosca, the dominance of the elite was due less to the psychological factors which Pareto singled out, but more to the organisational cohesion of the minority, the political class. In his book *Elementi di Scienza Politica* (*The Ruling Class*), Mosca focuses on two features:

- Organisational cohesion.
- The possession of some quality esteemed in that particular society.

Possession of both these factors determines the nature and power of the elite. Whether it is military skill in a warrior society, or political manipulative ability in a democratic society, the elite have more of that esteemed quality than the non-elite. In addition their ability to work together and be cohesive seals their dominance over the masses. Here again, for Mosca the mass is presented as passive and apathetic.

We can draw from Mosca's theory three core ideas: the idea of the political class (what Pareto called the governing elite); the idea of its organisational

miserable — przykry, żałosny, nędzny

cohesion and possession of particular qualities; and Mosca's fear of socialism related to his theory of the liberal-democratic state. Mosca believed that, in any society, effective power would be held by a ruling class, which he labelled the political class. This class was organised and cohesive, and its domination was hence irresistible. In addition, the power base of the elite was given by its superiority in some crucial respect, in a quality valued in that society.

What did this mean for a liberal-democratic society? In examining Mosca's thought we need to separate out his analysis and fear of *democracy* from his qualified approval of *liberalism*. Classical elite theory claims to be scientific. Mosca was offering what he thought of as a universal law of the impossibility of democracy. Yet this did not prevent him from issuing statements of a more normative nature, to the effect that an erroneous belief in democratic principles and an attempt to put them into practice would lead to harmful consequences, namely to socialism. He saw his task as revealing the iron necessities of political science. To the extent that people would accept and understand these necessities, the spread of democratic illusions would be halted. He saw socialism as a necessary consequence of such illusions.

Why did Mosca believe that socialism was a logical extension of democracy? Because the belief in popular sovereignty, giving power to the people, he thought, would entail satisfying their economic and social wishes as well as their political ones. It should be noted that this was not an argument peculiar to Mosca. It was a common assumption, both of those who welcomed the coming of democracy and of those who feared it. Democracy or popular rule was seen as entailing socialism. Demands for political equality were seen to give rise by the same token to pressures for social and economic equality. The linkage between the two was common currency among nineteenth-century liberals, socialists and conservatives. As noted in Chapter 1, it was the liberal thinker Alexis de Tocqueville who proclaimed that 'when the people is sovereign, it is rarely miserable', contrasting with Engels who exulted in 1845 that 'democracy, nowadays that is communism'. From the ranks of the conservatives, the Duke of Wellington warned that 'a democracy has never been established in any part of the world that has not immediately declared war against property'.[8]

It was the intellectual classes, Mosca believed, who were especially prone to believe in the illusions of democracy, and hence of socialism. Political democracy would turn into social democracy. It was the task of the social scientist to reveal what Mosca called 'the great constant laws' which rendered both democracy and socialism impossible illusions. As Mosca put it,

> In the world in which we are living, socialism will be arrested only if a realistic political science succeeds in demolishing the metaphysical and optimistic methods that prevail at present in social studies – in other words, only if discovery and demonstration of the great constant laws that manifest themselves in all human societies succeed in making visible to the eye the impossibility of realising the democratic ideal. On this condition, and on this condition alone, will the intellectual

classes escape the influence of social democracy and form an invincible barrier to its triumph.[9]

His appeal was thus addressed primarily to the intellectual elite, who could be convinced, Mosca thought, of the impossibility of democracy and hence of socialism. If nonetheless they fell prey to the illusions of democracy, or of its logical extension, social democracy, this would not and could not do away with the inevitability of elite rule. Indeed, socialism would bring about a fusion of political power and economic power to create a more powerful elite than any previously known.

The elitist project or argument was not entirely 'innocent': that is, it was not as neutral and objective as it claimed to be. In particular, the classical elite theorists were animated by a fear of socialism, even though they constantly proclaimed its scientific impossibility. They argued that 'the great constant laws' of political science proved that a society based on the rule of the people could never be achieved. Hence the socialist idea of a 'dictatorship of the proletariat' was an illusion, a Utopian dream, certainly if that dictatorship was envisaged along the participatory and decentralised lines which Marx celebrated in his text on the Paris Commune of 1871, *The Civil War in France* (see Chapter 5). There, Marx highlighted the Paris Commune's practice of recall and revocability of officials, which he saw as leading to a situation of popular power. Elite theory denied such a possibility. In the famous words of Max Weber, a socialist society would come to exemplify the dictatorship of the official, not of the proletariat.[10] Mosca, for his part, warned that

> if, then, all the instruments of production pass into the hands of the government, the officials who control and apportion production become the arbiters of the fortunes and welfare of all, and we get a more powerful oligarchy, a more all-embracing 'racket', than has ever been seen in a society of advanced civilisation.[11]

Socialism would reinforce elite power, rather than do away with it, because there would be one elite, rather than separate hierarchies in the spheres of economy and polity. Socialism would fuse these two elites into one, and thus enhance elite power over the mass. As Max Weber wrote, the two hierarchies, which were separate in a capitalist society, would be joined up in one all-powerful elite in a collectivist society.[12] Fear of collectivism was thus an important theme in the analysis of classical elite theory. The elitists announced the impossibility of socialism in any genuine form, yet feared the attempt to bring it about.

In the light of the reality of Soviet-type socialism, there are those who think that the elitist analysis has been all too clearly justified by the power structure of such systems. There, it could be argued, was realised the classic example of an all-powerful bureaucratic elite which disposed of economic power as well as political power, fusing both in a single political and economic ruling group. This would be, according to elite theory, the inevitable consequence of two 'laws' enunciated by that theory: first, the law of the circulation of elites, that a revolution cannot do away with elite rule as such, but instead merely changes the composition and nature of the elite (substitutes the Bs for the As, as Pareto put it); and second, that a socialist revolution intensifies elite power by its fusion of the hierarchies of economy and polity, separated as they are in a capitalist system.

The argument here revolves around the *inevitability* of such an outcome of socialist revolution. Elite theory announces such a situation as unavoidable. With respect to Soviet-style socialism, however, the question may be asked: to what extent did the rule of a Bolshevik or Communist elite emerge as a result of specific historical circumstances and a particular model of the revolutionary party, i.e. more contingent factors, rather than as a result of certain 'iron laws' valid at all times and in all places? This raises the key question of elite theory, its insistence on the unalterable determinacy of the theses which it enunciates. One may pose here a few counterfactual questions, to suggest alternative possibilities. What if human beings consciously take action to avoid the tendencies towards oligarchy or elitism? What if a socialist revolution had taken place in circumstances more auspicious to the socialist democracy envisaged in *The Civil War in France*? Would the outcome then have been no different? We shall return to these questions in our final assessment of elite theory.

The implications of Mosca's analysis for the study of the modern state can be summarised as follows. For him, there will always be a minority group which runs the state. Like Max Weber, he implied that much depends on the nature and character of this ruling group for understanding politics and the form of state. Weber suggested that the health or success of a particular political system depended to a large extent on the skills and capacities of the ruling group or political elite. The question was whether they were willing to take responsibility for political decisions, and accept their accountability to the people at elections, rather than shuffling off responsibility on to others, which was the behaviour appropriate to civil servants. Weber's antithesis between the politician and the civil servant is relevant in this connection. Weber argued that the behaviour expected from each was different. The civil servant had to follow policies decided on by democratically elected politicians and execute them dispassionately. The administrator acted in a hierarchy, at each level being responsible to his or her superior. The task of the politician, by contrast, was to propose and defend policies, to take responsibility for them, and to invite the electorate's judgement on the policies and on the politicians or leaders who proposed them. A healthy political system existed where there were politicians who had the qualities required for political leadership. Weber's fear was that, in the conditions of Imperial Germany before the First World War, the weakness of parliament contributed to the low level of political ability in the political system. He was concerned that there was no suitable training ground in the representative body to prepare leaders who were not afraid of defending policies, putting them to the masses, and taking responsibility for their success or failure.[13]

From our examination of elite theory so far, then, we can deduce the following conclusions. If elite theory is correct in its general line of analysis, in any society there will be a political class, separated from the mass, and this political class is in charge of that society's political affairs. Mosca suggests that this political class is broader than the government narrowly defined – it would include all those engaged in an active way in the exercise of power. Thus beyond the government it would include parliamentarians, at least the senior and more established ones, and bureaucratic, judicial and military elites: all those who form the state elite. This elite is not necessarily homogeneous, although Mosca did rather talk or write of it as a single group, animated by one will. There can be different sections of the political elite, competing for power. Elite theory here, as we shall see, can be reconciled with a form of pluralism.

What, then, is the role of the masses? Towards the end of his life, Mosca came to take a more favourable view of liberal-democracy. He thought that the elites in such a system could and should be responsible to pressure from below, that they would respond to the people, but that democracy was not possible in the stronger sense of the initiative flowing up from the people, from the masses. In a democratic system, as indeed in any other, it was still the ruling minority who controlled the system. In Mosca's words, 'what happens in other forms of government, that an organised minority imposes its will on the disorganised majority, happens also, and to perfection, whatever the appearance to the contrary, under the representative system'.[14] Nevertheless the organised minority might to some degree be responsive to the masses, and indeed this was the virtue or the superiority of the representative system of parliamentary democracy. Mosca wrote that the representative system could certainly not realise the rule of the popular majority, since that was impossible. However, as he put it in 1925,

> Although the representative system is not, as the official dogma has it, the rule of the popular majority, yet of all types of government it is the one in which the rulers on the whole will be affected by the sentiments of the majority, the one which furnishes the best means of judging and debating governmental acts. In other words, it is a rule of freedom, to the extent to which that term can still have real meaning in our time of super-states with their immensely complicated structures.[15]

Mosca thus saw that system as in a sense the best that one could hope for, and superior to a system of totally concentrated elite power, which he saw as the inevitable consequence of a socialist system.

We turn now to the third elitist theorist, Robert Michels, who enunciated the famous and grandly named 'iron law of oligarchy'. Michels' study *Political Parties* was first published in 1911. It was a case study of a particular political party, the German Social Democratic Party, before the First World War. On the basis of that study, he arrived at certain important conclusions, concerning the impossibility of democracy and, by implication, the necessary failure of

gulf — prepaid

socialism. Socialist revolution, he implied, would prove unattainable because of the emergence of an elite or oligarchy in the ranks of the mass socialist party. Thus from his empirical study of one political formation, the SPD, Michels drew far-reaching conclusions indeed. His stance, at least in *Political Parties*, was that of a disillusioned socialist, although as with all the elite theorists he also took the tone of the scientific and detached observer, concerned to tear away the masks of democracy and reveal the inevitable structure of elite power underneath.

The German Social Democratic Party was a mass working-class party committed to introducing socialism through democratic means into the authoritarian and hierarchical society of Imperial Germany in the period before the First World War. Yet, Michels argued, this party in its actual practice manifested characteristics at odds with its proclaimed goals. In this party of democratic socialism, where the leaders were supposed to be servants of the mass movement, representatives accountable to the sovereign party members, the opposite was the case. Michels exposed the continuing power of the leaders, stemming from their longevity in leadership positions. The stability of the leadership and the lack of challenges to their position, based on the veneration of the masses for their leaders, led to a growing gulf between leaders and led, representatives and represented, which counteracted the democratic and socialist principles which the party proclaimed. Thus Michels' investigation of this particular organisation revealed what he thought to be a general law, valid everywhere, for all organisations: here was the famous iron law of oligarchy, stating that 'Who says organisation says oligarchy.' His study claimed to show the inevitable domination of representatives over represented: in short, the impossibility of democracy or the realisation of the goal of popular sovereignty.

The implications of Michels' so-called law are far reaching indeed. His starting assumption was that democracy was impossible without organisation. To bring the masses into politics, which surely was the aim of democracy, involved the necessity of organisation, and of associations such as political parties. Yet if organisation resulted in a hierarchy, in a structure in which the people (or party members in this case) were inevitably subordinate to and dominated by the leaders, then organisation, that prerequisite for democracy, at one and the same time rendered democracy impossible. The means necessary for democracy were also factors blocking its achievement. Organisations like political parties involve representation, yet representation inevitably means oligarchy, the domination of the representatives over the represented. Hence elitism or the rule of the few arises out of the very mechanisms which are supposed to make democracy work.

We should emphasise that Michels saw his conclusions as valid for all times, for all places and for all large-scale organisations, and this led him to the conclusion that democracy was an impossibility. If democracy could not be achieved in the 'sub-systems' or organisations which were part of a democratic society, such as parties and pressure groups, then democracy in the society as a whole was likewise impossible. Michels was also insistent on the incompetence and passivity of the mass, in the classic elitist style. On this subject, the pages of *Political Parties* resound with clear and repeated statements: Michels wrote of 'the political immaturity of the mass', 'the organic weakness of the mass', 'the need which the mass feels for guidance' and 'the apathy of the masses and their need for guidance', and he concluded that 'The incompetence of the masses is almost universal throughout the domains of political life, and this constitutes the most solid foundation of the power of the leaders.'[16] This left no room for doubt that the rank and file was incapable of assuming the role of sovereign, and could not rise to the task which democratic theory, following on from Rousseau, assigns to it as the supreme body.

Of course, we need to establish *why* Michels was so convinced of the incompetence of the masses, and why he saw the experience of the German SPD as confirming this view. Democracy was seen by Michels as an impossibility for three reasons, which can be labelled as *technical, psychological* and *intellectual*. The technical reasons are rather practical. Michels argued that any large organisation requires representation. Direct democracy, permanent participation by the rank and file or by the people at large was impracticable and impossible. Representation is a matter of the economy of time – not all the people can participate all the time. Yet for Michels, such necessary representation opens up a gulf between those who are the representatives and those who are the followers, the led, the represented. The reasons for this development are partly psychological. In line with his low opinion of the mass, Michels emphasised the willingness of the mass to be led, their feeling of veneration for their leaders. Most people, it is implied, cannot be bothered about politics – or, in the case at hand, feel indifferent to the management and great policy decisions of the party. They are grateful to the leaders for taking the responsibility which they, the mass, feel neither the interest nor the willingness to accept. Thus the psychological dispositions of the mass, inherent in the non-elite, widen the gap between mass and elite.

Finally, the intellectual differences between mass and elite become a source of differentiation. Michels did not think that there was an inherent intellectual distinction between the oligarchy and the non-elite or mass. He did not argue that the former were innately more intelligent. But the analysis of *Political Parties* suggests how the leaders benefited from their positions in that they developed a wider range of skills than the rank and file of the party could ever hope to master. Nothing succeeds like success in the sense that those who had leadership positions developed knowledge and mental capacities which served only to deepen their separation from the 'ordinary' party members, who turned up for party meetings exhausted after a day's toil, and who did not have the energy or capacity to challenge the leaders. All these factors served to distinguish the leaders from the led.

The implications of Michels' 'iron law of oligarchy' are plain enough.

Democracy he described as an undiscoverable treasure: people might aspire to it, but the wish for democracy could never override the iron determinism of the laws of political science. By the same token, socialism too was doomed to failure, if Michels was right. He had started his political career as a syndicalist, and his book suggests a certain disillusionment with parliamentary socialism, which was later to carry him into the fascist camp. Michels ended his days as a supporter of Mussolini, and in 1928 he accepted a professorship in the fascist faculty of political science in Perugia, which he held until his death in 1936.[17] We should note that his analysis led to an idea of the inevitable 'deradicalisation' of socialism. He showed how the leadership of the socialist party distanced themselves from those whom they represented, and the logic of organisation predisposed them against any form of revolutionary politics. The elite group or oligarchy had achieved their leadership positions through the organisation of the party. Therefore they would be reluctant to risk the structure and survival of the organisation in forms of radical or revolutionary politics. Moreover, their whole attention was concentrated on the day-to-day tasks of maintaining the organisation. A process of displacement occurred, so that the means became the end: the organisational means loomed so large that they became an end in themselves. Tasks of organisational 'system mainten-ance' became overriding preoccupations, and any thought of social revolution was pushed aside. The professional oligarchy became a conservative force, not concerned any more with the politics of radical social transformation. In Michels' pithy words, 'What interest has now for them the dogma of the social revolution? Their own revolution has been effected.'[18] The working-class leaders or leaders of working-class organisations had become specialised professionals, having attained their positions through working their way up in the organisation. They were distinguished, and saw themselves as separate, from the rank and file: 'The proletarian leader has ceased to be a manual worker not only in the material sense, but psychologically and economically as well.'[19]

Michels' theory has come in for considerable discussion. Much criticism has focused on the wide-ranging conclusions he drew from one particular case study, the German SPD, and the confidence which he manifested in the 'iron' quality of the law which he asserted. It might be argued that his theory is much too deterministic and that he is unwilling to consider any counter-examples. One contemporary political scientist, A.H. Birch, argues that Michels' reputation is overrated, and suggests that 'the famous "iron law of oligarchy" that Michels produced is therefore much less significant than most of his admirers have claimed'.[20] Birch suggests that Michels makes sweeping generalisations on the basis of one particular case study, and that therefore such a generalisation 'can only have the status of a hypothesis to be tested in other cases, not the status of a law'. His further criticism is that Michels wrote as a disillusioned socialist, criticising the leaders of socialist parties for moderating initially radical socialist policies. Yet, says Birch, there is nothing necessarily undemocratic about this; indeed, Birch's criticism is that Michels was writing 'not as a supporter of democratic procedures concerned about the impact of bureaucratic organisation on them, but as a supporter of radical socialism concerned to point out that participation in the parliamentary process is likely to lead socialist leaders to moderate their policy commitments'. Birch notes that this moderation has been seen by some as a virtue, and that Michels is condemning what is an inevitable and possibly welcome feature of democratic politics. Nor has Michels, on this argument, established what he thought he had proved, the impossibility of democracy. In Birch's words,

> Democracy is a system in which rival parties compete for the support of the electorate. If the parties themselves are only partially democratic in their internal organisation, that may be a pity, but the system as a whole remains democratic so long as the choice between parties rests with the majority of adult citizens.[21]

This rather critical view of Michels suggests, first, that he generalised too much from one case, positing as a law what was really only a hypothesis to be tested in a variety of cases. Second, the critique is that the proof of oligarchy in a particular organisation, such as the SPD, would not establish the conclusion of the impossibility of democracy, because the conditions for democracy are to be found in the existence of a plurality of organisations. As long as there is the choice between different parties, a choice made by the electorate, then organisation may mean oligarchy, but oligarchy does not rule out democracy. Democracy is a choice between different elites, or oligarchies. As another political scientist, Giovanni Sartori, suggests, democracy stems from a dynamic between organisations, and is not made impossible by their oligarchic internal structure.[22] Finally, the suggestion is made by Birch that while Michels himself might have regretted the abandonment of revolutionary socialism by party leaders, their reformism might have been democratic in the sense that it responded to the wishes of party members and the electorate as a whole, rather than defying them, as the elitist hypothesis would require.

We can at this point sum up certain basic theses of elite theory. They will be evaluated in the final section of this chapter.

- In any political system, there is a minority which forms a political elite, or political class. Its nature and capacities are of crucial importance to the whole political system. This minority group holds effective power.

- As for the non-elite, they may not be totally without power. In a representative system, for example, their wishes may to some extent be taken account of by the political elite group or groups, and indeed a stable political system will be one where elite groups do precisely that, if only for their own self-interest and preservation. Nevertheless, the masses are 'out of it', spectators rather than players in the political game. The initiative flows from top to bottom, even if those at the bottom to some degree, at least in a representative system, have their wishes responded to.

- A socialist system only fuses elites which in a capitalist system are kept separate. It therefore could not achieve the goal of popular power or proletarian rule – those aims proclaimed by socialists and revolutionaries. It would furthermore establish more concentrated and oppressive elite power.

However, before coming to our final evaluation of the elite theory, we must consider attempts to combine elitism with democracy, and elitism with pluralism: the two go together in the so-called theory of democratic elitism.

The theory of democratic elitism

This section deals with the attempt to suggest the compatibility of elitism and democracy, the so-called theory of competitive democracy, as sketched out in the enormously influential argument of Joseph Schumpeter in *Capitalism, Socialism and Democracy*.

The thrust of elite theory was to deny the possibility of democracy by insisting on the inevitability of minority power. We can take from Birch again the convincing argument that while it might be a 'truism' to say that 'the rulers in a political system are few in number', this is not necessarily incompatible with democracy. 'Statements about the size of the office-holding group', Birch notes, 'tell us nothing about who they are, how they are appointed, or the relationship of the decisions they take to the views and interests of the rest of the community.'[23]

What has been called the 'theory of democratic elitism' or the idea of competitive democracy seeks rather to reconcile the discovery of elites with the reality of democracy. It is claimed that the existence of elites, the elitist hypothesis, is not incompatible with the working of a democratic society.

This theory of democracy and of the liberal-democratic state suggests that modern democracies, in large and complex societies, cannot work through the personal participation of all the citizens. There has to be representation, to achieve an economy of time and because interest in public affairs is not intense enough on the part of the whole population to meet demanding criteria of constant involvement. On this score the arguments of the elitists are accepted, to the effect that minorities are influential in the formulation of policy, and that the mass is relatively passive and uninterested in political affairs. The theory of competitive democracy accepts the existence of elites, but denies that this makes democracy impossible. The criteria of democracy must be made less demanding than the so-called 'classical theory', stemming from Rousseau, of direct citizen involvement and autonomy. A democratic society has only to meet the following two necessary and sufficient conditions. First, there must be several elite groups, or oligarchies, competing for power. In other words, as long as there is no one single oligarchical group, the anti-democratic implications suggested by the classical elite theorists do not hold. Second, not only must there be several elite groups competing for power, but it is the role of the people to choose between these groups at elections, to decide which particular group is vested with power.

Thus even if Michels' iron law of oligarchy is accepted as valid, or, to take an alternative version, Pareto's theory of the social pyramid is seen to be true, the crucial thing is that there are different 'peaks' or different pyramids, various oligarchies arising out of a plurality of organisations. In a democratic society, the people may not be the totally sovereign and rational body, but they are sovereign in the more limited sense that they have the deciding say as to which party (or parties, if there is a coalition) will be given power. In Birch's formula, worth repeating because it is succinct, 'Democracy is a system in which rival parties compete for the support of the electorate.'[24] Should these rival parties have the oligarchical structure described by Michels, this does not rule out democracy. This is because the elite groups have to respond to the will of the people in broad terms if they wish to gain or maintain power, and the electorate as a whole decides which elite group wins out in the struggle for power. Thus Sartori's idea is that democracy resides in the dynamic *between* organisations, rather than in the dynamic *within* them.[25]

The original version of this theory stems from the highly influential chapters on democracy contained in Schumpeter's book of 1943, *Capitalism, Socialism and Democracy*.[26] Schumpeter's claim was that this approach is a realistic theory of democracy, one which recognises the creative role of leaders and the passive role of the mass. He distinguished his theory from what he called the 'classical theory', creating, we may say, rather a 'straw man' against which to describe better his own theory. The classical theory, as he defines it, suggests a single will of the people, which the rulers or representatives, chosen by the people, put into effect. Schumpeter has an easy task in debunking this somewhat caricatured version of what he calls 'classical' democratic theory. His attack focuses on two issues. First, there is no unified will of the people: this is an abstraction, since people are split up into a variety of interests and groups. A unitary will does not exist. Second, Schumpeter emphasises the way in which people's political consciousness and interests, their perceptions of politics, are moulded from above; it is the political elites, the leadership teams, who are the creators of the agenda of politics.

Thus for Schumpeter and those following him in this tradition of democratic elitism, the elitist perspective is accepted in the sense that this is a 'top-down' perspective on politics: it is the elites who take the initiative, who form the political agenda, who propose policies to the passive mass. However, a system is democratic to the extent that the two criteria highlighted above are met, namely that there are several leadership teams, or elite groups, and that at periodic intervals, i.e. on election day, the choice is made by the mass (the public, the electorate) as to which group is vested with political power. After that, according to Schumpeter, the government (that elite group or leadership team vested with state power) should be allowed to get on with the job. In this vein .

way, there is what he calls a 'division of labour' between leaders and led: the leaders lead and govern, and the mass accepts this.

Democracy is thus defined by Schumpeter as a method – a method of producing a government. The role of the people, in this theory, is not to rule in the sense of directly exercising their sovereignty or having their 'will' prevail, nor does it involve any sustained direct participation. The role of the people is to produce a government through the process of electoral competition. The role of political elites is to offer to the electorate their policies and plans, and, if elected, to pursue those policies, relatively free from popular interference. The people keep out of direct involvement in government and let the leaders have a free hand until the time of the next election.

Schumpeter's theory has been much admired, and much criticised. It is impossible to deny the influence which his theory has had, or to ignore the fact that it is a highly realistic view of the workings of contemporary liberal-democracy. Its strength is that it sets out a theory which offers a convincing description of what could be called 'real existing democracy' in the modern world. This point is worth pursuing for a moment. The former East German dissident Rudolf Bahro coined the term 'real existing socialism' in his book *The Alternative in Eastern Europe* to suggest a distinction between the realities of Soviet-style communism ('real existing socialism', the regime which actually existed) and the socialist society such as Marx and Engels envisaged. In the same way, one could make a distinction between a theory like that of 'democratic elitism' as a theory of 'real existing democracy', and a theory more critical of the realities of liberal-democracy as it presently exists. Schumpeter's theory as an example of the general theory of competitive democracy has the following strengths.

As an explanatory rather than a normative theory, it offers a convincing view of the working of modern liberal-democracies, in which initiatives are taken by elite groups, and the masses are passive. People are called on to vote once every four or five years: in that sense the electorate is sovereign, but political matters are basically in the hands of a 'political class', as Mosca would put it.

In the same vein, the strength of this theory and the reality it describes is that it does not make great demands on the citizen body. It explains well enough the division of labour between rulers and ruled, and satisfies a minimalist conception of democracy, in that citizens have the right (and duty, possibly) to choose a government. Beyond that, there are no demands made on them, and defenders of this conception of democracy point to the positive aspects of this state of affairs. It contributes to stability, since too much involvement can lead to an irrational mob being stirred up by demagogues, as happened with movements of fascism. Thus with regard to the masses, the theory of democratic elitism offers them a role, congruent with contemporary realities, a role of choosing a government, yet nothing which is too demanding or which would lead to irrational mass action that could endanger democracy.

Finally, and again from the point of view of the realistic approach to real existing democracy, this theory of democratic elitism stresses, correctly it seems, that there is a plurality of elites in contemporary liberal-democratic society. The idea here is of what the French sociologist Raymond Aron called a 'differentiation of ruling hierarchies', and here too it seems highly realistic.[27] It paints a picture of a society somewhat akin to pluralism: there is a range of groups and associations, which we can imagine as distinct 'pyramids', each of them with an elite group at their peak. The fact of elitism does not rule out some degree of popular power, since the minimal definition of democracy ensures a choice between ruling elites at election time. The people are not totally passive, as is suggested in some extreme versions of elite theory (for example, in some of Michels' formulations noted above on the incompetence of the mass). To repeat the view of democracy which is given here, there are two or more competing elites, leadership groups of political parties, to which (though not in Schumpeter's version) could be added the idea of elite-led pressure groups. The people choose at periodic intervals which of these competing groups is to be vested with power, although the people do not decide the issues as such. The popular will is moulded by the elites. The fact, agreed by elite theory, that the people do not have the capacity actually to rule in any strong sense, to take the initiative and decide particular issues, does not really matter because this is not what democracy is about. Democracy in this sense involves the rulers having the initiative, but the people deciding who the rulers are.

Criticism of this view of democracy has often focused on its negative attitude to what is seen as the heart of classical democratic theory, the idea of popular participation. Defenders of a more participatory and developmental model of democracy suggest that democracy should be seen as a more normative concept, that democratic theorists should hold up criteria of what democracy should be, and then judge whether or not a particular system meets those criteria. The criticism is that the system described in the theory of democratic elitism is not a fully developed democracy, because it does not match up to the criteria of an active and developed, or rather self-developing, citizen body. As Arblaster notes, democracy is something still to be achieved.[28] There is a distinction, in our terminology, between the real existing democracy and what a genuine democracy should be.

In conclusion we can pose three areas of the theory which remain problematic. First, there is the question of one elite or several, and the question of whether, if there are several elites, these elites do in fact compete with each other, or are merely fractions of a relatively cohesive and coherent 'power bloc' or political elite. Second, there is the question of elitism and democracy: whether the situation of elite competition and mass choice at election time is adequately called democracy, or whether the term 'democracy' should be reserved for a system in which there is more initiative from below. Third comes the question of the power base of the elites: is the elitist theory convincing in explaining why these particular elite groups emerge and how they gain their power? Or are there deeper factors, a 'deep power structure', which in their different ways both Marxism and feminism grasp, but which is not perceived by pluralist and elitist-pluralist theories? That is the task of the next two chapters to investigate.

Notes

1. Mosca, G., *The Ruling Class (Elementi di Scienza Politica)*, trans. Hannah D. Kahn, McGraw-Hill, New York, Toronto and London, 1939, p. 50.
2. Bottomore, T.B., *Elites and Society*, Penguin, Harmondsworth, 1966, p. 15.
3. Pareto, V., *Sociological Writings*, ed. S.E. Finer, Pall Mall Press, London, 1966, p. 248.
4. Pareto, *Sociological Writings*, p. 266.
5. Mills, C.W., *The Power Elite*, Oxford University Press, New York, 1966.
6. Mills, *The Power Elite*, p. 296.
7. Pareto, *Sociological Writings*, p. 249.
8. White, R.J. (ed.), *The Conservative Tradition*, A. & C. Black, London, 1964, p. 155.
9. Mosca, *The Ruling Class*, p. 327.
10. Weber, M., 'Socialism', in Weber, M., *Selections in Translation*, ed. W.G. Runciman, Cambridge University Press, Cambridge, 1978, p. 260.
11. Mosca, *The Ruling Class*, p. 144.
12. Weber, M., 'Parlament und Regierung in neugeordneten Deutschland', in Weber, M., *Gesammelte Politische Schriften*, 3rd edition, J.C.B. Mohr (Paul Siebeck), Tübingen, 1971, p. 332, quoted in Beetham, D., *Max Weber and the Theory of Modern Politics*, 2nd edition, Polity, Cambridge, 1985, p. 83.
13. See Beetham, *Max Weber and the Theory of Modern Politics*, p. 99.
14. Mosca, *The Ruling Class*, p. 154.
15. Quoted in Meisel, J., *The Myth of the Ruling Class*, University of Michigan Press, Ann Arbor, MI, 1962, p. 324.
16. Michels, R., *Political Parties*, trans. E. and C. Paul, Dover Publications, New York, 1959, pp. 87, 56, 57, 205, 86.
17. See Beetham, D., 'From socialism to fascism: the relation between theory and practice in the work of Robert Michels', *Political Studies*, vol. XXV nos. 1 and 2, pp. 3–24 and 161–81.
18. Michels, *Political Parties*, p. 305.
19. Michels, *Political Parties*, p. 299.
20. Birch, *The Concepts and Theories of Modern Democracy*, Routledge, London and New York, 1992, p. 181.
21. Birch, *Concepts and Theories of Modern Democracy*, p. 180.
22. Sartori, G., 'Anti-elitism revisited', *Government and Opposition*, vol. 13, 1978, pp. 58–80.
23. Birch, *Concepts and Theories of Modern Democracy*, p. 169.
24. Birch, p. 180.
25. Sartori, 'Anti-elitism revisited'.

26. For recent discussion of Schumpeter, see *Journal of Democracy*, vol. 3, no. 3, 1992, special issue on 'Capitalism, Socialism and Democracy'.
27. Aron, R., *Progress and Disillusion: The dialectics of modern societies*, Penguin, Harmondsworth, 1972, p. 56.
28. Arblaster, A., *Democracy*, Open University Press, Milton Keynes, 1987, p. 105, quoting E.H. Carr.

5 | The Marxist view of power

Introduction: what is Marxism?

The purpose of this chapter is to present some of the main elements of Marxist theory and apply them to the power structure of the liberal-democratic state. The aim is to discuss the question of whether, and in what ways, Marxism is relevant to understanding the nature of the contemporary liberal-democratic state. This also involves comparing the main strands of Marxist theory with other theories studied in previous chapters.

The question of what is meant by 'Marxism' is not an entirely easy one to answer. The starting point is that Marxism is a large and diverse body of thought, and that there are many quite distinct versions of Marxism. In the first place, it is argued here that Marxism as a theory is not to be identified with a particular regime or political system, such as Soviet-style communism. It may be true that these regimes justified themselves and sought legitimation by claiming to exemplify or realise the theories of Marxism. However, these claims should be treated with scepticism, and certainly should not be accepted without further examination. The nature of the relationship between communist regimes and Marxist theory is itself a large and hotly debated topic, and it is further considered in Chapter 8, which deals with the communist system.

This suggests that the collapse of Soviet-type systems does not necessarily establish the conclusion that Marxism is of no relevance to contemporary liberal-democratic systems.[1] Marxist theory might still be valid as a critique and analysis of such systems, irrespective of the fate of those regimes that claimed to represent Marxist politics. In other words the collapse of communism does not necessarily mean the irrelevance of Marxist theory to the politics of our time.

Second, even when concentrating on Marxism as a body of thought, one should remember that terms like 'Marxism', as well as 'pluralism' or 'elitism', are abstractions, in the sense that they cover a wide range of thinkers or theorists, a long time span, and a spectrum of thought developed at different

times and in different places. Marxism can be used to refer to the writings of
Marx and Engels, or the ideas and political practice of Lenin, developed in
response to different conditions and in circumstances varying considerably
from those faced by the 'founding fathers' of Marxism. The tradition of
Marxism equally includes the theories of the Italian Marxist Antonio Gramsci,
the revolutionary strategy of Mao Tse-Tung, and a whole range of theorists of
the Second International (1889–1914) such as Karl Kautsky and Rosa
Luxemburg. This list could be extended even further to include more
contemporary Marxist traditions, referring to those who have been labelled
'Western Marxists', such as the Frankfurt School.[2] All these theorists can be
considered to some extent Marxist, yet there are important divergences
between them, not least because they wrote at different times, reflecting widely
varying situations or 'conjunctures'. The assumption made here is that
underlying or uniting these different theorists are certain core concepts,
acceptance of which justifies the label 'Marxist'. Such basic ideas include a
certain view of the significance of class and class struggle; analysis of the nature
of the state in general, and the liberal-democratic state in particular; a view of
capitalist society and its power structure; and finally certain ideas of reform
and revolution, a perspective which envisages the transformation of the
existing society.

There is also a distinction to be made between Marxism as theory, developed
by particular persons, and Marxism as a social movement. Marxism in the latter
sense refers to political and social movements animated or inspired by Marxist
theory, although here too the matter is not so simple. A recent historical study
of French Marxist thought in the period before the First World War reminds
us that 'Unfortunately, even the best studies of Marxism as a tradition have
emphasised the theoretical gymnastics of Marx's ideological progeny rather
than the doctrine's constitution as the collective discourse of mass socialist and
labour movements.' The same author suggests that 'Historians should
reconsider these priorities' and not substitute what he calls 'Marxology' for the
study of Marxism as a social movement: 'Marx may exemplify Marxist
socialism', this author notes, but he did not create it; 'Others of his time (and
before) independently reached his conclusions about the contradictions of
capitalism, the failures of the bourgeoisie, and the liberation of labour:
thousands of militants have become "Marxists" without reading Marx,
sometimes without awareness of his existence.'[3] One does not have to endorse
every line of this statement, but it is right to make a distinction between
Marxism as a body of theory, the writings of particular individuals, and
Marxism as the 'discourse' of mass movements and some political parties.

There are two basic issues which the following pages seek to address. First,
what are the main features of Marxist theories of power? What is the meaning
of some of the core concepts (class, state, revolution and capitalism) used
in the Marxist family of ideas? Second, the aim is to investigate whether
these concepts, and the theories which are based on them, are helpful in

understanding the politics of the contemporary liberal-democratic state. We are also concerned here with the question of comparison between Marxist theory and pluralist and elitist theory: in what ways do these theories differ from each other, and where does Marxist theory offer a different perspective? In short, the aim of this chapter is to expound and analyse some of the general themes of Marxism and to discover what it has to offer as a theory of power, applied to contemporary liberal-democratic politics. The question of the relationship of 'Marxism' and 'communism', or Soviet-type systems, is left until Chapter 7.

Class and class conflict

The starting point for the analysis of the basic Marxist concepts can be that Marxist theory in the broadest sense regards both pluralism and elite theory as inadequate theories of power; not so much wrong in themselves, but incomplete in failing to see 'the big picture', the overall structure of class power. Marxism as a theory of power is concerned to reveal a 'deep structure' of power, which is a system of class power. From Marxist perspectives, pluralist and elitist writers are not 'fantasising' when they describe a plurality of groups or, armed with the 'iron law of oligarchy', point to the emergence of controlling minorities within organisations. However, in the Marxist view, to understand fully this plurality of groups and the emergence of elites, one has to understand that group conflict and elite power exist within a wider context or structure. The starting point of wisdom, in Marxist eyes, is that pluralist and elite theories fail to recognise the context of class power which pervades the politics of liberal-democratic systems.

There is, then, a basic contrast between Marxist theories on the one hand and pluralist and elitist ones on the other. The former start from the fundamental proposition that liberal-democratic societies are capitalist societies. This means, among other things, that they are societies marked by significant inequalities of social and economic power which constitute a system of class power. This is the deep structure, the fundamental division, a dimension of power in its own right, which is seen in the Marxist tradition as the basic division underlying liberal-democratic society.

A contemporary political scientist, A.H. Birch, suggests that the Marxist claim is that 'democracy is a sham'. In Birch's view, Marxist theories emphasise the constraints on governmental power which stem from a particular structure of economic power. In his words, 'recognising the importance of practical constraints on governmental decision making does not necessarily involve acceptance of the Marxist claim that democracy is a sham'.[4]

One could suggest a more nuanced view here, not so much that democracy is a sham, but that genuine popular power, the ideas of democracy, the equality of citizens, their equal input into the 'decision-making process', cannot be fully or adequately realised in a society divided into social classes. In other words, there is a structure of social and economic inequality, a system of class power, which limits or constrains the democratic equality proclaimed by liberal-democratic systems. This system of class power stems from the division of society into classes, into a *ruling class* which owns and controls the productive resources of society, and one or more subordinate classes who are denied access to such economic power except on terms set by the dominant class, and who are thus subordinate to or controlled by the ruling class.

Such an analysis of society thus starts from an antithesis which is seen to characterise liberal-democratic societies. This antithesis is between the democratic equality among citizens which is claimed to prevail in the political sphere, and the social and economic inequality which is an integral part of a class-divided society. This class power is viewed as the foundation of a liberal-democratic system. Class power and class division are seen in the Marxist view not just as one source of inequality among others. Class division is seen as central and fundamental to liberal-democratic societies, and indeed to all societies which have preceded them, since they too were class societies. As one recent study of the concept of social class notes,

> Class structures constitute the central organising principles of societies in the sense of shaping the range of possible variations of the state, ethnic relations, gender relations etc., and thus historical epochs can best be identified by their predominant class structures.[5]

In contrast to pluralist and elitist perspectives, Marxist views see group competition and elite formation as somehow surface phenomena which mask a deeper and more fundamental reality. That reality is the division of society into opposing and contending classes. The social structure is marked by an opposition between the ruling class, which has control over the productive resources of society, the means of production in the Marxist language, and the subordinate class, which has to sell its labour power to the possessing and controlling class, on terms set in a general way by that class. The power base of the ruling class is its economic power, from which stem its political power and control over the state. These latter are based on class ownership or control of the means of production. This fact of class division is the 'secret' or deep structure of the liberal-democratic state, which exists in a capitalist society, which of course shares the feature of class division with all previously existing societies. In Marx's words, taken from Volume 3 of *Capital*,

> It is always the direct relationship of the owners of the conditions of production to the direct producers . . . which reveals the innermost secret, the hidden basis of the entire social structure, and with it the political form of the relation of sovereignty and dependence, in short, the corresponding specific form of the state.[6]

Thus our first task is to show how, in the Marxist view, this 'direct relationship of the owners to the direct producers' does indeed explain the 'innermost secret' of the liberal-democratic state and its politics, and to explain how the state is seen as situated within this context of class power. To explain this context more fully means identifying more specifically the owners of the means of production on the one hand and the 'direct producers' on the other.

The liberal-democratic state is situated within the context of 'capitalism', seen as a society divided into classes, of which the most important in Marxist terms are the bourgeoisie, the class which owns and controls the productive resources of the society, and the proletariat, the working class, which is excluded from such ownership and has nothing but its labour power to sell. It should be noted here that, while these two classes are indeed in the Marxist view the chief protagonists of capitalist society, they are not the only ones. Marxist theory in its different varieties has not failed to pay attention to what are seen as intermediary classes, such as the petty-bourgeoisie (i.e. the class of small proprietors and artisans, tradespeople and so on) and the peasantry, which are both seen as significant actors in particular situations. One example would be the role of the petty-bourgeoisie or 'small man' in supporting fascist-type movements, and this is discussed further in Chapter 8. Still, while it is important to recognise this, there is no doubt that Marxists have seen the two *main* classes as being bourgeoisie and proletariat.

By the same token, however, it is also important to recognise that these classes are not seen as homogeneous blocks, since their unity is sometimes fragmented and there are 'fractions' or subsections of classes which often play an important role in particular situations. To the extent that there is unity between the different 'fractions' or sections of either bourgeoisie or proletariat, this is not something naturally given, but is the result of a process of historical and political action. For example, the previously cited study of French socialism quotes a statement by the employers of the French textile town of Fourmies, reacting against the threatened May Day demonstrations of the workers:

> The undersigned industrialists, abandoning all the political questions or other matters which may have divided them during these grave circumstances, swear to defend each other with solidarity, and materially for the duration of the unjustified and undeserved war which has been declared against them.[7]

As the author comments, 'Much against their will, bourgeois Formiesiens had learned the meaning of "class consciousness" – the essence which, for Marxists, pervades social meaning as class conflict pervaded social structure.' In the same way, according to Marxist theory, for the subordinate class, the working class, unity and consciousness of common interests was a process which would be achieved historically through a process of class struggle, and was not something 'naturally' given. Nor was this unity and class consciousness something imposed from outside, at least not in the view of Marx and Engels, although Lenin's perspective on the question of class consciousness was different, as is discussed in Chapter 7.

The fact that in the Marxist view the politics of the liberal-democratic state is situated within a capitalist context, in which economic resources are owned and controlled by a group of persons, a ruling class, does not preclude recognition of the fact that capitalism as a system is constantly evolving, that it is a system now in its development far different from the capitalism of Manchester liberalism which Marx observed in his lifetime. One point, well made in a recent essay on the implications of the collapse of communist regimes by Bruce Ackerman, warns against the danger of failing to recognise that 'capitalism' can refer to widely differing systems:

> Does this label [of capitalism] describe Germany, with its elaborate welfare state and worker participation in industry? Or America, with its rigorous restrictions upon discriminatory employment practices and intrusive environmental controls on industry? Or Japan, with its aggressive state planning? Or Singapore, with its autocracy? Or a picture of laissez-faire England in the middle of the nineteenth century? Or the activist liberal's ideal of undominated equality?[8]

This point is well taken as a warning against using 'capitalism' as a label without being aware of the distinctions between different types of capitalism, of the historical evolution of capitalism, and of the different role of the state in various capitalist systems. Nevertheless, this does not amount to an argument against the use of the term 'capitalism' to suggest a system in which crucial decisions about employment, investment and production are in the hands of 'private' individuals and associations or corporations. Use of this term is also quite compatible with the recognition of the fact that in such systems the state also takes important decisions which affect the economy and its working. Hence the label of 'mixed economy' to refer to the nature of modern capitalism, in which economic power is shared between the state and private corporations.

The politics of liberal-democracy from the Marxist perspective is seen as determined, in a fundamental sense, by the basic 'structural' antagonism between conflicting social groups, namely classes. The power structure of liberal-democracy in this view may be described in the following four propositions:— *a proposal*

- Liberal-democratic states exist in a structure of class society.
- The classes of such a society are in a state of opposition and conflict.
- This opposition and conflict may be masked or veiled – the contending groups may not be fully conscious or aware of their antagonism and its full significance.
- The role of the state is to hold this antagonism in check, and to preserve the dominance of the ruling class.

Having identified this 'deep structure', which is seen as the key to the distribution of power within liberal-democracy, we need to explain three things: how, in the Marxist view, this structure is maintained; how, in that same view, it is challenged, through the dynamics of class conflict; and what relevance these ideas have to the present situation.

to hide

In the Marxist view, class structure exists as the basic framework of capitalist society, the structure within which the liberal-democratic state is situated. However, the extent to which people are aware of this underlying reality is a different matter. Marx and Engels certainly thought that this underlying reality was maintained and to some extent disguised by two basic institutions or forces. In the first place, it was maintained by the power of *ideology*, a set of ideas existing in any class society which veiled the reality of class power. In the second place, it was the task of *the state* to maintain the class structure of society, to function as an agent of class power in ways that need to be examined. The crucial point is that class structure, or the fact of class power, is seen in the Marxist view as not necessarily identical with the consciousness or awareness of that class division, still less with the desire to overcome it. The idea of the political equality of citizens in a liberal-democratic state, and furthermore the idea of their equality as consumers in a market place which is open to all, both serve as masking devices to hide the reality of class power and structural inequality. It was, however, the belief of Marx and Engels, and indeed other Marxists, that through the process of historical development there would be a coincidence between the deeper reality and awareness of that reality, that class-consciousness would develop on the part of the subordinate class or classes. They would become aware of their subordinate position and wish to challenge it and bring it to an end.

Before assessing how far these ideas stand up as an analysis of contemporary liberal-democracy, we need to explain the basic Marxist ideas of how the situation of class power would be ended. In the Marxist perspective there is a structure of class power, but also a dynamic of class antagonism and class struggle which is seen as leading to the transformation of the capitalist system and of the liberal-democratic state. This distinction between what we call here a 'structure of class power' and a 'dynamic of class antagonism' is similar to the distinction made by Erik Olin Wright in his recent study *Classes* between *class structure* and *class formation*. Class structure, he suggests, 'refers to the structure of social relations into which individuals (or, in some cases, families) enter which determine their class interests'. Class formation, on the other hand, is a process: 'class formation is defined by social relations *within* classes, social relations which forge collectivities engaged in struggle'.[9]

In the classical Marxist perspective, the subordinate classes would organise, would become aware of their true position and would seek to challenge it. There is thus a significant distinction between the two terms 'class structure' and 'class consciousness'. Again, Wright expresses similar ideas when he argues the distinction between class structure and class consciousness as follows:

> Class structure . . . constitutes the basic mechanism for distributing access to resources in a society, and thus distributing capacities to act. Class consciousness, in these terms, is above all the conscious understanding of these mechanisms: the realisation by subordinate classes that it is necessary to transform the class structure

to say freely sth like restriction

if there are to be any basic changes in their capacities to act, and the realisation by dominant classes that the reproduction of their power depends upon the reproduction of the class structure.[10]

He also notes that 'class formation . . . is the process by which individual capacities are organisationally linked together in order to generate a collective capacity to act, a capacity which can potentially be directed at the class structure itself'.[11] The Marxist expectation was that what Wright labels 'class formation' would be a historical process, generated by the very mechanisms of capitalism itself, which would indeed be directed at, or against, the class structure, aiming at its modification or transformation into a different structure – that of a classless society.

For Marxist theoreticians and for those engaged in the process of Marxist politics, the working class and its allies would develop its class consciousness and act in a revolutionary way. The socialist revolution would be the revolution of the majority of the population, who would seize hold of the state power and use that state power to introduce an entirely different system. Political action and organisation was seen as a necessary part of this process of social emancipation, as being the work of the majority of the population who would have, in the words of the *Communist Manifesto*, 'nothing to lose but their chains'.[12] Thus Marxism in its view of liberal-democracy asserts that not only is there a structure of class power, but this structure can be and will be overcome, through a process of class struggle. In a sense the politics of liberal-democracy is seen as the expression of class struggle, a process which will lead to a different structure of society and type of state.

In the Marxist perspective, the hitherto subordinate classes would develop a class consciousness which would reveal the true structure of society, and show up and indeed exacerbate the cleavages in society. Through the very process of capitalist production itself, the workers would be the agency of social change, the 'gravediggers' of the established order as the *Communist Manifesto* called them. The development of capitalism, for Marx and his followers, created an ever more homogeneous and cohesive mass, the working class. Certainly in the *Communist Manifesto* it was suggested that the working class would become a more disciplined and united force. Distinctions between skilled and unskilled workers, differences of trade, of ethnicity or nationality, of locality or religion, would all become less important with the unfolding of capitalism, which would fuse the working class into a more unified force, eventually organised on a national and quite rapidly on an international level. As the already cited study of French Marxism makes clear, in reality such assumptions of a united movement have often clashed with the stubborn social reality of a situation where divisions between sections of the workers have persisted, in terms of rivalry between skilled and semi-skilled, production and supervisory workers, not to mention antagonisms along national or ethnic lines. However, the expectation or the hope was that a revolutionary movement of workers would be developed through the very process of capitalist production itself. By grouping workers in larger factories, bringing them together, eventually spreading this sense of common interest across national boundaries, the capitalist system would create the force or the agency, a cohesive working class, that would overthrow the capitalist system.

On the basis of this process of economic development, the expectation of Marx and Engels, and of later Marxists, was that this economic underpinning would lead to cohesive class action, through the growth of a working-class movement which would become politically active and socially and economically combative. This process of the organisation of the working class would occur through political parties and trade unions taking action (class action) in the social and political sphere. The process of development from a disorganised mass into a cohesive class involved action in politics, such as the struggle to extend the right to vote. This was seen not as an end in itself, but as a means for developing the strength of the workers' movement and coming to power. Similarly, through action of the working class in terms of strikes and the formation of trade unions, the workers' movement would develop its organisation and cohesion.

The expectation of classical Marxism was thus that the working class would form the majority of society, that it would become cohesive and conscious or aware of common interests, overcoming intra-class divisions, and that this common interest would emerge through a process of class struggle not just in the political sphere but throughout society. Marxist theory does not neglect other sources of social conflict and identity, such as religion, or nationality, or ethnicity. Nonetheless, the expectation has been that these sources of identity would be subordinate to or overridden by class identity.

In the general theoretical treatises of Marxism, what Wright calls 'the characteristically polarised map of class relations' is presented, and this posits a confrontation between the two great forces, the two great camps of the main conflicting classes, workers and bourgeoisie. Yet this certainly did not preclude, in Marx's historical and political analyses of particular situations, what Wright calls 'a complex picture of classes, fractions, factions, social categories, strata and other actors on the political stage'.[13] Marx's analysis of _The Eighteenth Brumaire of Louis Bonaparte_ is a classic example of this, in which he showed the complex process through which Louis Napoleon, nephew of Napoleon Bonaparte, came to power in France in a _coup d'état_ on 2 December 1851, overthrowing the parliamentary republic. In this text Marx analysed class struggle not in the grand sweep of two classes competing with each other, but in a much more detailed way, focusing on a variety of groups or factions within classes, on the complex interweaving of events and on the role of classes other than 'bourgeoisie' and 'proletariat', notably the peasants and the petty-bourgeoisie.[14]

However, the general sweep of capitalist development, as presented in _Capital_, reveals with pitiless logic the polarisation of society into an ever larger class of workers, and a smaller class of capitalists presiding over means of production ever more centralised and co-ordinated. Intermediary classes would diminish in size and significance, and a socialist revolution would come about on the basis of two related factors, without which a socialist revolution was impossible.

The first of these two factors was the development of large-scale means of production, the product of capitalist society itself. In the *Communist Manifesto*, as elsewhere, Marx and Engels saluted the heroic mission of the bourgeoisie, in their conquest of nature and their development of the productive resources which alone would form the basis of a socialist society. Thus the first prerequisite for socialist revolution was the development of the material basis needed for a socialist society, a development which it was the historic mission of capitalist society to achieve.

The second prerequisite, equally essential, was a subjective factor, the emergence of a class of people, the working class, animated by the wish to create and achieve an alternative form of society, and united in the task of doing so by the very process of capitalist production itself. This involves the idea of what R.N. Hunt calls 'majority revolution', distinct from any project of minority insurrection.[15]

In the Marxist view the existing class structure would be challenged by class movements from below, and through political action and social action the working class would develop a cohesive movement aiming at the transformation of society, eventually accomplishing the revolutionary transition to socialism. The expectation was that through political organisation and other forms of action the working class would develop its political cohesion and class consciousness. But what form would that political organisation take? Certainly Marx and Engels envisaged that political parties were necessary, and this was one of the points of contention between them and their anarchist opponents such as Bakunin whom they confronted in debates within the International Workingmen's Association from 1864 to 1872. Furthermore, the development of class consciousness would emerge through political action, using the opportunities afforded by the existing state structure, including parliamentary politics where such institutions of representative government existed. In other words, Marx and Engels themselves were not 'abstentionists': they argued that the workers' movement would have to fight for the right of suffrage and use the liberties afforded in a parliamentary system in order to achieve power and develop their organisation.

The dominant tradition of the Marxist movement was to work within the structures of the liberal-democratic state and to seek to gain access to those 'bourgeois' institutions, if only for the purpose of eventually transforming them. This 'non-abstentionist' tactic really culminated in the period of the Second International of 1889–1914, with large and well-organised parties, primarily the German Social Democratic Party (SPD), apparently moving to electoral and political victory, and using the apparatus of the bourgeois state, not bypassing it.[16] Yet this created a dilemma, which is still relevant to contemporary politics. By participating, even if only 'tactically', in the institutions of the existing state, by seeking to use the suffrage as a means (though not the only one) of socialist transformation, the socialist or Marxist movement was stabilising the system, adding to the legitimacy of those very institutions which it was challenging. Participating in a process is a way of accepting the legitimacy of that process. The struggle for reforms within a liberal-democratic system strengthened the legitimacy of that particular state structure and gave its institutions greater stability. Furthermore, it resulted in a process of 'integration' of the working-class movement into 'its' own nation-state with its particular institutions, which the working class movement wanted to take over. In other words, we can see how revolutionary politics became, in the context of liberal-democratic regimes, a politics of reformism and piecemeal change, of working within a set of institutions accepted as legitimate.[17]

Marxism and the state

We have seen that the core of Marxist theory lies in its view of the deep structure of society, divided into classes which are defined in relation to one another. This relationship is seen as necessarily antagonistic, because of the exploitation by the ruling class of the labour power of the subordinate class, resulting in the appropriation of the products of its labour. Whether the situation is perceived as such by the members of the subordinate class is a separate question: class structure, we repeat, is different from class consciousness, although as we have seen the Marxist belief was or is that through the process of 'class formation' (Wright) the working class would develop a class consciousness leading to perception of the class structure of society and the wish to challenge it.

Where then does 'politics' fit into Marxist theory, and what is the role of the state? There are really two questions here: the more general one of how Marxist theory perceives the state in general, as an institution or set of institutions, and the more specific question of the liberal-democratic state, sometimes referred to by Marxists as systems of 'bourgeois democracy' or 'capitalist democracy'.[18] The aim is to compare theory and reality, in the sense of seeking to assess how useful Marxism is as a theory of the contemporary liberal-democratic state.

First, to explain the Marxist theory of the state in general, the starting point can be that contrary to what is often thought, the aspiration of Marxism is to a society free from the grip of the state. It is worth making this point because particularly in the light of the Soviet experience, with which Marxism is often wrongly identified, it is sometimes argued that the consequences of Marxism, and what it aspires to, necessarily involve the strengthening of state power. This was the anarchist charge against Marx, that Marxism in practice (and

indeed in theory) was committed to 'statism', that it was authoritarian. Some
modern writers or critics of Marxism echo this charge, seeing it as validated by
the experience of the Bolshevik Revolution and its development into Stalin's
totalitarianism. However, it is surely more accurate to suggest that Marx and
Engels envisaged the ultimate achievement of a society free from what Marx
saw as the dead weight of the state. It may be that this is a Utopian aspiration,
and certainly one which in the Soviet Union did not come to fruition. But at
least it must be recognised that the core of the Marxist view of political power
is to see the state as fundamentally a repressive force which exists to maintain
the structure of class power. The state is a necessary part of a society divided
into classes, and this is held to apply to all states, including the liberal-
democratic state with its ideas of citizen equality.

   The basic point, therefore, is that the state is seen as an instrument of class
rule, an apparatus of class domination. The corollary of this, naturally, is that
in a classless society there would be no need for the state. The modern state
is viewed in classical Marxism as a centralised and complicated apparatus,
growing ever more stifling and interfering. Its interference with the self-
regulation of society stems from its role in defending ruling-class power, and
from the state's concern to prevent subordinate classes from challenging that
power. One sentence from Marx's draft text on the Paris Commune of 1871,
The Civil War in France, gives a clear sense of the stifling and repressive nature
of the state. Marx wrote of 'the centralised state machinery which, with its
ubiquitous and complicated military, bureaucratic, clerical and judiciary
organs, entoils [enmeshes] the living civil society like a boa constrictor'.[19] The
task of the socialist revolution was to cast off this restrictive force.

   The state is therefore certainly not seen as a class-neutral agency performing
tasks of common social interest. The Marxist view of the state recognises that
the state may indeed fulfil some common social purposes, but these shared
functions are realised through an agency, the state, which is superimposed on
society, and which exists as a repressive institution (or set of institutions) to
maintain a system of class power. The common social tasks are taken out of
the hands of society and carried out by the state. This organisation is not class-
neutral or impartial but exists in a context of class power which it is the state's
purpose to maintain.

   The Marxist view of the state is thus in sharp contrast to the liberal view,
which sees the state as a necessary evil whose purpose is to secure individual
rights, including notably property rights, and whose power has to be restricted.
The Marxist view also sees the state as the guardian of property rights, of class
property, but as a necessity only in class-divided societies. Compared with the
pluralist view, it denies that the state is a neutral agency for policy formation
which is equally responsive to the demands of the various pressure groups of
society. In other words, Marxism rejects what we earlier called the 'pincushion'
view of the state.

   We can thus sum up the Marxist view of the state in the following

function of the state from marxist

propositions, which also move us on to consider the problem of the Marxist view of one particular form of state, liberal-democracy.

1. The state is seen as a necessary institution, in all class-divided societies. The purpose of the state is to defend a structure of class power.

2. The state, therefore, whatever its form, is not 'neutral' as between the different social classes in civil society; it exists primarily and fundamentally to secure the interests of one class and repress those of another.

3. The state is an apparatus which maintains class rule through repression and coercion, against those who challenge the power of the ruling class. This does not mean, however, that force is the only means through which the state operates. We have to consider the power of ideology. For example, the ideology of the liberal-democratic state disseminates the belief that all are citizens and that 'everyone counts for one and no-one for more than one'. This is one aspect of the ideology which the state along with other institutions in society propagate as a means of defending the existing order.

4. The modern state is an apparatus of ever greater complexity, a means of domination which assumes more sophisticated forms of surveillance. The state is superimposed on society as an apparatus which is separate from society and relatively autonomous from 'civil society'. Marx criticised the view of the German philosopher Hegel, who argued that the state represented a universal common interest, over and above the antagonisms and 'particularities' of civil society. In Marx's view the state could never attain this universality, despite its autonomy from society, because it was still a representative of a class interest and not of a common or general interest. There is thus a sort of paradox in the Marxist view. The state is over and above society, separate from it. However, and this is the next point, this autonomy or separation is only a relative one. At one and the same time the state is an apparatus of domination autonomous from society and with interests of its own, but it is also linked to society, and safeguards the interests of the economically dominant class in that society.

5. This presents the next point, which is that this autonomy is only relative. There is, in the Marxist view, a crucial link between state power and class power. The two are not the same, but the former is the means of propping up the latter. Those who hold state power (those who were referred to in an earlier chapter as the state elite) have a certain independence from the economically dominant ruling class, but it is an independence constrained by the class structure of society and the economic power which that gives to the ruling class. The core problem of Marxist political sociology is the link between class power and state power, the ways in which the two are connected. In this way the state is not neutral. *units?*

The concept of the 'relative autonomy of the state' has been used to describe the way in which the holders of state power are not just puppets of the ruling class, are not directly controlled by them, but are still constrained by the structure of economic or class power. There is, in the Marxist view, a

ruling gp ≠ economically → dominant? rich?

distinction between the ruling group which controls state power, and the economically dominant class. There are tensions between the former group, referred to by Marx at one point as a 'governing caste' (*regierende Kaste*), and the latter, whom he labelled as the economically 'ruling class' (*herrschende Klasse*).[20] The holders of state power must have a certain freedom of action, or autonomy, from the economically dominant class in order for the state elite to function effectively as defenders of the status quo. For example, the holders of state power might be the agents of reforms, such as the Factory Acts or the US New Deal, which were resisted by the capitalists themselves, even though such reforms stabilised the system and thus were in the long-term interests of the economically dominant class. The suggestion here is that the bourgeoisie itself might not see its own long-term interest, that the state can be the agent of reforms to maintain class power, and for that purpose the state needs a certain freedom of manoeuvre, or relative autonomy.

Under certain circumstances this relative autonomy of the state might take heightened forms, as in the Bonapartist state, when state power was held by Louis Napoleon and his cronies, people quite different from the property-owning classes, the bourgeoisie. A similar situation could be analysed with respect to the fascist state. However, the Marxist view is that even in such extreme situations of heightened state autonomy, this autonomy still remains 'relative', since the power of the state elite remains constrained by the structure of class power and economic control. There is thus a fundamental link between state power and class power, yet also a tension between those who wield the former and those possessed of the latter. This tension goes to the limit in certain situations: for example when state power is held by those who wish to reform the structure of economic power, as when socialist or social democratic governments come to power.

6. This point moves us on to consider the idea of different forms of state. So far we have expressed some general propositions which are true of all forms of state. However, the Marxist view recognises different forms of state, of which the liberal-democratic state is one. This form of state is sometimes referred to by Marxist writers as a system of 'bourgeois democracy'. The significance of this term is that it suggests the contradictory nature of that form of state, or as Miliband puts it, 'the tension, in a capitalist society such as Britain, between the promise of popular power, enshrined in universal suffrage, and the curbing or denial of that promise in practice'.[21]

Marxist theory in general is far from denying the significance of those rights and liberties which are part of the liberal-democratic state, and which differentiate it from authoritarian forms of state, such as fascism or military dictatorship. Just because they are all seen as class states does not mean that the distinctions between them are of no importance. Indeed, it could be said that Marxist theorists have valued the opportunities which the liberal-democratic system affords for the development of working-class politics and democratic action, and indeed for more general reasons. Moreover, Marxist political analysis has classically shown how, in situations where those rights and liberties afforded by liberal-democratic states appear to endanger the economic or social power of the ruling class, the latter have been in some circumstances willing to abandon liberal-democracy and install a 'strong state' or forms of authoritarian politics. Such systems of strengthened executive power, of what Poulantzas has called 'the exceptional state',[22] abolish the democratic elements of the liberal-democratic state, the political as well as the economic and social organisations of working-class politics, i.e. socialist or social democratic parties and trade unions, and indeed, as with fascism, all forms of pluralistic politics. They install what could be called a top-heavy and repressive state. Examples of such a move to authoritarian forms of state include the overthrow of the Second French Republic by Louis Bonaparte, described by Marx in *The Eighteenth Brumaire of Louis Bonaparte*; the move towards fascism in inter-war Europe; and more recently the *coup d'état* by the Greek colonels in 1967 and the overthrow of the Allende government in Chile in 1973.

Thus the Marxist view of the liberal-democratic state stresses the differences between that form of state and authoritarian state forms. Marxists from Marx onwards have sought to explain the breakdown of democracy and the installation of an authoritarian system in terms of the dangers which democracy and the representative state are seen as posing, under certain conditions, for the property-owning classes. In situations of severe economic and social crisis, the ruling class may be tempted to resort to authoritarian politics to negate the gains made by the working class under conditions of 'bourgeois democracy'.

We can conclude our review of the Marxist theory of the state by again suggesting its nuanced nature. The liberal-democratic state is seen as a class state, as are all states, but it is differentiated from other types of state, such as authoritarian forms of the bourgeois state, and due recognition is paid to those institutions and features which account for this differentiation. It should be pointed out, however, that within the corpus of Marxist theory and practice there have been different attitudes to the liberal-democratic system, which in many ways reflect the ambiguity within Marx and Engels' own writings. As M. Levin points out in his recent study, Marx and Engels themselves did not have much experience of liberal-democratic systems, which were relatively few in their lifetime.[23] Indeed, with the possible exception of America and perhaps Holland, and allowing for the other exception of the short-lived Second French Republic (1848–51), there was no system in Marx and Engels' lifetime in which male, let alone universal, suffrage, had been achieved. However, Engels was impressed by the possibilities of peaceful electoral advance opened up by the albeit limited and distorted franchise in Germany. He saluted the advances made by the German Social Democrats. In his famous 1895 Preface to Marx's text *Class Struggles in France*, Engels sketched out a scenario for revolution through steady electoral advance, in which the socialists would come to power through the ballot rather than the barricade, in the manner of 'an irresistible

natural process' as he put it. The time of street fighting was over, and the
revolutionaries were benefiting from legality: it was the defenders of the
established order who feared that 'La légalité nous tue', legality was killing
them.[24] This attitude was taken further by the 'revisionist' Eduard Bernstein
in his book *The Preconditions of Socialism*, or, in an earlier English translation,
Evolutionary Socialism, which sketched out a similar process of peaceful and
gradual parliamentary transition to socialism.[25]

By contrast, Lenin took a much more contemptuous attitude towards
parliamentary democracy, emphasising in *The State and Revolution* (1917) that
parliament was merely a talking-shop given over to the task of 'fooling the
common people', and that the task of the socialist revolution could not be
achieved through such institutions. They must be 'smashed' and replaced by
institutions of true popular power, the soviets or councils. This strand of
theorising on the state is considered further in Chapter 7, which deals with the
formation and development of the communist regime.

The relevance of Marxism to the contemporary liberal-democratic state

How convincing and how relevant is Marxist analysis to the reality of
contemporary liberal-democracy? Three problem areas can be highlighted.

1. The first issue concerns class structure and revolution. The polarisation
of classes has not taken place, it could be argued, and the division into 'two
great hostile camps' envisaged in the *Communist Manifesto* has not revealed
itself as the shape of the present society. In so far as there are social classes,
there is rather a continuum or spectrum ranging from top to bottom, with
infinite gradations, rather than the stark contrast which the *Manifesto*
envisaged as the inevitable outcome of the contradictions of capitalism. And
it might further be adduced that the idea of a revolutionary working class has
not materialised either. The proletariat, the subordinate class, defined as those
with nothing to lose but their chains, has in general terms sought reforms not
revolution. Rather than the collective class consciousness anticipated by
Marxists, it has been an individualist consumerist consciousness which has
triumphed. Freedom has been seen not in terms of revolution and achieving a
collectivist society, but in terms of individual prosperity and consumption.
Indeed, there are those, like Gorz, who argue that the very concept of the
proletariat no longer applies, at least not with the connotations which Marx
gave to the term.[26] The idea of the working class as a universal class, whose
exploitation and alienation would propel it to revolutionary activity, has been
made irrelevant by the development of history, including reforms and other
action by the state.

It could also be added to this critique of Marxism that, despite the difference
noted earlier between Marxism as a theory and the Soviet communist regime,
Marxism came to be identified with an authoritarian and statist system as

represented by the ex-USSR. Hence the appeal of socialist and Marxist ideas has been correspondingly less and the legitimacy of liberal-democracy correspondingly greater.

2. Second, it has been argued that Marxism was too deterministic, and saw revolution as the only possible outcome of the contradictions of the capitalist system. However, this neglected a number of political factors which changed the facts of the situation. The history of liberal-democratic systems has been one of reforms, which have resulted in concessions to the working-class movement, limiting exploitation and admitting workers to the benefits of citizenship. Citizenship has come to represent an alternative to the polarisation of classes and class antagonism which was the future of capitalism as Marx saw it. The argument of people like T.H. Marshall could be used to suggest that the politics of liberal-democracy has resulted in a process of integration of the working class into the nation.[27]

This argument is directed against the Marxist view of the state as expounded above. The liberal-democratic state was seen by Marxists as a set of institutions that were not neutral, which were used to maintain a class-divided society. The counter-argument here would be that the Marxist view of the state as an agent for 'managing the common affairs of the whole bourgeoisie' has long been out of date, given the achievement of universal suffrage and the formation of working-class or social democratic parties which have been able to capture state power and introduce far-reaching reforms that have redressed the balance of power between capital and labour. In addition, this argument would suggest that the weight of the state in a mixed economy has taken power away from the capitalist class, to the extent that it is doubtful whether one can speak of a capitalist economy any more.[28] According to some critics, the system has fundamentally changed, and Marxist theory has failed to take these changes into account. This critique argues that, in both the political and the economic sphere, the analysis of Marxism has been outmoded by the development of the capitalist system and the adaptability of the liberal-democratic state.

3. A third set of problems or objections raises the further point that Marxism as a theory of power might perhaps 'privilege', i.e. give too much emphasis to, economic or class power. It could be suggested that there are other divisions which are no less important, possibly more significant, such as gender divisions or ethnic and national divisions, or even the distinction between creative elites and the passive mass, the shapers and doers at the top and the recipients or governed at the bottom, the eternal cycle of elites that Pareto and others analysed. Finally, 'post-modernist' critiques of Marxism suggest that the idea of the proletariat as the subject or agent of history is irrelevant to the reality of post-modernist society, in which there is no single project, no single agency, and everything is fragmented and disassociated. The time of 'grand narratives' is past, and the idea of the proletariat and its political agencies as the wave of the future and the force of modernity is a myth which is no longer, if it ever was, appropriate to contemporary reality.[29]

From a somewhat different line, there is the criticism that Marxism suffered from taking the Enlightenment project too seriously. In other words, the critique is that Marxism operates with an inflated view of the possibilities of human action and capacity. Critics suggest that the project of human beings knowing and controlling their own society is fundamentally flawed. Kolakowski concludes his three-volume study of Marxism with the criticism that this whole body of thought shares the illusion of the 'Promethean' creed, which holds that social life could be made transparent and come under human control. Such a myth, Kolakowski argues, can only lead to one outcome, a form of tyranny: 'the self-deification of mankind, to which Marxism gave philosophical expression, has ended in the same way as all such attempts, whether individual or collective: it has revealed itself as the farcical aspect of human bondage'.[30] Kolakowski also accuses Marxism of being a form of Utopianism, stemming from its heroic or 'Promethean' belief that all social problems are capable of resolution through human political and social action:

> Marxism takes little or no account of the fact that people are born and die, that they are men or women, young or old, healthy or sick; that they are genetically unequal, and that all these circumstances affect social development irrespective of the class division, and set bounds to human plans for perfecting the world.[31]

It is somewhat hard to respond to all these criticisms of Marxism, especially as our task here is to concentrate on the relevance of Marxism to the contemporary liberal-democratic state, and on Marxism as a theory of power. What follows therefore, is a provisional conclusion with reference to Marxist perspectives on the contemporary liberal-democratic state and its social context, comparing those perspectives with pluralism and elitism.

In the first place, it may be useful to make a distinction between Marxism as critique, and Marxism as a programme of social movements and model of an alternative society. In terms of Marxism as critique, it can be said that the fundamental contribution of Marxism to the analysis of the state was to broaden the scope of analysis, to see the state and political power in general in a wider context of social, or rather class power, imposing structural constraints on what the holders of state power could achieve. This does not mean that Marx dismissed democracy as a sham, but it does suggest that the ideals of the democratic or liberal-democratic state (as sketched out in Chapter 2 – ideals of autonomy, equality and collective decision making of citizens) are threatened or thwarted by the realities of economic and social power: in other words, by the class inequality which is still a reality of liberal-democratic systems.

Furthermore, Marxist theory offered a broader critique of the capitalist society in which the liberal-democratic state was situated. The *Communist Manifesto* points out how, in capitalist society, everything becomes a commodity, the commodification of all properties is seen as inescapable and all human relations are measured with 'the cash nexus'. This 'commodification' spreads to all aspects of the life of such societies. The Marxist critique was of a system of 'reification', in which relations between people are seen as unalterable relations between things. In the Marxist tradition it was Georg Lukacs, especially in his book *History and Class Consciousness*, who drew out more explicitly some of the implications of this line of thought.[32]

The essence of the Marxist critique could be said to be of a system which escapes conscious control by the human beings subject to it, and in which the continued existence of a structure of social inequality casts doubt on the claims made by liberal-democratic societies. Those claims are of 'people power', of citizen equality, of a state equally responsive to the demands of the people, as suggested by pluralist theorists who invoke the idea of equal access to the centres of power. The Marxist tradition focuses on the problem of the link between class power and state power, and how state action cannot be understood in abstraction from the context of class power. Exactly how constraining are the pressures on those who hold state power? How much room for manoeuvre is there for members of the state elite who wish to transform the social structure in the direction of greater social equality? These are the questions posed by Marxist perspectives on the state and power. The experience of the Mitterrand government of France from 1981 and its change of policies furnishes an instructive example of constraints on the holders of state power.[33]

It can be further asserted that Marxist perspectives are essential in pointing out the limitations of both pluralist and elitist views of power. It seems hard to deny that there are 'structural' inequalities in capitalist societies, stemming from their class structure, and that these economic and social inequalities affect the nature of politics and of key institutions in such systems, for example political parties. One recent case is the payment to the (British) Conservative Party of several million pounds by people who, it appears, were not citizens of the United Kingdom, yet who spent vast sums in order to help secure the return of a government favourable to their economic interests. As one political commentator noted on this matter, making a comparison between modern parties and eighteenth-century patronage politics, 'In modern democracies, political parties are changing from the mass organisations which typified the early twentieth century into more exclusive networks, of influence, wealth and connection.'[34]

Thus the Marxist view points to the structure of wealth and economic power as an indispensable part of the power structure of liberal-democratic societies. It also suggests that what is involved here are networks of economic power, structures of wealth and influence which to a certain extent elude conscious control by those subject to them. Currency exchanges, as witnessed by the famous example, again in Britain, of 'Black Wednesday' on 16 September 1992, suggest the relative powerlessness of supposedly sovereign and elected governments faced with economic forces they cannot control. These forces (e.g. international currency speculation) themselves seem mysterious 'reifications', referred to as 'the market'. They are apparently the impersonal result or sum total of hundreds, or rather thousands, of individual decisions which collectively determine individual fates. Thus two core Marxist ideas, the idea of a deep structure of economic power, stemming from class divisions, and the idea of forces apparently uncontrollable, are highly relevant to the reality of contemporary liberal-democratic systems, and to the realities of human fate at the present moment.

Of course, this does not necessarily mean that, because Marxist views in this sphere are valid, the Marxist projection of the revolutionary role of the proletariat and of class polarisation has also been borne out in contemporary politics. Classical Marxism has indeed 'privileged' class divisions, seeing those as the key to political and social development, a source of division more important than any other. This did not mean that other sources of conflict were totally ignored or marginalised. For example, with respect to national divisions, Marxists starting with Marx himself have recognised the existence and force of nationalism, and have grappled with its implications as a force often cutting across or overriding social or class divisions, sometimes indeed reinforcing them.[35] Marx himself ridiculed his son-in-law Lafargue for suggesting the immediate abolition of nations, and he proved himself well aware of the significance for the class struggle in England of the conflict between English and Irish workers. Nevertheless, it is an open question what the relationship is between different identities, or different levels of discrimination or oppression. Other identities, whether national, racial/ethnic or gender identities, or one's identity as an individual consumer on the market, or as a citizen, a supposedly sovereign voter: these are all important, are cultivated in different ways, and have been significant in 'mobilising' people for forms of action sometimes different from the socialist revolution which Marxists have envisaged, albeit in different ways. In this sense, one could say that pluralists have a point: that 'identity' is constructed in different ways, and the idea that people would think of themselves primarily as members of conflicting social classes and act accordingly in politics does not seem to have been borne out in reality. For example, in current conflicts in former Yugoslavia identities have been shaped or reshaped along ethnic lines, as people come to see former neighbours as members of ethnic groups rather than fellow citizens.[36]

The shape of politics in the twentieth century has indeed assumed forms very different from those envisaged by classical Marxism. The three lines of criticism outlined above referred to the headings of class/class structure; politics and the state; and the question of agency and identity. Our argument here is that the evolution of the class structure in liberal-democratic systems has been different from the tendency of society to polarise into the 'two great hostile camps' as suggested by Marxism. In part this was precisely because of ideas of citizenship, and the achievement of reforms, both political and social. These reforms were initiated or approved by a state responsive to working-class pressure, and also, it has to be said, by a state wishing to preserve social peace and cohesion, even if the price to be paid for this was reforms which limited capitalist power and privilege. Hence the ever-present danger that such capitalist groups might resort to authoritarian politics if they felt the liberal-democratic state was too 'concessionary' (this issue is discussed below in Chapter 8, which deals with fascism). The reforms enacted by the state certainly took the sting out of radical socialist or Marxist protest. These reforms included social reforms, such as the creation of the National Health Service and the Welfare State in Britain, and reforms at the workplace to lessen the arbitrary power of 'hiring and firing' and to improve working conditions. It does seem to be the case that, while Marxist theorists were not blind to sources of conflict other than class, the emphasis was placed on this division as overriding all others, as giving people the basic identity which would inspire them to action on (predominantly) class lines.

While giving due recognition to these lines of criticism, our conclusion here is that they in no way rule out the relevance of Marxism to the politics of contemporary liberal-democratic systems. These systems are marked by inequalities of economic power, which have a crucial impact on the political sphere, and which have serious implications for the ideas of citizen equality and participation celebrated by the liberal-democratic state. If those who are in lower socioeconomic positions are also those least knowledgeable about and participatory in the politics of liberal-democracy, this suggests that subordinate economic and social positions are correlated with effective exclusion from the citizenship sphere. This casts a different light on the politics of liberal-democratic societies, giving credence to the Marxist critique of 'bourgeois democracy'.[37] The dynamics of capitalist society, with their liberal-democratic state, may have turned out differently from the prediction offered in Marx's own writings, but Marxist analyses of the power structure of society are still relevant, indispensable even, to the understanding of contemporary reality.

As for the relationship between Marxist theory, pluralist theory and elite theory, the Marxist view of the politics of liberal-democracy is that the process of class struggle is primary. Historically speaking, contrary to the order in which the topics are treated in this book, in a certain sense both pluralism and elitism can be seen as responses to and critiques of Marxism. Pluralism, while of course having antecedents in liberalism and the liberal tradition, is a view of society or of politics which holds that liberal-democratic systems are marked by a host of sources of conflict or antagonism, cutting across class cleavages. Pluralism therefore denies the primacy of class, and not only points to other sources of division, but suggests that these are all equally important – people can enter into conflict over religion or ethnicity, and they can express antagonism over regional issues, so there is no single overriding central division (the class division) which lies like a geological 'fault line' in capitalist society.

Elite theory, on the other hand, took a different line in challenging Marxism. It sought to argue (as we saw in the section on Michels) that the Marxist or socialist movement would give rise to an elite, and that the movement of history was one of a struggle for elite power and not one which could or would achieve a classless society. The comparison between the different theories is taken up in Chapter 10 while the next chapter takes up feminist perspectives on liberal-democratic societies and their power structure.

Notes

1. Callinicos, A., *The Revenge of History: Marxism and the East European revolutions*, Polity, Cambridge, 1991; and Blackburn, R. (ed.), *After the Fall: The failure of communism and the future of socialism*, Verso, London and New York, 1991.
2. Anderson, P., *Considerations on Western Marxism*, New Left Books, London, 1976.
3. Stuart, R., *Marxism at Work: Ideology, class and French socialism during the Third Republic*, Cambridge University Press, Cambridge, 1992, pp. 22 and 28.
4. Birch, A.H., *The Concepts and Theories of Modern Democracy*, Routledge, London, 1993, p. 194.
5. Wright, E.O., *Classes*, Verso, London, 1985, p. 31.
6. Marx, K., *Capital*, Vol. III, Lawrence and Wishart, London, 1974, p. 791.
7. Stuart, *Marxism at Work*, pp. 76–7.
8. Ackerman, B., *The Future of Liberal Revolution*, Yale University Press, New Haven, CT, and London, 1992, p. 34.
9. Wright, *Classes*, p. 9 (structure) and p. 10 (formation).
10. Wright, *Classes*, p. 28.
11. *Ibid.*
12. Marx and Engels, *Communist Manifesto*, in Marx, K. *The Revolutions of 1848*, ed. D. Fernbach, Penguin, Harmondsworth, 1973, p. 98.
13. Wright, *Classes*, p. 7.
14. See Marx, K., *The Eighteenth Brumaire of Louis Bonaparte*, in Marx, K., *Surveys from Exile*, ed. D. Fernbach, Penguin, Harmondsworth, 1973.
15. Hunt, R.N., *The Political Ideas of Marx and Engels*, Vol. I, Macmillan, London, 1975.
16. Kolakowski, L., *Main Currents of Marxism, Vol. II: The Golden Age*, Clarendon Press, Oxford, 1978.
17. See van den Linden, M., 'The national integration of European working classes (1871–1914): Exploring the causal configuration', *International Review of Social History*, vol. XXXIII, 1988, pp. 285–311.
18. Miliband, R., *Capitalist Democracy in Britain*, Oxford University Press, Oxford, 1982.
19. Marx, *The Civil War in France*, in Marx, K., *The First International and After*, ed. D. Fernbach, Penguin, Harmondsworth, 1974, p. 246.
20. Marx, K., 'Parties and cliques', in Marx, *Surveys from Exile*, p. 279.
21. Miliband, *Capitalist Democracy in Britain*, p. 1.
22. Poulantzas, N., *Fascism and Dictatorship*, New Left Books, London, 1974.
23. Levin, M., *Marx, Engels and Liberal Democracy*, Macmillan, London, 1989.

24. Engels, F., Introduction to Marx, K., *The Class Struggles in France 1848 to 1850*, in Marx, K. and Engels, F., *Selected Works in Three Volumes*, Progress Publishers, Moscow, 1969, Vol. 1, p. 202.
25. Bernstein, E., *The Preconditions for Socialism*, ed. H. Tudor, Cambridge University Press, Cambridge, 1993.
26. See Gorz, A., *Farewell to the Working Class: An essay on post-industrial society*, Pluto, London, 1982.
27. See Marshall, T.H., 'Citizenship and social class', in Marshall, T.H., *Sociology at the Crossroads and Other Essays*, Heinemann, London, 1963, pp. 67–127.
28. See Crosland, C.A.R., *The Future of Socialism*, Jonathan Cape, London, 1976; and Shonfield, A., *Modern Capitalism: The changing balance of public and private power*, Oxford University Press, Oxford, 1965.
29. Callinicos, A., *Against Postmodernism: A Marxist critique*, Polity, Cambridge, 1989.
30. Kolakowski, L., *Main Currents of Marxism: Vol. III: The Breakdown*, Clarendon Press, Oxford, 1978, p. 530.
31. Kolakowski, L., *Main Currents of Marxism: Vol. I: The Founders*, Clarendon Press, Oxford, 1978, p. 413.
32. Lukacs, G., *History and Class Consciousness*, Merlin, London, 1971.
33. Ross, G., Hoffman, S., and Malzacher, S. (eds), *The Mitterrand Experiment: Continuity and change in Modern France*, Polity, Cambridge, 1987; and Singer, D., *Is Socialism Doomed? The meaning of Mitterrand*, Oxford University Press, New York, 1988.
34. Kettle, M., 'Paying the price for party politics', *Guardian*, 19 June 1993.
35. See Schwarzmantel, J., *Socialism and the Idea of the Nation*, Harvester Wheatsheaf, Hemel Hempstead, 1991.
36. See Glenny, M., *The Fall of Yugoslavia: The Third Balkan War*, Penguin, London, 1992.
37. Miliband, R., *Divided Societies: Class struggle in contemporary capitalism*, Clarendon Press, Oxford, 1989; and Miliband, *Capitalist Democracy in Britain*.

6 | Feminism and the state: gender power, feminism and power

Introduction: gender power

This chapter deals with the question of gender power and the state. Our concern is to explain how feminist perspectives are relevant to the topic of power in general, and how they are essential to understanding the nature of liberal-democracy and the distribution of power in that form of state. The approach taken here presents feminist perspectives as offering a critique of 'politics' as traditionally defined, and as pointing to a dimension of power ignored by other theories. Feminism in its broadest sense raises crucial questions about the nature of participation in modern politics, the 'gendered' nature of the state and political activity in liberal-democratic and other systems, and the significance of aspects of life hitherto shunted off into the sphere of 'the private' and hence considered irrelevant to the distribution of power.[1]

This is not to say that feminism is the only perspective from which such problems could be considered, but that it raises central questions concerning the definition of politics and the nature of power. These form an essential element in thinking about politics in our time. There are other theoretical perspectives which criticise undue attention on the state, such as anarchism; and other dimensions of power apart from the gender dimension which limit participation and access to political power, such as racial and ethnic divisions. Nevertheless, feminism as theory and movement goes to the heart of basic questions concerning the nature of politics and state power, and along with Marxism it situates pluralist group conflict and elite analysis in a wider context of power, male power or patriarchy.

We start from the premise that feminist perspectives involve a critique of all the other perspectives on power and on the liberal-democratic state which have been considered so far. These other theories are, from a feminist perspective, considered inadequate in that they neglect a fundamental dimension of power, namely gender power, the power of men over women. To the extent that they fail to consider this dimension of power, they give a distorted view of the power structure of liberal democracy, or any other form of state. Feminist perspectives, then, reveal the inadequacies of other theories of power, but their contribution goes further. Not only are they effective as a critique, but they involve fundamentally different views on the definition of 'the political', and cause us to question the whole way we look at politics and the state.

A useful point of comparison can be made between feminism and Marxism, as theories of power in general and more specifically of liberal-democracy. In the first place, just as 'Marxism' is an abstraction, because there are different versions of Marxism, and a whole range of varying and sometimes conflicting Marxist theorists, the same can be said of feminist perspectives. They share the common theme of emphasising gender division as a dimension of power, but differ in their explanation of the causes of the power of men over women, how this dimension of power relates to other dimensions of power such as class division, and the strategies and actions through which this power structure can be transformed. There is thus a variety of feminist perspectives, and there is no such thing as *the* feminist view.

The parallel with Marxism can be pursued further. Both feminism and Marxism take a common stance, in that both are concerned to reveal what we earlier called a 'deep structure' or power dimension which exists in the liberal-democratic state and the society which surrounds it, and in other forms of state and society as well. This power dimension is in both cases seen as a 'fault line' or basic division which is to some extent hidden from view. Both views of power are concerned to unmask or reveal a source of power or inequality which is concealed by the rhetoric of democracy and citizen equality typical of liberal-democracies. This is held to undermine or call into question the surface appearance of liberal-democracy and its invocation of equality.

Of course, the 'deep structure' which Marxist views of power and feminist perspectives are concerned to reveal is different in each case. From the Marxist point of view, the contradiction in liberal-democracy is between the idea of citizen or political equality and the facts of class division which lead to economic and social inequality. Feminist perspectives see the opposition as one between the claims of equal access to power and citizen equality on the one hand, and sexual or gender inequality on the other. The liberal-democratic rhetoric of equality is seen to be misleading, because it masks real inequalities of power between men and women. These inequalities are seen both at 'elite' level, in terms of the participation of women as opposed to men at key levels of decision taking, and also at the 'mass' level, in terms of the relative exclusion of women from political activity, their underrepresentation or even 'invisibility'. The analysis is first of women's exclusion, historically speaking, from membership of the citizen body at all, and second, even after inclusion in the citizen body, of their relative marginalisation as active citizens. The claim is that the ideas of democratic autonomy and equal participation are not realised because of inequalities stemming from gender divisions and a hidden line of domination of men over women. Feminist perspectives thus point to the fact that whatever may be claimed in the celebration of liberal-democracy and its invocation of democratic values, democracy in a genuine sense has still to be achieved. This dimension of inequality may be obscured in modern society because of apparently equal citizenship rights and legal rights, but it persists in more subtle ways, and denies the surface appearance of liberal-democratic equality.

Furthermore, as regards the similarities and differences between Marxism and feminism, both see pluralism and elitism not so much as wrong in themselves in their analysis of power, but as incomplete, failing to include the hidden dimensions of power which stem from class or gender inequality. However, the relationship between class inequality and gender inequality, the relationship between each of them as dimensions of oppression, is a problem in its own right. Marxist perspectives, as we saw in Chapter 5, see class division as not the only, but as the most fundamental division and source of inequality. Class struggle is the basic antagonism which moves history along, from one epoch to another. Feminist perspectives at least qualify this claim, if they do not reject it altogether. Socialist feminist perspectives qualify the primacy of class antagonism by bringing into play the dimension of sexual or gender inequality. Other forms of feminism see this latter dimension of power (gender division) as replacing class division as the candidate for the primary division that accounts for social and political conflict and moves history on.

The relationship between these, and other, forms of domination and inequality is a source of debate and controversy. Both Marxism and feminism may be alike in unveiling a structure of inequality veiled by the surface appearance of democratic equality. Yet they disagree on what that structure is, and on the relationship between class and gender inequality. In addition, within each camp there are disagreements as to the way in which the situation of inequality can be transformed. Some varieties of feminism see the antagonism between women and men as equivalent to the class struggle between bourgeois and proletarians, and they talk of 'sex classes' as the equivalent to Marxist social classes.[2]

We can thus define what we call here 'feminist perspectives' in the broadest sense as that body of thought which holds that there is a fundamental division within liberal-democratic societies, and indeed in all societies, between men and women, and that this division stems from a situation of structural inequality between men and women which creates a structure of male power. Feminist perspectives seek not only to reveal this somewhat hidden structure of inequality, but also to analyse its sources and ways in which it can be transformed. Only then, it is argued, could the promise of liberal-democracy, or democracy in general, be fully realised. if men & women will be equal.

We can note two other general aspects of feminism with respect to the question of power, and the nature of liberal-democracy. The feminist claim is that the exclusion of women from political power signifies the denial of the promise of autonomy or self-determination held out by the ideals of liberal-democracy. Here again the parallel with Marxism might prove illuminating. Marx contrasted the surface appearance of liberal-democracy and its rhetoric with deeper processes which went on beneath the surface. He contrasted the overt and public sphere of the sale of labour power, that 'very Eden of the innate rights of man', where 'Freedom, Equality, Property and Bentham' were the sole ruling forces, with the deeper processes of a social structure where the capitalist confronted the labourer, and the true source of inequality was revealed:

> He, who before was the money-owner, now strides in front as capitalist; the possessor of labour-power follows as his labourer. The one with an air of importance, smirking, intent on business; the other, timid and holding back, like one who is bringing his own hide to market and has nothing to expect but – a hiding.[3]

Without pushing the parallel too far, we can say that feminist theory makes a similar contrast between the appearance of democracy in liberal-democratic society and its denial or limitation in practice, because of a structure of male power – a system of patriarchy. This structure of male power is seen not as stemming primarily or solely from the political sphere as conventionally defined, but as pervasive in, perhaps originating from, what is sometimes called the 'private' sphere, the sphere of the family and home. Feminist theory is thus concerned not merely to unveil the existence of this context of gender inequality, and to reveal its implications for democracy. It has the purpose, too, of seeking to account for this structure of inequality and of questioning the distinction between the 'public' and 'private' sphere.

Traditionally, the 'public' sphere has been seen as the realm of politics, concerned with the broad questions of public interest and common affairs of the whole body politic. This has been from Aristotle onwards contrasted with the 'private' sphere, the sphere of household and family, dealing with partial specific matters of interest only to the individuals in that household, as opposed to matters of general concern to all citizens. According to Daniela Gobetti in her study *Private and Public*, the distinction between public and private involves three dimensions. In Aristotle's thought, the distinction involved the contrast between a private sphere characterised by a 'natural' *hierarchy* and a public sphere characterised by *equality*, an equality of fellow citizens. Second, the public sphere aimed at a general good, distinct from the individual good, whereas in the household the general good of the household was inseparable from the particular good of the male head of household. His dependants' view of what that good was did not count. Third, political association aimed at the highest good, which involved justice and the alternation between ruling and being ruled. This pursuit of the highest good was not possible in the narrow confines of the household or private sphere.[4]

The point to be made here is that traditionally this public sphere, involving politics and the pursuit of a common interest, the sphere of the political, has been held to be, and for many centuries indeed was maintained as, the sphere of men, excluding women. Debates within feminist theory about ways of ending this situation of exclusion and subordination again have certain parallels with debates within the Marxist camp. Those holding Marxist perspectives insisted that the achievement of political and legal rights for the proletariat was an important but not a sufficient element in the process of proletarian, or rather human, emancipation. So too within the feminist perspective there are those who argue that the achievement of political equality and legal rights was to some extent formal and limited. Such political and legal rights would not be adequate in themselves to ensure social equality between men and women and an end to patriarchy.

Inclusion and exclusion

If such is the nature of feminist theory, in the broadest sense, we need to explain the nature of the fundamental power division, or system of male dominance, and how this affects the nature of politics in liberal-democratic systems. We operate here with the basic concepts of inclusion and exclusion, and we are concerned with the implications of feminist analysis for the power structure of liberal-democracy. The feminist challenge to liberal-democracy is broadly to question the extent to which the liberal-democratic state lives up to the ideas of citizen equality which it proclaims and which were sketched out in Chapter 2. The feminist challenge is to call for what Anne Phillips has named the 'engendering of democracy'.[5] This is a good slogan, in that it suggests that the creation of a proper democracy cannot be achieved until sexual or gender equality has been attained. Of course, it is true that feminism should not be reduced to or defined simply as the pursuit of equality. What this slogan suggests, however, is that feminist theory points out the gender biases in the working of democracy, and seeks to identify their origins and ways of transforming them. Creating democracy, in the sense of a full democracy living up to its promise, means 'engendering' it by breaking down the exclusion of women from full political life.

A defence of liberal-democracy could argue that in this respect liberal-democratic systems have responded to the feminist challenge. After all, it could be maintained, the entry of women into the citizen body has been achieved, and their participation extended in the ranks of the political elites. Therefore whatever goods, in the literal and metaphorical sense, are available to men in liberal-democratic systems are open to women too. The logic of this argument would be that feminist perspectives have nothing to offer in terms of a critique of contemporary liberal-democracy.

The fight to achieve a democratic society by widening the ranks of the citizen body involved the extension of political rights to 'half the human race', to women. Liberal-democratic societies were marked by a protracted and difficult struggle to achieve this. In the United Kingdom it was only after the First

World War that women were successful in gaining the vote, that basic and minimum requirement for effective citizenship. Not until after the Second World War was that goal reached in France, home of the French Revolution and of the tradition invoking the 1789 Declaration of the Rights of Man and Citizen. In Switzerland it was not until 1971 that women achieved the right to vote in the cantonal elections.[6]

For a long period of their existence supposedly democratic regimes in which the idea of popular sovereignty was invoked saw 'the people' as defined in exclusively male terms. Democratic regimes were regimes of exclusion, denying a variety of categories of people the status of 'citizen'. These exclusions, as we noted in Chapter 2, were based on gender, on property and on age, and sometimes on ethnicity and race. The overcoming of exclusion based on gender has been and perhaps remains a central part of the politics of liberal-democratic systems.

We could thus say that feminism has acted as a protest against a false universalism which invoked the rights of the human being, but 'constructed' those rights in practice as exclusively male rights. The critique of this false universalism is similar to the critique practised by Marxism, seeking to debunk or qualify the claims made by liberal-democratic regimes by revealing inequalities hidden beneath the surface.

Gender bias

Feminist perspectives reveal a dimension of power which other theories do not fully consider, if they consider it at all. That dimension of power is, of course, what we have called here the gender dimension. The crucial issue is what that gender dimension really is, in the sense of how it manifests itself in the political life of liberal-democratic societies, at the level of elites, and more broadly in terms of participation in politics and citizenship. The interesting and challenging questions which feminism poses go beyond the mere statement of this dimension of gender power. There are three questions which need to be confronted:

1. What factors are responsible for this gender division, this power dimension, which must severely qualify the extent to which liberal-democratic societies live up to their claims of citizen equality and autonomy? And how exactly, in what ways and at what levels, does this gender division show itself in contemporary politics?
2. What is the relationship between this dimension of power and others, such as class division, or the elite/mass distinction, which have been explained in earlier chapters?
3. How can this dimension of gender power be overcome? Through what strategies and movements can it be transformed? And what are the

implications of such movements of feminism for the power structure and nature of liberal-democracy, and indeed for the very concept of politics?

Our starting point here can be the realisation that the historical achievement of citizenship, at least at the formal level of the vote, which was itself a very protracted process, has not in fact brought about equality of participation and sharing of power between men and women, despite the rhetoric of democratic equality and human rights. Not only did it take many years of struggle to extend the vote to women, but this inegalitarian state of affairs was accepted as natural by political theorists, with a few honourable exceptions, like J.S. Mill. The feminist critique of traditional political theory has seen the traditional canon of political thought as male dominated, written by men for men, acknowledging women, when it did so at all, as represented by their husbands. Indeed, the established tradition of political thought has at times gone further than this, suggesting that because of their emotional and irrational nature, women were not even fit subjects to be represented by others, let alone citizens in their own right. The more 'moderate' position, of women as suitably represented by fathers or husbands, was clearly stated by James Mill, father of John Stuart Mill, in his essay on 'Government'. Writing of 'the principles which ought to guide in determining who the persons are by whom the act of choosing ought to be performed', meaning choosing representatives, James Mill stated:

> One thing is pretty clear, that all those individuals whose interests are indisputably included in those of other individuals, may be struck off without inconvenience. In this light may be viewed all children, up to a certain age, whose interests are involved in those of their parents. In this light, also, women may be regarded, the interest of almost all of whom is involved either in that of their fathers or in that of their husbands.[7]

Hence, the *main*stream of political theory and indeed of political science has been condemned or criticised as *male*stream, accepting without question the exclusion or at best marginalisation of women from political life.

John Stuart Mill, writing in *The Subjection of Women* in 1869, pointed out that the state of affairs regulating the relationship of men and women remained, at the time he was writing, an anomaly in the modern world. At that time, as he clearly indicated, it was not just that women were denied the vote, that minimal condition of entry into the public sphere. They were denied basic legal rights, and in all essentials their autonomy was not recognised, since they could not be property owners in their own right, and they were in all essentials commanded by, and legally and politically subordinate to, their husbands. Mill noted that this was entirely at variance with the beliefs to which the modern (i.e. post-French Revolution) world paid homage. There was an anomaly here which Mill identified very clearly: in no other sphere of life, he observed, did a mere accident of birth disqualify people from competing for and entering certain occupations. As he put it,

At present, in the more improved countries, the disabilities of women are the only case, save one, in which laws and institutions take persons at their birth, and ordain that they shall never in all their lives be allowed to compete for certain things. The one exception is that of royalty . . . The disabilities, therefore, to which women are subject from the mere fact of their birth, are the solitary examples of the kind in modern legislation. In no instance except this, which comprehends half the human race, are the higher social functions closed against any one by a fatality of birth which no exertions, and no change of circumstances, can overcome.[8]

He noted this as 'an isolated fact in modern social institutions; a solitary breach of what has become their fundamental law; a single relic of an old world of thought and practice exploded in everything else, but retained in the one thing of most universal interest'.[9]

Now, over one hundred years later, it could be said that these legal and political anomalies have been removed, and that liberal-democratic societies assert the fundamental equality of women with men, so that if Mill were writing today he would not be able to point out that what he called 'the higher social functions' were closed to women purely because of their gender. Yet the feminist critique of liberal-democracy is that, despite the achievement of this formal political equality, and undoubted progress in legal equality, there still exists in liberal-democratic societies, not to speak of others, a dimension of inequality which has implications for the politics of this kind of system.

The feminist challenge to liberal-democratic societies is well summed up by Jenny Chapman who points out that, despite this formal equality, the presence of women in key positions of power is undeniably thin. As she puts it, 'With a very few and arguable exceptions among industrialised nations, women remain outside the centres of decision-making throughout the world and the forms of status, influence and power which are available to men continue to elude them'.[10] This raises the question of why this is so, and what light it sheds on the politics of liberal-democratic systems.

The study carried out by Jenny Chapman demonstrates what she calls two 'almost iron' laws which determine the participation, or lack of it, of women in the political elite of modern liberal-democratic systems. Just as Michels enunciated his 'iron law of oligarchy', we have here a feminist equivalent, seeking to explain not the unalterable fact of elite domination, but in this case the predominantly male nature of the elite and the exclusion of women from politics. Chapman claims that the two laws are as follows:

1. That wherever political rewards exist which are desirable to men, relatively few women will be found seeking, and even fewer securing them.
2. That wherever there is a hierarchy of such rewards, then the higher up the hierarchy we look, the smaller the proportion of women will be.[11]

There is thus what could be called a universal gender pattern which works to create a male-dominated elite. This pattern seems true for a variety of political systems, liberal-democratic or not, and poses the questions noted above – what are the reasons for it, and how can it be changed? The answer suggested by Chapman seems to be that the recruitment to elite positions is controlled for the most part by those who are already well ensconced in such positions, namely men. The explanation offered here is one of a self-perpetuating elite, which controls entry and assigns top positions on the basis of qualities which they themselves esteem. In the words of Chapman, 'wherever women are seeking access to political elites they are doing so through the medium of institutions created by men', on the basis of qualities which men are more likely to possess: 'whatever the attributes may be which are valued by men, women in a male-dominated society are less likely to possess them'. Chapman's own explanation for the facts that she presents is what she calls the scissors theory, to the effect that 'whatever is associated with success among men, women will have less of it – the first blade of the scissors. Whatever women have that men do not will be of no use to them in competition with men – the second blade.'

Thus the implications of feminism for the power structure of liberal-democratic societies are not merely that there is a deep structure of gender power, but that this affects the nature and composition of the political elite in these societies. Furthermore, this structure of power has not been fundamentally transformed by the acquisition of formal political and legal rights. These rights may be a necessary but are certainly not a sufficient condition for the achievement of genuine equality between men and women. To the extent that this power dimension exists, liberal-democratic societies deny their own principles.

The feminist challenge

We have seen that feminist perspectives in their most general sense point to the long time it took for women to be admitted to the ranks of the citizen body in liberal-democratic societies. Studies of political theory also note how this situation was seen as natural, indeed in some cases was celebrated, by a long line of political theorists in the European canon of political thought.[12] The thinker who was cited in Chapter 2 as the representative democrat, Jean-Jacques Rousseau, appears in a somewhat different light when his views on women are considered. Seeing women as bringing disorder and passion to the commonwealth, Rousseau seems to have had an essentialist notion of their nature as emotional and passionate, i.e. irrational. Thereby he disqualified them from being good citizens, or indeed from being citizens and bearers of political rights at all.[13]

The implications of such by now familiar 'readings' of the classic canon of political thought go beyond the revelation of a deep-rooted sexism in 'the great thinkers', or some of them, of the Western tradition. Our concern here is with what this reveals about the politics and theory of the liberal-democratic state, and the categories appropriate to understanding its power structure. Accounts

Thereby

of the democracy of the Greek city-state make the obvious point that the highly participatory nature of the polis rested on a narrow set of criteria for citizenship, excluding women, not to mention slaves and foreigners.[14] By the same token, the theme of exclusion and inclusion is sounded, as we have seen, by feminist perspectives on liberal-democracy. The acquisition of the right of universal suffrage, itself a difficult and prolonged process, has certainly not led to equality of representation in the ranks of the political elites in liberal-democracies, as we have seen from Jenny Chapman's study. But more than that, the feminist critique is that the gender bias of liberal-democracy bites deeper. It is not merely a question of barriers to the entry of women into the political class of the decision-takers. The feminist challenge is that the conditions for more general participation, indeed the opportunity to be a 'good citizen', are unequally available, and more difficult to achieve for women than for men. This deep inequality again is seen to be hidden under the rhetoric of citizen equality, and is bound up with a particular concept of politics which is associated with some central features of liberal-democratic politics.

This can be explained as follows. At the simplest and most obvious level, if active participation in politics requires time, and if within the family, or in what has traditionally been seen as the 'private' sphere, tasks are unevenly distributed between women and men, then this limits entry into the political sphere, in any active sense, to those who are relatively liberated from child-care and domestic responsibilities. As Anne Phillips notes, 'the very notion of the active citizen presumes someone else is taking care of the children and doing the necessary maintenance of everyday life'.[15] If that 'someone else' is normally a woman rather than a man, this skews or distorts the whole system of entry into the sphere of active citizens. The feminist perspective seeks to unveil a private sphere with its dimension of power which casts in a new light the equality of citizens, and accounts for effective exclusion of women from active political life. It raises the question of how, and with what significance, this 'private' sphere has been constructed and defined, since there is a structure of male power here with important consequences for entry into the 'public' sphere of political activity.

Thus the feminist critique of liberal-democracy seems to have various elements. First, there is the underrepresentation, if not invisibility, of women in the ranks of political elites in liberal democracies. Second, despite formal political equality, there are a number of systematic barriers limiting political involvement on the part of women. These barriers are constituted by an unequal distribution of tasks or a sexual division of labour in the family, and by 'patriarchal' attitudes generally, imparting a systematic bias to the whole political system of liberal-democracy. The bias stems from the social context, a context of gender power. The implication is that what was traditionally referred to as the private or non-political sphere has important implications for politics: indeed, in a sense it is not 'private' at all, since it affects people's availability for political activity. There is a system of 'patriarchy at work' which imparts a gender bias to the whole political system of liberal democracy.[16]

It should be noted in passing that this analysis is not limited to or specific to liberal-democracy. The study by Jenny Chapman contains data comparing two liberal-democratic systems (USA and UK) with the USSR. Her conclusions point to the ways in which 'dominant parties in three very different political settings are a vital part of the process which converts male status in one sphere into resources in the other, and how women, without status in either, cannot be beneficiaries'.[17] Her somewhat pessimistic analysis establishes that it is socioeconomic resources which are crucial to entry into the ranks of the 'political class'. Because women generally have less of these than men do, entry into politics is more difficult for women. Where there are movements or parties, such as Social Democratic or Labour Parties, which challenge this dominance of the higher socioeconomic class, this does not make things much better either, because traditionally such movements have favoured male industrial workers for promotion and nomination as candidates: 'the criteria of selection never work to the advantage of women, irrespective of whether their tendency is to reinforce or to modify the standard model of recruitment among men'.[18]

However, feminist perspectives are concerned not just to analyse this state of affairs (patriarchy), but also to change it. Our subject here is the way in which feminist perspectives and movements shed a new light not just on the power structure of liberal-democratic systems, but more generally on the definition of what is 'political', the nature of politics and problems of power. The feminist challenge is to suggest that liberal-democracy is in some deep sense 'flawed', because the composition of the political elites and access to the ranks of active citizens remain deeply affected by the gendered nature of power, despite the achievement of equal rights in the political and legal spheres. The political elite, indeed the very nature of the state itself, is consequently affected. The state in a liberal-democratic society is a 'male' state, because of the gender of the personnel who primarily compose its ranks, and hence this imparts certain systematic biases to policy outputs.

This, however, raises certain theoretically interesting and practically important questions, which again go to the heart of the politics of liberal-democratic systems. Seeing the state in feminist terms as a male state rests on certain assumptions, which touch themes of equality and difference. To speak of feminist perspectives is indeed an abstraction, since there are different feminist theories which each have contrasting views on how the 'maleness' or patriarchy of the existing system of liberal-democracy is to be overcome. Many currents of feminism have seen feminist movements as exemplifying a totally different style of politics, which contrasts with the 'atomism' of traditional liberal-democracy. It is argued that women as women have interests and concerns common to them. These do not get expressed in the political system of liberal-democracy, which is thus unresponsive to certain issues; they are excluded from consideration. This is due in part to the 'maleness' of the political elite, but the matter goes deeper than that. The very structures of the liberal-democratic state are, or at least traditionally were, lacking in structures or movements which put these issues on the agenda of politics. The politics of liberal-democracy thus involves a 'mobilisation of bias' – to use the term coined by Schattschneider, although not used by him in connection with feminism – which systematically marginalises or excludes a range of issues relating to women as women.[19] Thus the politics of liberal-democracy remains, so to speak, skewed or distorted. A dimension of power exists which, while not exactly immune from criticism, persists in an obscured and hidden form.

The system of liberal-democratic pluralism includes a range of groups which express particular interests, mainly ones stemming from people's (usually men's) role in employment or in the productive sphere. The male nature of these groups has, however, excluded certain issues from being considered, and is related to the unrepresentative gender composition of the political elite both as cause and consequence. Here again the feminist critique would be in some respects parallel to the Marxist view – that the state is not neutral, some interests are dominant, and this contradicts the notions of equality and responsiveness to citizen interests which supposedly underlie the liberal-democratic state.

These considerations lead to discussion of the nature and content of those issues which traditionally have been kept off the agenda in liberal-democratic systems, and the related topic of the means through which this situation of exclusion or marginalisation might be transformed. In this connection it is necessary to discuss the question of feminism as movement, and the implications of feminism for the nature of participation in the liberal-democratic state.

With reference to the first question, a useful enumeration can be made following the demands of the first Women's Liberation conference held at Ruskin College, Oxford, in 1970. According to Lovenduski and Randall, four issues were raised: equal pay; equal education and opportunity; 24-hour nurseries; and free contraception and abortion on demand. To these issues were added, four years later, demands for financial and legal independence for women; and an end to discrimination against lesbians and the call for a woman's right to choose her own sexuality. Finally, in 1978 there was a demand for freedom from intimidation by threat or use of violence or sexual coercion, and 'an end to all laws, assumptions and institutions which perpetuate male dominance and men's aggression towards women'.[20] These issues were placed on the agenda of the politics of liberal-democratic systems by the women's liberation movement, a new force in the politics of this form of state.

The feminist challenge to liberal-democracy was to point out that these issues were not being expressed or articulated in the liberal-democratic system, and that to change this situation a new type of movement was required, a women's movement which would express a new form of politics. The significance of the feminist movement is thus twofold: a critique of what were seen as the inadequacies of liberal-democratic politics, and the affirmation of a more spontaneous and participatory kind of movement, both social and political, extending the boundaries of the political.

Feminism can be seen as a movement *different in kind* from the more traditional groups, movements and parties which had previously arisen in liberal-democratic systems. In this sense feminism can be seen to be operating with a different concept of politics, emphasising themes of participation and spontaneity. It involves a critique of hierarchy, which some feminist perspectives have seen as typical of male-dominated and traditional movements in the political and social sphere. Thus the challenge was to develop a new style of politics which would overcome the alienation which seemed to be inherent in bureaucratised and large-scale movements. Those existing social and political movements seemed to be prime candidates for Michels' iron law of oligarchy. The aim here was to develop movements which would operate in different ways, not merely raising different issues, but acting and organising differently, to achieve a style or form of politics based on more direct forms of participation and spontaneity.

The feminist critique of the politics of liberal-democracy at this point involves a critique of the 'distancing' of liberal-democracy and its politics from everyday life. In particular, the critique is that participation for most people, unless they are especially active citizens, is limited to the act of voting in local and national elections at regular intervals, an intermittent act seemingly often remote from everyday concerns. The feminist emphasis on movements of a new type was seen to validate and exemplify a much more immediate type of politics, compared with which the role of citizen offered by the electoral politics of liberal-democracy, important though that was, seemed rather dreary and unsatisfying, as well as spasmodic.

Anne Phillips has shown well how the exaltation of spontaneity and direct ongoing participation raises certain problems. This form of highly participatory politics, whether in feminist or other forms, makes heavy demands on those committed to it, and creates its own forms of inclusion and exclusion. There are those, in any social movement of this type, who are able and willing to practise this 'total' politics, and those who are not, and who find themselves excluded from such movements because they are not willing to make such heavy commitments, or are unable to do so. Furthermore, this raises a central problem of democratic theory, that such movements give more weight to the 'intense' activists, those who do have the time and energy for such activity. In French syndicalist theory these were called the *minorités agissantes*, the active and creative minorities who were supposed to spur on and mobilise the rest, and wake the other workers or unionists from their lethargy. The theoretical problem that this raises is the question of whether such commitment or energy can count as an 'entitlement' to have a greater say than those who, for whatever reason or inclination, do not take the step towards the activist and highly participatory model. This creates a new division between activists, a possible minority, and 'the others'.

The strength of the liberal-democratic mode of involvement, although possibly its weakness too, is that it does not make too high or heavy demands on citizens. In the voting booth, the votes of all count equally, whether they are activist or not, whatever their degree of involvement. The positive side of the voting model, if it can be called that, is that 'The higher the demands placed on participation, the more inevitable that it will be unevenly spread around; the more active the democratic engagement, the more likely it is to be carried by only a few.'[21] However, the other side of the coin of this liberal-democratic mode of involvement is that it does not take any account of activism, or give intensity of preference any weight. It should be made clear that these problems are not specific to feminism; they are raised by all movements which promote and seek to justify a more activist and participatory mode of politics than is afforded by 'normal' liberal-democratic politics.

A further argument is that such spontaneous and participatory movements afford opportunities for developing awareness of identity and shared interests which the 'atomised' mode of involvement of the ballot box does not allow. The feminist critique of liberal-democracy thus focuses on certain strengths and weaknesses of the participation, limited though it is, which is the 'normal' mode of involvement in such systems.

It was not just a new mode of organisation or participation that feminist movements put forward. While they were not the only type of such movements, they can be taken as exemplifying what have been called the 'new social movements', one of whose characteristics has been the attempt to develop alternative modes of participation. Beyond that, however, it is a redefinition of the 'political' which is involved here. The feminist challenge was that certain issues had been kept off the agenda of politics: issues relating to the sexual division of labour. These issues are ones which were previously defined as non-political or 'private', relating purely to the domestic sphere. The contribution of feminism was that it brought into the political sphere issues that formerly were not considered political at all.

The importance of the feminist critique is therefore that it highlights the problematic nature of what is meant by the sphere of the political. The nature of power relationships in the so-called private sphere clearly has implications for questions of 'politics' in the traditional sense. The dimension of power in the 'private' sphere, as traditionally constructed, of the family affects people's 'availability' for political activity, and in that way determines the broader question of who participates in politics and with what results. The gender dimension of power thus influences quite strongly the nature of the 'public' sphere, and in that way the functioning and health of the liberal-democratic system. Of course, the danger here is that this extension or redefinition of the sphere of the political can lead to a 'politicisation' of all aspects of life which is not necessarily welcome. Yet what is meant by the slogan 'the personal is political' is rather that political participation and the formation of political elites cannot be divorced from, or remain unaffected by, the dimension of power in the wider society. In this respect feminism identifies a system of male dominance, or patriarchy, which other theories of politics do not take into account.

We should note here that there is a further problem with feminism as a movement. It really raises the question of how what we have called the 'gender dimension' of power relates to other forms of power and division, such as class or ethnic relationships. For at least some versions of feminist theory, it can be said that gender divisions play the role which class divisions hold in Marxist theory. In neither case is the particular power dimension under question (gender in the feminist theory, class in the Marxist one) seen as the *only* division in society; nor is politics reduced just to the expression of gender divisions or class divisions. But it may be said that in each case the division in question is seen as the fundamental one, and the model (of feminism or Marxism) highlights that particular division or 'fault' as the basic one in society. In feminist perspectives, this then entails the view that women as women have important interests in common, as an oppressed group – interests opposed to those of men. Part of the purpose of feminist movements, part of the process of what has been called 'consciousness raising', has been to develop awareness of this unity of interests. The critique of liberal-democratic societies, as we have seen, was that these interests were ignored or marginalised by the power structure of liberal-democratic societies, and the purpose of the women's movement was to remedy this situation. However, as the account by Lovenduski and Randall of contemporary feminist politics in Britain makes clear, feminist politics, like Marxist politics, has not been immune to divisions and cross-cutting issues which fragment the movement.

Lovenduski and Randall point out that, with the development of feminist politics in Britain, the initial assumption that women as women had interests in common came under challenge because of other issues and divisions. They note that 'The starting point of the WLM was the belief that women had a common interest in challenging their male oppressors. But, almost immediately, the different political backgrounds of feminists began to fracture the movement's unity.'[22] This was partly a matter of women in different class positions, or in different racial or ethnic groups, claiming that there were significant differences between and among women which had to be recognised. For example, according to Lovenduski and Randall, black women 'criticised a feminist movement which claimed to speak for all women, but which made virtually no attempt to involve black women or to reflect their special concerns'.[23]

The interesting point here is that this suggests that in understanding the power structure of liberal-democratic societies, or indeed any system, one needs to be open to the possibility of different dimensions of power and inequality which cut across each other, which is a point made in pluralist perspectives. Thus, just as socialist politics has in practical terms had to cope with movements or ideas such as nationalism which cut across class lines, or movements of religious affiliation which do the same, so too has feminist politics come to develop ideas of people having a variety of identities – for example, as women, or as people in particular class or ethnic positions – identities which may in a particular situation conflict with each other. What is known as the politics of identity seems to be a developing branch of political science, highlighting the way in which people have a variety of identities and interests, each of which can be tapped or mobilised by particular movements and ideas.

In this respect, the question of feminist movements and the way they propose to challenge the fact of male domination is also of central importance for understanding the politics of liberal-democracy. We noted earlier that feminism in some of its varieties has defended and articulated ideas of spontaneous, non-hierarchical movements. But this is by no means the only form of feminist politics, and various observers have noted a shift away from the more participatory 'grass-roots' attitude and from its hostility to more 'orthodox' forms of politics. This has changed to a more favourable attitude to engagement in the politics of liberal-democracy, and to involvement in its established institutions, such as representative assemblies and mainstream political parties. Anne Phillips observes a development or transformation away from what she calls 'the first moment in feminist thinking' which emphasised the themes of direct democracy and participation. Such concerns gave way to a somewhat different concern with themes of citizenship:

> In the first phase, feminists concerned themselves with what we might call the micro-level of democracy inside a movement, and democracy in everyday life. In the second phase, we have turned to the macro-level of women's membership in the political community: exploring questions of inclusion and exclusion, and dampening down the universalising pretensions of modern political thought.[24]

More empirically minded observers note that at least in Britain, with reference to the period after 1979, 'many British feminists became active in the traditional institutions of political competition – parties, unions and local government'.[25] The problem here, as with all radical movements, is the danger of institutionalisation, the problem of integration into existing institutions. This resulted in a division between those feminists who wanted a greater degree of direct participation and spontaneity, and those women who felt that, for anything to be changed, access had to be gained to existing institutions and centres of power. There was an antagonism between those sections of the women's movement which were committed to a 'new' conception of politics, pointing to the limitations of the traditional representative institutions of liberal-democracy, and those who with a greater or lesser degree of reluctance saw the terrain of activity or pressure as lying within the key institutions of liberal-democracy, notably in terms of the existing parties, unions and, in some cases, sympathetic local government. This raises questions of tactics and strategy which are not our chief concern here.

These debates and dilemmas parallel the dilemmas of socialist and working-class movements, faced with the problem of whether or not to participate in the existing institutions of the 'bourgeois' state, or alternatively to practise a politics of 'abstentionism', avoiding the dangers of integration in those very same institutions. The politics of feminism raises the same question of the extent to which liberal-democratic institutions have the capacity to absorb or neutralise opposition. The final section of this chapter reviews the different tendencies in feminist politics, concentrating on another crucial aspect of feminist politics: how can the system of male domination be changed?

Feminism and the politics of liberal-democracy

It was noted above that feminism cannot be considered as one undifferentiated block, since there are very different strands within it. They may all agree in pointing out the gender dimension of power, and the gender bias of the state in liberal-democratic and in other systems of power. However, they differ in what are seen as the causes of that male power or patriarchy, and also in the means seen as necessary to transform the structure of male domination. There are also differences between the various forms of feminism in the way they conceptualise the relationships between this dimension of power (patriarchy) and other forms of power, such as class.

The conventional distinction, which is made in most books on the subject, is into three strands of feminism, which are labelled 'liberal', 'socialist', and 'radical'. It may, however, be doubted whether this division is so helpful in understanding what feminist perspectives have to contribute to the analysis of power in liberal-democratic systems. Liberal feminist perspectives, as usually defined, concentrate on legal and political inequalities preventing women as individuals from entering the public sphere. The obvious corollary of this, in terms of strategies to change the structure of male domination, is that there should be equality of opportunity, absence of discrimination on gender lines, and that the extension of those 'Rights of Man and Citizen' proclaimed by the French Revolution's Declaration of 1789 should in reality be extended to all citizens – that women no less than men should have effective rights of access to the public sphere.

Historically, this liberal feminism underwent the same fate as liberalism in general. It was challenged by socialism. Socialist feminists took up the challenge that the acquisition of legal and political rights was insufficient as a means of sexual or gender emancipation, since it left untouched what was the real cause of sexual inequality, namely the economic context, the ownership of property. This was seen as the real underpinning of gender division, with the corollary that sexual equality could only be attained once a socialist revolution had taken place. The implication in at least some versions of socialist feminism was that women's emancipation would have to wait until the 'great day' of socialist revolution, and thus a politics of deferment was in order. This subordination of the politics of feminism to socialist politics was not endorsed by later socialist feminists, who have developed a more subtle analysis of the relationship between class inequality and gender inequality.

Finally, radical feminism has been used as a label to denote a more heterogeneous strand of feminist theory which cannot be placed either in the 'liberal' or the 'socialist' streams of feminism. This strand of radical feminism holds that it is neither legal nor political discrimination, neither inequality of rights nor economic inequality, which forms the bedrock of gender power, but a much more subtle and pervasive form of power, labelled 'patriarchy', which is manifested through a variety of social and political institutions, indeed through the whole culture of society, both in liberal-democratic and in other societies. Such patriarchy may well be propped up by, and in its turn contribute to, inequality of legal and political rights and economic inequality, but 'patriarchy' forms a structure of power in its own right, and cannot be reduced to or seen as dependent on other forms of inequality, as is held by both liberal and socialist or Marxist forms of feminism.

In some of its forms, radical feminism seems to hold that there are essential differences between men and women, which cannot be eradicated, and that these differences have to be 'celebrated'. Men are seen as destructive, violent and negative, and a political system based on male power is seen as correspondingly endowed with these qualities. However, not all forms of radical feminism take this line. In many respects, radical feminism can be seen as a critique of the inadequacies of other forms of feminism, seeing liberal feminism and socialist feminism as not going far enough in touching on the real causes of sexual inequality, and failing to grasp a 'deep structure' of male power: in other words, giving too superficial an account of the causes of male domination and the means necessary to overcome that. In the radical feminist perspective, neither the extension of legal rights and the achievement of the suffrage, nor radical socioeconomic transformations, would be enough to secure the eradication of patriarchy, important though such transformations and changes might be. To achieve a transformation of gender relations would be 'the longest revolution', as Juliet Mitchell calls it, which would entail changes in all spheres of life, and changes in the way people see each other. It would above all entail changes in the sphere hitherto and still considered 'private', the sphere of the family and the sexual division of labour, which still imposes an unequal burden on women and which, as we saw above, has important implications for their entry into the public or political sphere. As Susan Moller Okin points out, 'An equal sharing between the sexes of family responsibilities, especially child care, is "the great revolution that never happened".'[26]

It could thus be said that radical feminist perspectives really widen the concept of the political, and indeed the idea of what is meant by revolution. Political transformations and the attack on the dimension of gender power depend primarily not on a change in the holders of political power, but on much wider transformations in the family, in the sexual division of labour. These transformations are seen as highly relevant to changes in the political sphere, narrowly defined. Changes in the wider context are seen as necessary preconditions for altering the nature of the political elite and the nature of politics in modern societies.

The problem with this conventional tripartite distinction into three forms of feminist political analysis – liberal, socialist/Marxist and radical – is that it is at one and the same time too vague and over-general, and also suggests that the three categories are mutually exclusive when perhaps they are complementary as modes of analysis.[27] They can all be seen as approaches to understanding what we have here called the gender dimension of politics, but they are approaches which need not be mutually exclusive. There seems no reason to think that legal or political discrimination, economic inequality and the broader phenomenon of 'patriarchy' could not be seen as different facets of one dimension of power, the power of men over women.

This leaves untouched the wider question of how this gender dimension of power is to be transformed. Many accounts of feminism which use this tripartite distinction point out that each variety or strand of feminism offers a different perspective on the appropriate means for challenging gender power. Socialist feminists would, obviously enough, see the success of such a challenge as in some sense bound up with the fortunes of a socialist movement, whatever form that might take. Here it could be pointed out not only that such perspectives risk making feminism a sort of hostage to another type of movement, but that socialist challenges to the existing order, to the extent that they are possible in the present situation, would still prove capable of provoking a capitalist backlash which might undermine the chances of success of both socialism and feminism.[28] Radical feminist perspectives would see an autonomous women's movement as an important precondition for an effective and sustained challenge to patriarchy and for the transformation of male power. This then raises the question, noted above with reference to contemporary British feminism, that there is a tension between an autonomous women's movement and a possible 'integration' into established institutions. At least there is the problem of finding a 'space' within existing institutions, and the danger of the absorption of an independent movement.

The problem with these statements is that they are highly general. They do, however, show that talk of an undifferentiated feminism is not very helpful, considering the variety of distinct and often opposed feminisms. We need to sum up by showing what feminist perspectives in their variety suggest about the power structure of liberal-democratic systems, and why feminist theory provides insights and a perspective different from the other theories covered above.

We noted above that feminism is important as critique, as an exposure in the first place of the male nature of the political elite, and the barriers to full citizenship which impede women from full citizenship autonomy. In theoretical terms, feminist perspectives are also a critique of all the other theories of power considered so far in this book, criticising them for being blind to one crucial dimension of power. Pluralist theories emphasise group conflict and the pressure from civil society on the state. Feminist perspectives point out a number of ways in which this pluralist theory ignores several features that limit or distort the pluralist perspective. The question arises whether the male nature of these pluralist pressure groups, and of the state elite too, relegates or marginalises women's participation in politics, and prevents issues which women as women have in common from being part of the political agenda. Defenders of pluralist politics could, it is true, claim that the women's movement is an exemplification of pressure group politics, of the emergence of issues which were not previously on the agenda, and maintain that this shows the openness of the political system.

However, this answer is too facile, since it neglects the continuing predominantly male character of the political elite and other elites in liberal-democratic systems. Feminist perspectives thus cast doubt on how truly representative liberal-democratic systems are, and they function as a critique both of pluralism and also of elitism. Feminism suggests that pluralism neglects the gender dimension of politics, by turning a blind eye to the male nature of the elites of pressure groups. By the same token, feminism can be seen as a critique of elitism. While elite theories accept, or even defend, the inevitability of minority rule, they fail to recognise the predominantly male composition of the political elite in liberal-democratic societies and its implications. The implications are severe in terms of the nature of liberal-democracies as representing the interests of their citizens. It is of course true that 'representing one's interests' and 'being representative of', in the sense of reflecting the nature or identity of people, are two separate senses of representation. In other words, it could be said that the male nature of the political elite does not matter because they could be as good or as capable as women of representing women's interests, even though by their gender they did or do not represent women in the sense of reflecting their characteristics. However, it is at least a reasonable presumption that representation in the sense of 'reflecting the characteristics of' is to some degree a necessary condition for representation in terms of 'representing the interests of'.[29] Thus the overwhelmingly male nature of the political elite in liberal-democracies can be held to undermine the representative nature, and hence the democratic credentials, of contemporary liberal-democracy.

Second, as far as elitism is concerned, feminism can be seen as a critique in the sense of defending movements which were anti-elitist, anti-hierarchical in their structure, thus casting doubt on the elitist thesis of the inevitability of structured minority domination. Of course, the existence of these 'new social movements', of which feminism is one, movements of a participatory and non-hierarchical kind, does not necessarily disprove elitist theories of oligarchical tendencies and pressures, but it does suggest at least the possibility of movements organised in different ways, opposing the iron law of oligarchy.

As far as Marxism is concerned, both Marxism and feminism can be seen as concerned to unveil a deep structure of power which was hidden from view by the superficial appearance of liberal-democratic systems. Feminism and Marxism thus in a way go together at least in their approach to the analysis of the power structure of liberal-democracy. They wish to probe beneath the surface appearance. However, feminism can also be seen as critical of Marxist theory in at least some of its versions for practising a politics of 'deferment', for being somewhat blind to the gender dimension of politics, and for being too 'reductionist' in the explanation of gender inequality. In addition, some feminists might suggest that, while at least for some people it may be possible through social mobility to 'escape' from their subordinate class and the oppression that this subordinate status brings, 'escaping' from one's position as a woman is not possible, even though gender inequalities may be to some extent 'compensated' or disguised through a higher socioeconomic position.

The crucial question is to see what the feminist perspective offers which other perspectives on politics do not offer. Here our concluding words could be that it is not so much the nature or composition of the elite which is important, but the widening of the definition of the political, to include matters hitherto deemed to fall outside the political sphere. This has important implications for understanding the nature of politics in liberal-democratic systems, and indeed in all forms of state. It suggests that power is not restricted to the sphere of the state, and that there is a dimension of power in civil society which is not grasped by those theories of politics which limit themselves to the interaction between state and civil society. This dimension of power has to be grasped to understand the issues with which politics in liberal-democratic societies is concerned, and those which are excluded from the agenda. There is a structure of power in the family, a sexual division of labour, which not only limits the freedom and emancipation that are promised by the defenders of liberal-democracy, but also has crucial implications for the idea of citizenship, limiting the capacity for effective citizenship, and hence autonomy, of half the population of liberal-democracies. Feminist perspectives include not only the uncovering of the existence of this dimension of power, but discussion of ways to transform it, and the relationship of this dimension of power to other forms of power and inequality which exist in liberal-democratic society.

Notes

1. Randall, V., *Women and Politics: An international perspective*, Macmillan, Basingstoke, 1987; and Sassoon, A.S. (ed.), *Women and the State: The shifting boundaries of public and private*, Routledge, London, 1992.

2. See Burstyn, V., 'Masculine dominance and the state', in *The Socialist Register 1983*, ed. R. Miliband and J. Saville, Merlin, London, 1983, pp. 45–89.

3. Marx, K., *Capital*, Vol. I, Lawrence & Wishart, London, 1954, p. 172.

4. Gobetti, D., *Private and Public: Individuals, households and body politic in Locke and Hutcheson*, Routledge, London and New York, 1992, pp. 14ff. See more generally, Elshtain, J.B., *Public Man, Private Woman: Women in social and political thought*, 2nd edition, Princeton University Press, Princeton, NJ, 1993.

5. Phillips, A., *Engendering Democracy*, Polity, Cambridge, 1991.

6. See Lovenduski, J., *Women and European Politics: Contemporary feminism and public policy*, Wheatsheaf, Brighton, 1986, p. 233.

7. James Mill, 'Government', in Mill, J., *Political Writings*, ed. T. Ball, Cambridge University Press, Cambridge, 1992, p. 27.

8. Mill, J.S., *The Subjection of Women*, in Mill, *On Liberty*, ed. S. Collini, Cambridge University Press, Cambridge, 1989, p. 137.

9. Mill, *The Subjection of Women*, p. 137.

10. Chapman, J., *Politics, Feminism and the Reformation of Gender*, Routledge, London and New York, 1993, p. xi.

11. Chapman, *Politics, Feminism and the Reformation of Gender*, p. 4.

12. See Coole, D., *Women in Political Theory*, 2nd edition, Harvester Wheatsheaf, Hemel Hempstead, 1993; and Okin, S.M., *Women in Western Political Thought*, Princeton University Press, Princeton, NJ, 1979.

13. See Pateman, C., *The Disorder of Women: Democracy, feminism and political theory*, Polity, Cambridge, 1989.

14. See Hornblower., S., 'Creation and development of democratic institutions in Ancient Greece', in Dunn, J. (ed.), *Democracy: The unfinished journey 508 BC to AD 1993*, Oxford University Press, Oxford, 1992.

15. Phillips, A., 'Must feminists give up on liberal democracy?', in Held, D. (ed.), *Prospects for Democracy*, Polity, Cambridge, 1993, p. 100.

16. Walby, S., *Theorizing Patriarchy*, Blackwell, Oxford, 1990.

17. Chapman, J., *Politics, Feminism and the Reformation of Gender*, p. 73.

18. Chapman, J., *Politics, Feminism and the Reformation of Gender*, p. 70.

19. See Schattschneider, E., *The Semi-Sovereign People*, Holt, Rinehart & Winston, New York, 1960.

20. Lovenduski, J., and Randall, V., *Contemporary Feminist Politics: Women and power in Britain*, Oxford University Press, Oxford, 1993, p. 10.

21. Phillips, 'Must feminists give up on liberal democracy?', p. 101.

22. Lovenduski and Randall, *Contemporary Feminist Politics*, p. 65.

23. Lovenduski and Randall, p. 80.

24. Phillips, 'Must feminists give up on liberal democracy?', p. 94.

25. Lovenduski and Randall, p. 133.

26. Okin, S.M., *Justice, Gender and the Family*, Basic Books, New York, 1989, p. 4.

27. Bryson, V., *Feminist Political Theory*, Macmillan, London, 1993, p. 4.

28. Beetham, D., 'The limits of democratization' in Held, D. (ed.), *Prospects for Democracy*, p. 69.

29. Pitkin, H.F., *The Concept of Representation*, University of California Press, Berkeley, CA, 1967; Pitkin, H.F. (ed.), *Representation*, Atherton Press, New York, 1969.

Part II

Rivals to the liberal-democratic state

7 | The communist state and its collapse

Introduction

This book has as its purpose the investigation of the power of the modern state, and the analysis of theories explaining and assessing its power. It was noted in the introduction that, in the conditions of late twentieth-century politics, the liberal-democratic state appears to have 'seen off' its two main rivals, those state forms which for much of the twentieth century offered different models of the state, namely communist regimes and fascist systems. This chapter seeks to explain the main features of the first of those two rival systems, and some of the problems raised by the collapse of communism.

First, however, we need to explain the framework within which communist systems or regimes are being dealt with here. In the first instance, the aim is to show a different model of the state, which contrasts with liberal-democratic systems in various ways. The purpose of doing so is partly to cast more light on the nature of the liberal-democratic state, by comparing such 'pluralistic' states with those dominated by a monopolistic state party. From the perspective of pluralism, the communist state illuminates or exemplifies the totalitarian state, a state form which sought to achieve the full politicisation of society, the ultimate idea of total control. How far such a characterisation of the communist state is valid is considered further below.

More generally, the analysis of the communist state and its collapse is relevant for the following reasons. It suggests the appeals of a form of state which claimed both to offer a model of democracy or an idea of popular power different from the model of liberal-democracy, and to satisfy demands for social equality and an alternative to 'bourgeois society'. A brief historical survey of this form of state, notably in the form it took in the Soviet Union, illuminates both the original appeals of such a model of political power, and its failure to achieve the goals it proclaimed. Those goals were political, the idea of a new state structure (the Commune state), and social and economic, in terms of the model of a collectivist and, in some senses, more egalitarian economic structure. In addition, Gorbachev's attempt at reform of the Soviet system, or *perestroika*, is one of the most striking attempts at what could be called 'in-system reform' of modern times – and one of the most unsuccessful ever.

Second, discussion of what we call here communist regimes is also highly relevant to the question of the nature of Marxism and its importance in the twentieth century. It was noted in Chapter 5 that there is a fundamental distinction between Marxism as a critical theory, and the nature and structure of those communist regimes that claimed to realise the principles and goals of Marxism. Such systems claimed also to have achieved a higher form of democracy than was possible in the class-dominated systems of liberal-democracy. Examining the principles underlying such communist systems and their historical evolution is a necessary element in understanding the fate of Marxism in the twentieth century. There are indeed fundamental differences between the theory of Marxism and the practice of communist regimes. However, it is difficult to deny that the existence of those systems of what have been labelled 'real existing socialism' and their claim, however distorted, to represent or realise Marxism in practice, had a huge influence on modern politics. Opponents of Marxism claimed that the undemocratic and even totalitarian nature of such systems revealed a fundamental truth about Marxism, and showed what its theory meant in practice. The association of Marxism with systems in which effectively unchecked power came to be concentrated in the hands of a party–state elite meant that Marxist alternatives to liberal-democracy had much less appeal in those societies. The Marxist critique of such systems of 'bourgeois democracy' carried less conviction, given the apparent connection of Marxism with systems which could be described as repressive and undemocratic. Thus the second reason for investigating the nature of such systems is to cast some light on the fate of Marxist politics, and the way in which Marxism came to be put into practice, albeit in a distorted form, in a context quite different from that which Marx and Engels had envisaged as 'ripe' for socialist revolution, and with results very different from what they envisaged as a socialist society.

One final preliminary observation relates to the comparison between communist regimes and fascist ones. They are each dealt with here in consecutive chapters under a general heading of 'rivals to the liberal-democratic state'. However, this does not imply that these rival systems to liberal-democracy are fundamentally the same, or that they represent the *only* possible alternatives to liberal-democracy. The differences between fascist and communist regimes are crucial. Moreover, there are numerous other types of state in the modern world which are not liberal-democracies but do not fall under the heading of either 'communist' or 'fascist'. In particular, authoritarian regimes, such as military dictatorship or forms of clerical conservatism, have been important in twentieth-century politics, not to speak of earlier times, yet they lack the 'totalitarian' and all-pervasive drives characteristic of both communism and fascism. The differences between authoritarian and totalitarian regimes are discussed further in Chapter 8. The differences between the two systems of fascism and communism remain, however, especially in the fact that the communist regime emerged as a revolutionary challenge to liberal-democracy and to the idea of a market society. Fascist systems, in all their complexity, developed out of a crisis in liberal-democracy, seeking to defend the private ownership of productive resources from a threat, real or imagined, from the Left.

The treatment of communist systems offered here is thus to be seen as illuminating the nature of liberal-democracy, as casting light on the politics of Marxism and, beyond that, as contributing to a deeper understanding of theories of pluralism and elitism. It involves some historical material dealing with the emergence and development of the communist regime, so that this chapter contains a sketch of the historical background of the Soviet system.

Liberal-democracy and communist systems compared

In seeking to understand the nature of the communist system and its features, comparing them with liberal-democracy, we can take as a starting point two obvious and central points of contrast. The first is between the nature of communist systems as systems of *one-party rule* and the 'pluralistic' competition between parties and pressure groups characteristic of liberal-democracy, celebrated in pluralist theory. Second, the contrast lies in the different social and economic context of the two systems. Communist or Soviet-type systems operated with a system of a *planned economy* (or a command economy), in which the resources of society were in overwhelming proportion collectively owned and administered. This contrasts with the liberal system of a mixed economy, in which, however modified by some degree of state ownership and intervention, economic decisions are taken through the mechanisms of the market.

Two other features can be added to those already mentioned. They refer, first, to the propagation in communist systems of an official ideology of Marxism-Leninism, by which decisions were supposed to be justified, and second, to the control by the single party of 'civil society' and its institutions. In the words of one text defining communist systems, 'the range of institutions which in Western societies were more or less independent of the political authorities, e.g. press, trade unions, courts, were in the communist states effectively under the direct control of the party hierarchy'.[1] In other words, the separation between 'state' and 'civil society' which is held to characterise 'pluralist' systems did not apply in communist systems. Civil society was controlled to a considerable degree, if not totally, by the single party, a characteristic which in the eyes of some analysts of this system merited the label 'totalitarian'. This term describes the attempt of such regimes, albeit not realised completely, to achieve the 'politicisation' of all areas of social life, the idea that 'nothing was private'.[2] Compared with liberal-democratic societies, which are marked by a range of groups and associations, independent of the state and of each other, such groups in communist systems were regarded as 'transmission belts' for party commands, means for sealing the single party's control over society. For this reason, movements of opposition in communist societies, such as the trade union Solidarity in Poland, initially attempted to carve out for themselves a sphere of independent action, to gain autonomy from the control of the party.

Thus communist systems were characterised not merely by the control of the state by a single party, but also by the pervasive nature of political power, the 'invasion' of civil society by the state. Those who use the label 'totalitarian' to describe such societies point to the attempt to 'mobilise' the population in active support of the single party and its ideology. Critics of this label, on the other hand, suggest that while the term 'totalitarian' might possibly describe the Soviet system under Stalin, after 1953 Soviet systems moved to a more pluralistic form, in which elements of opposition and dissent manifested themselves, even if in a covert form within the higher echelons of the ruling party.[3]

The purpose of the following exposition is to survey the historical evolution of the Soviet system, and to analyse the ideas underlying it. There are really three issues to be considered here, which structure the material that follows: first, the historic evolution of the Soviet system, as exemplified by the case of the USSR; second, the features of the 'classic' Soviet system, in which 'the leading role of the party' was the basic element of the state structure; and third, the unsuccessful attempt of Gorbachev in his 'perestroika project' to remodel the system, and the implications of that failure not just for Marxist theories but more generally.

The Bolshevik Revolution

In contrasting the liberal-democratic and the communist state, the starting point can be the historical observation that the Soviet system in Russia was the prototype or model for this type of state system. This system emerged from the revolutionary overthrow of Tsarism in February 1917, followed some eight months later by the Bolshevik seizure of power in the October Revolution. The communist system thus emerged out of a revolution made in the name of Marxism against the newly born and weakly implanted liberal-democratic regime of Russia, installed after the collapse of Tsarism in the February Revolution of 1917.

The first problem here is the obvious one that the Bolshevik Revolution of October 1917 took place under circumstances very different from those analysed by Marx as prerequisites of socialist revolution. For Marx and Engels a socialist or communist revolution would be possible only on the basis of a mature and ripe capitalism, in which the working class would form the majority of the population, and where the polarisation of classes had resulted in a situation in which the 'two great hostile camps' confronted each other. In the words of Marx and Engels' text *The German Ideology* (unpublished in their lifetime), a communist revolution could be achieved only once capitalism had maximised its productive powers. The 'estrangement' of capitalism, they wrote, could be abolished only given certain '*practical* premises':

> It must necessarily have rendered the great mass of humanity 'propertyless', and produced, at the same time, the contradictions of an existing world of wealth and culture, both of which conditions presuppose a great increase in productive power, a high degree of its development.

In bold words, they noted that 'Empirically, communism is only possible "all at once" and simultaneously, which presupposes the universal development of productive forces and the world intercourse bound up with communism.'[4]

From the very time of the Bolshevik seizure of power, both critics of Bolshevism and more friendly observers noted that this prerequisite for socialist revolution was not satisfied in the case of the Bolshevik Revolution. Lenin and the Bolshevik party set up the Soviet state in circumstances quite different from those indicated in the above quotation. Some critics of Bolshevism, such as Karl Kautsky, the chief Marxist theoretician of what before the First World War had been a united socialist and Marxist movement, argued that the attempt to create a socialist state and society in such circumstances was doomed to failure. It would lead only to the tarnishing of the socialist project as a whole. In his pamphlet *The Dictatorship of the Proletariat* published in 1918 Kautsky suggested that the Bolshevik Revolution could result only in dictatorship. This would not be the dictatorship of the proletariat as envisaged by Marx (in his text *The Civil War in France*), since such a 'dictatorship' was only possible where the workers constituted a majority of the whole population and exercised democratic rights of universal suffrage through a parliamentary system. Kautsky insisted that:

> In other words, the social revolution must not for the time being proceed further than the majority of the population are prepared to go. This is because however desirable the immediate realisation of its objectives may seem to far-sighted individuals, the social revolution would not meet with the necessary conditions for establishing itself permanently.[5]

His core idea was that 'The dictatorship of the proletariat admits of no other definition than the rule of the proletariat on the basis of democracy.' The question, of course, was what was meant by 'democracy'. Kautsky's understanding was that democracy meant a representative parliamentary republic, with open mass parties, based on universal suffrage. Lenin's understanding of the post-revolutionary state or what he called the 'Commune state' was, as we shall see in the following section, quite different.

The implication of Kautsky's argument was clearly that the Bolshevik Revolution could not make good its claim to introduce a state form more democratic than the liberal-democratic state. Because of the conditions under which Bolshevism came to power, and the Bolsheviks' disregard for multi-party democracy and rights of opposition, Kautsky suggested that it would be a dictatorship *over* the proletariat and not the democratic majority rule of the workers that would result. In such a situation the goal of socialist revolution could not be met. The aspiration of classical Marxism was to create a planned economy in which the workers, the direct producers, would be able to exercise effective control over the productive resources, and in which social and political relations would come to be 'transparent', controllable through conscious human action. This seems to be the picture Marx sketched of a future communist society, although he did not portray it in any detail, only in very broad outline.

The Bolshevik response, as articulated by their leaders Lenin and Trotsky, was to dismiss the charge of people like Kautsky. The Bolsheviks maintained in 1917 that socialist revolution throughout Europe was possible. Lenin saw Russia as the weak link in the imperialist chain, arguing that making a socialist revolution in Russia in 1917 would be the spark that would set off similar revolutions throughout a Europe radicalised by the misery and slaughter of the war. This perspective was set out in Lenin's famous 'April Theses' of 1917, which proclaimed the imminence of revolution throughout Europe, and the urgency of proceeding in Russia from the 'bourgeois' stage of the revolution to the next stage of 'socialist' revolution. The Bolshevik hope and expectation therefore was that revolution in Russia would not be an isolated event, and that the Bolsheviks would not have to take power cut off from the more advanced economies of Western Europe.

Neil Harding in his study of Lenin's political thought has shown convincingly that Lenin's theory of state monopoly capitalism formed the theoretical background to the Bolshevik seizure of power in October 1917.[6] The analysis was that, on a worldwide or at least European scale, the capitalist system had indeed reached the point of maturity which Marx had postulated as necessary for socialist revolution. The Bolshevik Revolution would be part of a European process, and would unleash socialist revolution throughout Europe. The aim was to introduce into Russia a new type of state, far more democratic than any liberal-democratic system. This state Lenin described in his pamphlet *The State and Revolution* as the Commune state, in reference to Marx's praise of the Paris Commune of 1871.

The Bolshevik Revolution was thus carried out in the expectation of its extension to Europe as a whole. Lenin's perspective was one of what the Hungarian Marxist Georg Lukacs calls the 'actuality of the revolution', a belief in the imminence of revolution throughout Europe. Lenin wrote in September 1917 that 'socialism is now gazing at us from all the windows of capitalism'.[7] Kautsky, on the other hand, in his already-cited polemic against Lenin, criticised the Bolsheviks for staking everything, as he put it, on a throw of the dice, taking the risk that the revolution would not be confined to Russia – a gamble which in the event did not pay off.

Democracy and dictatorship: the Commune state

We noted above that one of the fundamental virtues claimed by defenders of the liberal-democratic state was that such systems achieved, in a feasible and realistic form, an input of the popular will into politics. The choice and competition between parties and the device of elections meant that political leaders had in some sense to represent the popular will and pursue policies approved of by the people, if the leaders wished to remain in power.

The claim made by Lenin and the Bolsheviks in creating the Soviet system was that a new type of state had been created, which would achieve a proletarian democracy far more worthy of the name 'democracy' than anything which liberal-democracy could achieve. This new type of state Lenin called the Commune state, and its realisation was the aim of Bolshevik politics in and immediately after the revolution of October 1917. In such a form of state, it was held, the people would be genuinely self-governing. The Commune state would exemplify a form of popular power which would revive the direct participation found in the ancient Greek city-state, extending it to the broad mass of the population. As one student of Lenin's thought and practice notes, 'For a brief period of perhaps nine months after the October Revolution in 1917, the Bolsheviks committed themselves to the most audacious attempt at transforming the vocabulary and the practice of politics since the French Revolution of 1789.'[8]

The Bolsheviks thus claimed to have achieved a form of democracy superior to and more 'participatory' than that of liberal-democracy. The theory of this state was expounded in two works by the leader of the Bolsheviks, Lenin. These works were *The State and Revolution* and *The Proletarian Revolution and the Renegade Kautsky*, in which latter work he rebutted the criticisms which Kautsky had directed against the Bolshevik seizure of power. The first of these two works was written just before the October Revolution, and the second shortly after, in the summer of 1918. Both works expressed a view of the state which drew on Marx's description of the Paris Commune of 1871. Especially in *The State and Revolution*, Lenin made much of Marx's statement that 'the working class cannot simply lay hold of the ready-made state machinery and wield it for its own purposes'.[9] In his writings on the Paris Commune, Marx had saluted that short-lived experiment, the self-government of Paris under siege conditions from March to May 1871, as an attempt to realise the goal of society governing itself, free from the grip of the centralised and repressive state. In the words of one of his draft versions of the finished text, he wrote of the Paris Commune that:

This was, therefore, a revolution not against this or that Legitimate, Constitutional, Republican or Imperialist form of state power. It was a revolution against the *state* itself, this supernaturalist abortion of society, a resumption by the people for the people of its own social life. It was not a revolution to transfer it from one fraction of the ruling classes to the other, but a revolution to break down this horrid machinery of class domination itself.[10]

The same spirit was shown by Lenin's texts on the state in this period, described by some commentators as a sort of 'honeymoon', lasting from October 1917 to the beginning of the Civil War in the following year. Lenin rejected any accommodation with the state form of liberal-democracy. The existing state, the liberal-democratic parliamentary state, was nothing but a fraud or a façade, and had to be smashed. As Lenin wrote in *The State and Revolution*, parliament was just a talking-shop given over to the task of fooling the common people, and the liberal-democratic system was nothing but a mask to veil the domination of the ruling class, the bourgeoisie. Therefore, the task of the revolutionary movement was to destroy this form of state and replace it by another.

This 'other' form of state was precisely what Lenin called the 'Commune state', modelling it on Marx's presentation of the Paris Commune. Marx had singled out as the chief feature of that form of state the destruction of the standing army and its replacement by a militia, the people in arms. He also emphasised the destruction of the state as a separate apparatus over and above society. The state had to be made the servant of society by devices such as the recall of officials, who would be paid no more than workmen's wages. The stifling apparatus of the state had in Marx's view reached its highest point in the regime of Louis Bonaparte, installed through the *coup d'état* of 1851. The Bonapartist state represented the autonomy of the state: the state appeared to 'be suspended in mid-air', bearing down on society. The self-government of Paris from March to May 1871, under siege conditions in the aftermath of the Franco-Prussian War, was seen by Marx as the antithesis of the Bonapartist state, that centralised and bureaucratic body. The Paris Commune represented a revolt of society against the state itself, the aspiration to reduce and perhaps annul completely the gap between state and society. It was, for Marx, the 'political form at last discovered under which to work out the economical emancipation of labour'.[11]

For Lenin, too, the state form of parliamentarism and liberal-democracy had to be 'smashed', and replaced by the Soviet state, which would exemplify the features of the Commune model. It is ironic that a regime which under Stalin came to create what Robert Tucker rightly calls a 'hypertrophied state' started life with these highly libertarian ideas.[12] The view of the state which Lenin advanced in October 1917 was that the new state form was based on institutions of popular power, namely the soviets (councils) of workers, soldiers and peasants. These institutions could realise forms of much more direct popular power than could be achieved under any system of parliamentary ('bourgeois') democracy.

Lenin's invocation of the soviet state was therefore an appeal to the masses to take power for themselves. It was based on a number of assumptions, some of which came quite rapidly to be discarded after the seizure of power. These assumptions were that the operations of the state were basic and simple, and could be carried out by any literate person. Further, the optimistic perspective was that this new state was one which itself would fairly soon 'wither away'. Lenin rejected the anarchist argument that the state apparatus could be dispensed with immediately, but he nevertheless maintained that, once the revolution had been secured, even this new and ultra-democratic state would start its process of withering away and become redundant. In this sense the anarchist goal of the disappearance of the state could be realised, not immediately but in the foreseeable future, and society would then rule itself.

Lenin and the Bolsheviks could scornfully reject Kautsky's criticism of their project. Lenin dismissed Kautsky as a 'renegade', as someone defending the system of bourgeois democracy, which was no more than a figleaf covering the economic and social dominance of the bourgeoisie. What was being created in Russia, he argued, was a system which would recreate some elements of primitive democracy, and hence establish a system of 'proletarian democracy', a thousand times more democratic than the parliamentary democracy which Kautsky was defending. And even this genuine democracy was a form of state which before too long would be redundant.

The charge has been levelled against Lenin that these perspectives on the state seem totally 'Utopian'. In the first place, they clearly bear little relation to what happened in Russia after the revolution. It was not long after the revolution that Lenin changed his perspective, insisting that the dictatorship of the proletariat was to be instituted through the party, not through the soviets. He changed his perspective from the libertarian one of October 1917 to one in which the role of the party loomed much larger. Lenin subsequently came to doubt even the capacity of the party to contain enough devoted and capable persons for the task of constructing socialism in Russia. Indeed, Harding suggests that at the end of his life, 'in the last pamphlets he wrote in this his political testament, Lenin became a Jacobin . . . even the Party had fallen prey to careerism, the legacy of the past and the cultural level of petty-bourgeois Russia'.[13]

Noting the fact that this idea of the Commune state was not realised in practice once the revolution had taken place, or at least its implementation was exceedingly short-lived, some observers suggest that Lenin's invocation of popular power was purely 'instrumental', designed to stir up the masses for the purposes of rallying them behind the Bolshevik Party, and that the libertarian Lenin is not to be taken seriously. Others, like A.J. Polan, take the view that Lenin, intolerant of dissent and pluralism, really put forward a perspective which involved 'the end of politics', and that this Utopian perspective hid what was later to become a dictatorial attitude to politics.[14]

The crucial question is whether the attempt to establish the 'Commune state' was a serious effort to create a democracy deeper than that realised in a liberal-democratic system, and whether this model of direct and participatory democracy could accommodate difference, and tolerate conflict and individual rights. In a challenging article, Neil Harding poses the problem of the relationship of Leninism to Marxism, and the broader question of Marxism and democracy. Asking the question of whether Marxism-Leninism exhibited what he calls 'a fundamental antagonism to democracy', Harding's claim is that:

> Leninism was an authentic Marxism. As an ideology it faithfully reflected Marx's own impoverishment of the Western tradition of politics, limiting its scope, its permanence, and the richness of its vocabulary and distinctions. It also faithfully reflected Marx's own deep ambivalence towards and suspicions of democracy.[15]

If these criticisms are correct, then it is not worth examining the Commune state perspective. This alternative to liberal-democracy, it could be argued, did not work in Russia in 1917, but neither could it work anywhere else. It neglects the need for a specialised and separate apparatus of power, a differentiated state – which is a necessity in a complex modern society, marked by diverse interests that need reconciliation and hence that require an apparatus to some extent over and above society to perform this function. Certainly, it is impossible to deny that, in the Bolshevik project as carried out in the conditions of Russia in 1917, the initial commitment to the Commune state went along with a belief in the role of the 'vanguard party' as the instrument of revolution, and this needs to be explained in assessing the evolution of the communist state.

The role of the party

The basis of the communist system as it evolved until the coming to power of Gorbachev and *perestroika* was the idea of 'the leading role of the party', encapsulated in Article 6 of the constitution of the Soviet Union until its repeal by Gorbachev in 1991. This statement has to be qualified with reference to the period of Stalin's domination, from the end of the 1920s until 1953, when the role of the party was subordinated to Stalin's personal control, backed up through purges enforced by the apparatus of state terror. Still, if the 'leading role of the party' characterised the power structure of communist regimes for most of their existence, we need to examine the meaning of this term and its historic origins and development.

We noted above that Bolshevism in Russia came to power invoking a highly democratic, indeed ultra-democratic, view of the state. Bolshevism in theory and practice was very much the creation of Lenin, and one of its defining characteristics was the emphasis on what he termed the 'vanguard' role of the party. Bolshevism arose out a split in the Russian Social Democratic Labour

Party at their congress of 1903 in Brussels and later London, a split between those who came to be known as the Bolsheviks (the majority) and the Mensheviks (minority). This split took place over two issues, the first being the nature and organisation of the revolutionary political party, and the second the nature of the (forthcoming) Russian revolution.

If the revolution was to be, as both factions agreed, a 'bourgeois' revolution whose main purpose was the overthrow of Tsarism, then what was to be the relation between this revolution and the subsequent socialist revolution? The Mensheviks argued in line with 'orthodox' Marxism that once Tsarism had been overthrown there would have to be a protracted period before capitalism could mature, and the working class come to power in a socialist revolution. Bolshevik perspectives, by contrast, insisted that, because of the timidity of the bourgeoisie in Russia and Eastern Europe generally, the working class and the peasantry would be the forces acting for the overthrow of Tsarism. Therefore there would be a shorter interval between the two revolutions than the Menshevik analysis implied. Indeed, Lenin wrote in 1905 that those popular forces which had made the bourgeois revolution would 'begin immediately . . . to make the transition to the socialist revolution. We stand for uninterrupted revolution. We shall not stop half way.' He thus put forward a theory not so different from Trotsky's view of 'permanent revolution'.[16]

However the crucial significance of the Bolshevik/Menshevik split concerns the question of the party. The Leninist idea of the party imparted a particular stamp to Bolshevik politics, which had fateful consequences for the type of state system that was to emerge once the revolution had taken place. Before the split of 1903, Lenin had expounded his views on the role of the party in *What is to be Done?* published in 1902. In this book Lenin set out the model of a party of a new type, effective in combating autocracy, and very different from the mass socialist parties of Western Europe. Lenin was the creator of Bolshevism, and it was through the instrument of a tightly organised conspiratorial party that the Bolsheviks came to power in 1917. When considering the question of the nature of the Soviet state, and indeed the question of its collapse, it is crucial to understand the pivotal role of the Bolshevik Party in the creation and (later) running of that state system.

Lenin assigned a crucial role to the party in forming the consciousness of the working class, and he thought that only a tightly organised party of professional revolutionaries would be adequate to the task of leading the working class. In both respects, it can be argued, Lenin diverged from Marx, although this is a matter on which there is considerable disagreement. While there are those, like Kolakowski, who insist on the crucial and disastrous transformation which Lenin wrought in the theory and practice of Marxism through his ideas on the party, others like Harding take a somewhat different view, arguing that it is subsequent events which have given the ideas expounded in *What is to be Done?* their resonance. Harding suggests that Lenin's views on the role of the party were entirely consonant with what passed for 'orthodox Marxism' at the turn of the century, as represented notably by Kautsky.[17]

Lenin insisted that in a social democratic or Marxist movement the party performed a crucial leading function. He made the basic and important distinction between two forms of class consciousness. Lenin distinguished between what he called 'economism' or 'trade union consciousness' on the one hand, and 'social democratic consciousness' on the other. The former type of consciousness was limited, in the sense that it involved consciousness of the necessity to fight for better conditions for the sale or hire of labour power. Workers imbued with such consciousness would not envisage the necessity of political struggle, at least not in the sense of a fundamental transformation of the political system and the struggle to achieve a different kind of society altogether. There was for Lenin, as indeed there was for Marx, a fundamental distinction between action to improve conditions within the capitalist system, and action imbued with 'social democratic consciousness' to change the nature of the whole system. This involved political action going beyond the sphere of the economy and trade union action, important and necessary though these were. Lenin's essential point was that, left to its own devices, the working class would attain only what he called 'trade union consciousness'. The mediation of the party was necessary to develop the full social democratic consciousness in the ranks of the working class and bring about a socialist revolution. In his famous words,

> The history of all countries shows that the working class, exclusively by its own efforts, is able to develop only trade-union consciousness, i.e. the conviction that it is necessary to combine in unions, fight the employers, and strive to compel the government to pass this or that necessary labour law, etc.[18]

He went on to contrast such consciousness with the theory of socialism: 'The doctrine of socialism, however, grew out of the philosophic, historical and economic theories elaborated by educated representatives of the propertied classes, by intellectuals.' Endorsing the words of Kautsky, indeed quoting them explicitly, Lenin agreed that 'socialist consciousness is something introduced into the proletarian class struggle from without', words of Kautsky which Lenin described as 'profoundly true and important'. The implication was clear: the party had to be a collective intellectual; it was the party which had the task of introducing socialism to the working class. Without the party to do this, working-class struggles would be 'spontaneous', which for Lenin meant remaining at the level of trade unionist politics: 'the spontaneous working-class movement is trade-unionism, is *Nur-Gewerkschaftlerei*, and trade unionism means the ideological enslavement of the workers by the bourgeoisie'.[19]

In addition, Lenin specified the type of organisational structure that was necessary to overthrow the Tsarist autocracy. The party had to be centralised and secretive, and could not function along the lines of Western European parties as an open mass party, because that would lead only to its suppression by the forces of autocracy. Therefore the organisational weapon which Lenin created and which he described in *What is to be Done?*, the Bolshevik Party, was a centralised and secretive party of professional revolutionaries, different from the looser, more open, more 'Western' parties which the Mensheviks advocated. It was over this issue that the split of 1903 occurred.

Lenin's view of the party was criticised both by his contemporaries and by later commentators. There are those who see it not merely as a departure from the Marxism of Marx and Engels, but as being elitist, dictatorial and centralist. It has been seen as making possible, perhaps inevitable, the Stalinist dictatorship that followed. On the other hand, commentators such as Harding maintain that the arguments of *What is to be Done?* should not be exaggerated or wrenched out of context. In his words, 'In 1907 Lenin insisted that the arguments and organisational principles of *What is to be Done?* were not intended as general statements of ever-lasting applicability but were, on the contrary, pertinent to a particular situation faced by the Russian movement at a particular moment of its development.'[20] Lenin himself wrote in 1907, five years after the publication of *What is to be Done?*:

> The basic mistakes made by those who now criticise *What is to be Done?* is to treat the pamphlet apart from its connection with the concrete historical situation of a definite, and now long past, period in the development of our party.[21]

As far as the response of contemporaries to Lenin's ideas is concerned, the sharpest criticisms came from Rosa Luxemburg and, at least at one 'pre-Bolshevik' moment in his career, Trotsky, who was to be the joint leader with Lenin of the October Revolution.[22]

These controversies still remain relevant to the politics of our time, because whatever Lenin's insistence that the ideas set out in his text *What is to be Done?* were never meant to be immutable prescriptions for a fixed model of party organisation, it was the Bolshevik Party which planned and organised the October Revolution. This, unlike the February Revolution, was by no means a spontaneous revolution, but was carefully prepared and led by the Bolshevik Party. Furthermore, despite the theory of the Commune state, in the reality of post-revolutionary Russia it was the Bolshevik Party which held the reins of power. The soviets became ineffectual institutions that were subject to party control, and the party itself lost any vestiges of inner-party democracy. The ban on factions which was announced at the 10th Party Congress in 1921 can be seen as a turning point in the fortunes of Bolshevism, accompanied as it was by the secret 'Point 7' which allowed for expulsions from the Bolshevik Party.

There is clearly a tension within Lenin's thought, and in the whole nature of Bolshevism, between its libertarian proclamations of the Commune state and its emphasis in both theory and practice on the role of the Bolshevik Party. Lenin's view of the party as bringing socialist or revolutionary consciousness to the masses put a far greater emphasis on the role of the party than was the case in the thought of Marx. The party had been the instrument for the seizure of power, and after the revolution it became the fundamental governing institution in the society. This led to the emergence of a bureaucratic party–state apparatus, to which there was no countervailing power. This monopolistic control by one party fundamentally marked the character and nature of the communist state, in its Russian or Soviet variety, and in other Soviet-type systems which imitated this fundamental characteristic of the 'leading role of the party'.

In the Soviet Union, the swelling of the party–state apparatus and its bureaucratization were phenomena already clearly visible before the death of Lenin in February 1924. Lenin's 'last struggle', as Moshe Lewin has called it, was a desperate and ultimately unsuccessful action against the spirit of careerism and bureaucratism which he saw as stifling or strangling the revolutionary impetus.[23] One need only read the writings of Lenin near the end of his life – for example, his text *Better Fewer But Better* – to detect a sense of failure. The despairing and pessimistic tone of these texts expresses Lenin's realisation that the Soviet state was in no way, as he put it, 'worthy to be called socialist, Soviet, etc.'.[24] The contrast is obvious between this pessimism and the defiant tone in which Lenin replied to Kautsky in 1918, defending the new state system of the soviets as a million times more democratic than the parliamentary systems of liberal-democracy.

Whether the promise of a genuine socialist democracy which Lenin held out in 1917 could ever have been realised is a difficult question to answer. Given the conditions in which the Bolshevik Revolution took place, the idea of a society moving rapidly towards the withering away of the state was clearly an impossibly Utopian aspiration. In this sense the elitist critique, that socialism gives rise to the 'dictatorship of the official' rather than the dictatorship of the worker, might seem justified. Developments after 1917 could be taken as a vindication of Michels' 'iron law of oligarchy', discussed in Chapter 4, as showing the inevitability of the bureaucratisation of the party apparatus and the impossibility of sustaining democracy. However, the problem with this interpretation is that it suggests that no alternative was possible after 1917 to the rapid erosion of the model of soviet democracy and to the destruction of at least some degree of inner-party democracy. This would be too simplistic a conclusion. The particular circumstances under which the Bolshevik Revolution took place, and the contingent fact that there were alternatives to the concentration of power in Stalin's hands, suggest that the creation of the Soviet party–state was not an inevitable outcome of socialist revolution, as elite theory seems to indicate.

The October Revolution had received mass backing from a population that wanted bread, land and peace, and the Bolsheviks were the only party that responded to those demands. Yet the result of the revolution was a state system in which one party ruled, not the libertarian state sketched out in Lenin's vision of *The State and Revolution*. By the time of his death in 1924, Lenin had to some extent been responsible for the erosion of democracy within the party, because of the ban on factions of 1921 and the destruction of democracy outside the party, as apprehended already in 1918 by Rosa Luxemburg. In her pamphlet on the Russian Revolution she had warned that the dissolution of the Constituent Assembly in January 1918, the famous episode when it was reported that 'the guard is tired' and the Assembly was dissolved, was a dangerous step and could lead to a form of dictatorship by a small controlling minority.[25]

In the period of Stalinism any vestiges of democracy within the party, not to mention outside it, were destroyed. The Stalinist state can be seen as the polar opposite of the Commune state sketched by Lenin in *The State and Revolution*. Stalinism, as a term used to describe the period of Stalin's personal rule – starting with the beginning of collectivisation in 1928 and marked by his destruction of the Bolshevik Party as an instrument of rule – has been described as 'revolution from above'.[26] It involved the forced collectivisation of agriculture, rapid industrialisation and the emergence of a stratum of bureaucratic rulers to form a new ruling group, dependent on Stalin for advancement. Stalinism has been described by Robert Tucker as a 'state-building process' leading to what he calls 'the construction of a powerful, highly centralised, bureaucratic, military–industrial Soviet Russian state'.[27]

The concept of totalitarianism has been used to describe the Soviet system under Stalin. In fact, most uses of the concept, which is discussed more fully in Chapter 8, extend the term to cover not just the Soviet system after Stalin as well as under him, but fascist systems as well. The problems with this concept are discussed below, but certainly the idea of almost total power, the 'politicisation' of all spheres of life and the denial of any 'private' sphere are aspects of the totalitarian 'syndrome' which apply to the Stalinist state. So too was the imposition on to the mass of the population of an ideology, a creed for which all people had to manifest enthusiastic endorsement. Furthermore, the Stalinist system was characterised for at least some of its life by the unrestrained use of terror directed in the first instance against the party, those who could form an alternative 'old guard' to Stalin and his hand-picked associates and followers. Yet the Stalinist terror extended to much wider circles, and became more broadly and randomly directed at people outside the party, reaching its peak in the unrestricted purges of 1937.

The Soviet model

This section seeks to describe and briefly assess what we call here the 'classical' Soviet system as a form of state, comparing it with liberal-democracy. By the 'classical' Soviet system is understood the system as it developed in the period between the death of Stalin in March 1953 and Gorbachev's accession to the post of General Secretary in March 1985. The chief feature of this form of state was the 'leading role of the party', enshrined in the 1977 Soviet Constitution. Article 6 of that constitution, repealed in 1991, ran as follows:

The Communist Party of the Soviet Union shall be the guiding and directing force of Soviet society, the core of its political system and of [all] state and social organizations. The CPSU shall exist for the people and shall serve the people. The leading and guiding force of Soviet society and the nucleus of its political system, of all state organs and public organs, is the CPSU (Communist Party of the Soviet Union).

Armed with the Marxist-Leninist teaching, the Communist Party shall determine the general perspective of the development of society and the lines of the internal and foreign policy of the USSR, direct the great creative activity of the Soviet people, and impart a planned, scientifically-founded character to its struggle for the victory of communism.[28]

Within that party, moreover, power was hierarchical and centralised, organised on the principles of democratic centralism. This principle supposedly combined election to leading party posts, the democratic element, with the idea of centralised and united execution of decisions democratically arrived at. In theory, the principle involved the formal election of all leading party bodies, yet through the *nomenklatura* system these elections were controlled from above. This system meant in practice that the higher party organs had lists of those deemed suitable for key positions in the apparatus of party and state, and such candidates were selected in advance and then presented for election, i.e. ratification, by the lower levels of the party–state apparatus. This *nomenklatura* has been described as forming the Soviet ruling class, a party–state elite which became self-perpetuating. In the words of one historian of the Soviet Union, 'Through this by now highly developed and sophisticated *nomenklatura* system of patronage, this Central Committee [of the CPSU] supervised in principle every single appointment of any importance in any walk of life, delegating these powers to lower-tier party organisations for appointments lower down the hierarchy.'[29]

The leading role of the party had two consequences: the centralisation of power in the hands of the state–party elite; and the extension of that power throughout the pores of civil society. The tasks of the party included the organisation of economic growth and development, the maintenance of the ideology of Marxism-Leninism, and the supervision and encouragement of a form of political participation which did involve millions of citizens in both party and state (Soviet) activities, although this was a participation strictly regulated and 'guided'. In this sense, the Soviet system aimed at the mobilisation of the masses, as the totalitarian model suggests, yet it was a mobilisation led by and guided by a party structured along the hierarchical lines we have noted.

Most analyses of the power structure of the Soviet system in the period before Gorbachev's reforms of the 'unreconstructed' state system concentrate on the evident fact of a bureaucratic state–party elite, in whom power was concentrated. Marxist-type perspectives on these systems were concerned with the problem of whether this ruling group could be considered as a 'ruling class' in the Marxist sense. Given that the party–state elite did not themselves legally own the means of production, but only administered them, it seemed to make more sense to talk of a bureaucratic stratum which possessed effective control over economic resources and political power. This line of analysis was given classical expression in Trotsky's study of the Stalinist system, *The Revolution Betrayed*.[30] This argued that a bureaucratic elite, necessarily arising in the conditions of scarcity under which the Bolshevik Revolution had been made, arrogated to itself ever more power and set itself up as a differentiated power group, dominating society. In certain respects the later analysis of the German theorist Rudolf Bahro came to a similar conclusion. He saw Soviet systems, which he described as those of 'real existing socialism', as marked by 'subalternity', a division of power between a commanding elite and a passive mass, a form of society which he viewed as totally different from the socialism desired by Marx and Engels.[31]

What all these accounts or analyses of the Soviet system left as an open question was not so much *whether* the system would change, but rather *how* it would be transformed. Trotsky's analysis spoke of a new revolution which would mobilise the workers in such systems to take power away from this bureaucratic elite, while preserving the collective ownership of the economy. The analysis of people like Bahro and Roy Medvedev, who could be called 'party reformers', was less apocalyptic, in that they seemed to see the possibility of reform from within the party apparatus. 'Modernisers' would arise within the party who would be willing to loosen the grip of the party over civil society, and relax the ban on factions within the party, so that a form of 'socialist pluralism' could develop.[32] The question remains of the degree to which these perspectives have been validated or refuted by the actual course of events, and the last section of this chapter attempts a brief survey of the Soviet system during the time of *perestroika* or restructuring.

Soviet systems in the age of *perestroika*

When Gorbachev came to power in 1985, there had already been attempts to reform or restructure Soviet-type systems, although not in the Soviet Union itself. Such attempts were seen in Hungary in 1956, in Czechoslovakia in 1968, and in Poland through the trade union Solidarity in 1980. The movements of opposition came from a variety of sources: from intellectuals, as in Czechoslovakia with Charter 77; from workers, as with Solidarity in Poland; and both from within the ruling party (Czechoslovakia) and outside it (Poland). While generalising about such a variety of different attempts is hazardous, it can be said that they all had a sort of 'minimum programme' which involved moves towards a form of socialist pluralism. The demands were for groups in civil society to have their own 'space', a degree of autonomy from the control of the party. In practice, this would have meant challenging 'the leading role of the party', although movements like Solidarity in Poland were cautious about doing so explicitly. Such attempted transformations of the power structure of Soviet systems came to nothing chiefly because of the repressive power of the USSR.

A further stage of the transformation of these systems began in 1985 when Mikhail Gorbachev became General Secretary of the CPSU. While it is very hard to sum up briefly this vast historic process of *perestroika* and failed reform, it seems that initially Gorbachev's scheme was limited to economic reform, in order to modernise and make more efficient the economic structure of the USSR in a changed world.[33] Yet Gorbachev came to realise that this 'revolution from above' or economic restructuring would not be successful without political reform, without making the participation claimed by the Soviet system into something genuine and not a ritualistic process in the grip of the party. Thus 'democratisation' (*democratsiya*) came to be placed on the agenda – at first a democratisation paradoxically urged on or sponsored from above. From this followed a number of far-reaching consequences which totally transformed the power structure and nature of Soviet-type systems, eventually leading to their collapse.

The transformation of *perestroika* aimed initially at limited reforms and changes, albeit extending from the economic to the political sphere. Hence institutional changes were made which were designed to create forms of pluralism and genuine participation from below, notably the total transformation of the representative structure of the soviets. This involved the replacement of the hitherto exclusively formal structure of the Supreme Soviet by more genuine representative bodies. In March 1989 there were elections to a newly formed Congress of People's Deputies. This body was elected through open and contested elections very different from the *nomenklatura* ratification which had passed for elections in the old-style Soviet system. It is true that measures were taken to preserve for the Communist Party its privileged position, by giving it special advantages in the nomination of candidates and guaranteeing it a proportion of the seats in the newly formed representative assembly.[34] However, these provisions were ultimately unsuccessful in preventing the erosion of party dominance. Thus the process of reform undertaken by Gorbachev involved a move from economic reform to political reform. His aim seemed to be an attempt to preserve the leading role of the party, while simultaneously mobilising popular support for reform by *glasnost*, openness. The Congress of People's Deputies in turn elected the Supreme Soviet, which had a number of committees that were intended to function as an effective check on executive power. The intention was to achieve a separation of party and state, to make the soviets independent of the grip of the party. This marked a move away from the notion of a one-party state to a form of state modelled on Western-style systems of representative democracy, with ideas of separation of powers, procedural guarantees against abuse of power, the rule of law, and checks on executive power: in other words, a move away from the notion of a party–state in which the Communist Party was the crucial and only effective centre of power.

The core aims of *perestroika* can be described in general terms as involving an attempt at democratisation and the creation of a 'space' for civil society to be independent of the party–state. Furthermore, it led to the opening up of pluralism within both the Communist Party and the wider society, as well as economic reform in the sense of moves away from a command economy towards a greater degree of market relations. The aim was to achieve greater autonomy of productive units and some degree of control from below. Finally, within the sphere of the USSR as a whole, the project of *perestroika* necessarily led to confrontation with the nationalities issue, something which loomed ever larger throughout Gorbachev's tenure of office and showed the force of nationalism. This issue is examined further in Chapter 9.

Our concern here is with the broad question of the transformation of the 'old-style' Soviet system, based on the idea of the leading role of the party, into a different form of state, formally resembling a pluralistic Western-style democracy. The interpretation which is given here suggests that *perestroika* went through different stages: initially designed as economic transformation, then as political transformation with the slogan of democratisation, with Gorbachev's aim being to overthrow obstacles from the party bureaucracy by appealing to the people. The interesting question is why this process of reform of the system failed so totally, in what must be one of the most unsuccessful projects of political reform of all time. The aims of *perestroika* were bold. Gorbachev announced to the 28th Party Congress on 3 July 1990 that:

> The Stalinist model of socialism is being replaced by a civil society of free people. The political system is being radically transformed; genuine democracy is being established, with free elections, a multiparty system and human rights; and real people's power is being revived . . . Life has become fuller, more meaningful, more interesting.[35]

One fundamental reason for the failure of such a vision was that the process of democratisation, and indeed of *perestroika* as a whole, developed a dynamic which broke the framework within which it was initially conceived. Life became 'more interesting' in ways rather different from the ones envisaged by the initiators of *perestroika*. What started out as reform, perhaps even revolution, 'from above', designed to rejuvenate the one-party system, developed as a flood of demands from civil society which could not be steered in one direction. In November 1989 Gorbachev claimed that 'the interests of consolidating society and of focusing all its healthy forces on the accomplishment of the difficult tasks of restructuring make it advisable to maintain a one-party system'.[36] However, once the lid of one-party rule maintained by force had been lifted, a Pandora's box was opened releasing forces which went in many different directions.

This was especially true of the national question.[37] This raises a large topic which is discussed more fully below, the question of nationalism as a significant force in modern politics, both for maintaining or legitimating states and, with respect to the multinational system of the USSR, for undermining the established order. The prospects of limited reform and genuine democracy were impeded because of the pressure of national demands and ethnically based nationalist fervour.

It is difficult to sum up such a complex process, and draw out general lessons for the theory of the modern state. *Perestroika* started out as an attempt to reform communism, but ended with its fall. It started as an attempt to democratise the existing system, first within the context of single-party rule, then through reviving the soviets, turning them into genuine organs of popular power and control, and the opening up of civil society to forms of pluralism. What began as an attempt to modify the forms of one-party rule finished with the destruction of the whole system after the failed coup attempt of August 1991. This left on the agenda an attempt to create a Western-style democracy, a liberal-democratic structure, in a social and economic context not very favourable to such an attempt, and marked by nationalist conflict which threatens to undermine it.

One central reason for the collapse of the one-party system of the communist model was that, despite its structured and ritualised forms of mass participation, the system was not democratic: it did not allow choice, or genuine control from below. Nor did it satisfy national, or nationalist, grievances. In its classic form, the Soviet system was able to survive because of the suppression of dissent, and its relative success in building up an advanced economic infrastructure. However, in later conditions of a more advanced economy, economic performance was poor, and the system did not allow for the expression of dissent or genuine popular power. And whereas Lenin in 1921, at the 10th Party Congress of the Bolshevik Party, announced the ban on factions and the intention to put the lid *on* opposition, the reform programme of Gorbachev took the lid *off*. He created a state structure which was an uneasy compromise between the old-style version with the leading role of the party still intact, and a new-style version with a representative organ, the Congress of People's Deputies, and marked by forms of pluralism. The American political scientist Gail Lapidus has expressed well the difficulty of the whole project, writing of 'the tension between the need to increase social initiative to revitalise the Soviet system and the fear that increased social autonomy will threaten central control'.[38]

In the event, the 'revitalisation' of the Soviet system unleashed forces which could not be contained within the framework of single-party communist rule. Its complete and utter failure led to the collapse of communism and the disappearance of one of the main rival forms of state to liberal-democracy. The implications of this are explored in the final chapter. For the moment we have to turn our attention to the other main rival to liberal-democracy in the twentieth century, which was also a bitter enemy of the communist system.

Systems of fascism and other forms of authoritarian rule, such as military regimes, have been important and remain so in the politics of our time. This is the material for the following chapter.

Notes

1. White, S., Gardner, J., Schöpflin, G., and Saich, T., *Communist and Postcommunist Political Systems: An introduction*, 3rd edition, St Martin's Press, New York, 1990, p. 5.
2. An influential definition of a 'syndrome' of totalitarianism was given by Friedrich, C.J., and Brzezinski, Z.K., *Totalitarian Dictatorship and Autocracy*, Praeger, New York, 1961, p. 9.
3. Brown, A.H., 'Political power and the Soviet state', in Harding, N. (ed.), *The State in Socialist Society*, Macmillan, London, 1984.
4. Marx, K. and Engels, F., *The German Ideology*, Lawrence & Wishart, London, 1965, p. 46.
5. Kautsky, *Selected Political Writings*, ed. and trans. P. Goode, Macmillan, London, 1983, p. 122. See also Salvadori, M., *Karl Kautsky and the Socialist Revolution 1880–1938*, New Left Books, London, 1979, Chapter 8.
6. Harding, N., *Lenin's Political Thought*, Macmillan, London, 1983, Vol. 2, Chapter 3.
7. Harding, N., *Lenin's Political Thought*, Vol. 2, p. 75. See also Lukacs, G. *Lenin: A study in the unity of his thought*, New Left Books, London, 1970.
8. Neil Harding, 'The Marxist-Leninist detour', in Dunn, J. (ed.), *Democracy: The unfinished journey 508 BC to AD 1993*, Oxford University Press, Oxford, 1992, p. 164.
9. Marx, K., *The Civil War in France*, in Marx, K., *The First International and After*, ed. D. Fernbach, Penguin, Harmondsworth, 1974, p. 206.
10. Marx, *First International and After*, p. 249.
11. Marx, *First International and After*, p. 212.
12. See Tucker, R.C., 'Stalinism as revolution from above', in Tucker, R.C. (ed.), *Stalinism: Essays in historical interpretation*, Norton, New York, 1977, p. 95.
13. Harding, *Lenin's Political Thought*, Vol. 2, p. 307.
14. See Polan, A.J., *Lenin and the End of Politics*, Methuen, London, 1984.
15. Harding, N., 'The Marxist-Leninist Detour', p. 157. The implications of this are considerable. If Harding is right, then Marxism, in its Leninist or possibly any other form, has nothing to contribute to the analysis of liberal-democracy.
16. See Carr, E.H., *The Bolshevik Revolution 1917–1923*, Macmillan, London, 1950, Vol. I, Chapter III, for these debates, p. 56 for quote from Lenin.
17. Harding, *Lenin's Political Thought*, Vol. 1, Chapter 7.
18. Lenin, V.I., *What is to be Done? Burning questions of our movement*, in Lenin, V.I., *Collected Works*, Foreign Languages Publishing House, Moscow, 1961, Vol. 5, p. 375.
19. Lenin, *What is to be Done?*, p. 50.
20. Harding, *Lenin's Political Thought*, Vol. 1, p. 161.
21. Quoted in Harding, *Lenin's Political Thought*, Vol. 1, p. 161.

22. For Luxemburg's criticism, see Luxemburg, R., 'Organizational questions of the Russian social democracy', in Luxemburg, R., *The Russian Revolution*, ed. B. D. Wolfe, University of Michigan Press, Ann Arbor, MI, 1961. For Trotsky, see Deutscher, I., *The Prophet Armed: Trotsky, 1879–1921*, Oxford University Press, Oxford, 1970, p. 90.

23. Lewin, M., *Lenin's Last Struggle*, Pantheon, New York, 1968.

24. Lenin, *Better Fewer But Better*, in Lenin, V.I., *Selected Works in One Volume*, Lawrence & Wishart, London, 1969, p. 701.

25. Luxemburg, *The Russian Revolution*.

26. See Tucker (ed.), *Stalinism*, especially the essay by Tucker, 'Stalinism as revolution from above'.

27. Tucker, 'Stalinism as revolution from above', in Tucker (ed.), *Stalinism*, p. 95.

28. Unger, A.L., *Constitutional Development in the USSR: a guide to the Soviet Constitution*, Methuen, London, 1981, p. 234.

29. Hosking, G., *A History of the Soviet Union*, Fontana/Collins, London, 1985, p. 375.

30. Trotsky, L., *The Revolution Betrayed: What is the Soviet Union and where is it going?*, Pathfinder Press, New York, 1970.

31. Bahro, R., *The Alternative in Eastern Europe*, New Left Books, London, 1978.

32. Medvedev, R., *On Socialist Democracy*, Macmillan, London, 1975.

33. White, S., *Gorbachev and After*, 3rd edition, Cambridge University Press, Cambridge, 1992.

34. See on these elections White, S., '"Democratisation" in the USSR', *Soviet Studies*, vol. 42, no. 1, 1990, pp. 3–25.

35. *Current Digest of the Soviet Press*, vol. XLII, no. 27, 1990, p. 2.

36. *Current Digest of the Soviet Press*, vol. XLI, no. 48, 1989, p. 20.

37. Motyl, A.J., 'The sobering of Gorbachev: nationality, restructuring, and the West', in Bialer, S. (ed.), *Politics, Society and Nationality inside Gorbachev's Russia*, Westview Press, Boulder, CO, and London, 1989; Hajda, L., and Beissinger, M. (eds), *The Nationalities Factor in Soviet Politics and Society*, Westview Press, Boulder, CO, and London, 1990; Smith, G., *The Nationalities Question in the Soviet Union*, Longman, London and New York, 1990.

38. Lapidus, G., 'State and society: towards the emergence of civil society in the Soviet Union', in Bialer (ed.), *Politics, Society and Nationality inside Gorbachev's Russia*, p. 124.

8 | The fascist and the authoritarian state

Introduction

There are a number of reasons for dealing with the problem of fascism and fascist states, and setting this in the context of authoritarian regimes in general. In the first place, with reference to the historical and political experiences of the twentieth century, from the early 1920s to the end of the Second World War there developed a challenge to the liberal-democratic state from mass movements of a fascist kind. Such movements, arising out of situations of deep crisis in liberal-democratic systems, achieved state power in Italy (in 1922) and in Germany (in 1933). In ideological terms, these fascist and national-socialist regimes declared their hostility to the principles and ideas underlying the liberal-democratic state. Fascism announced itself as the foe of the principles of 1789, and waged war, both metaphorically and then literally, against political systems basing themselves on ideas of liberty, equality and fraternity. In short, fascism as movement and fascism as regime were opposed to the ideas and institutions of the liberal-democratic state. For part of the twentieth century it seemed possible that these systems of mass-based authoritarianism, represented by fascist and Nazi regimes, would succeed in overthrowing liberal-democratic systems. If only for the sake of understanding liberal-democracy, we need to understand what one author has called 'the appeal of fascism', and the way in which fascist movements developed and came, in some cases, to attain state power.[1]

The fascist challenge in one sense came to an end in 1945, with the military defeat of fascist Italy and of Hitler's Germany. Shortly afterwards, with the onset of the Cold War, it seemed that the world was divided into the two rival blocs of liberal-democracy and Soviet-style communism, with fascism rapidly becoming a distant historical memory. However, in more recent times, there seems evidence that fascist-type movements are experiencing a resurgence, and form a renewed threat to the liberal-democratic state in a variety of contexts, including newly unified Germany, Italy, France and also some countries of Eastern and Central Europe in the context of post-communism.[2]

161

As Brecht wrote in his play *The Resistible Rise of Arturo Ui*, 'the womb from which that emerged is still fecund' (*der Schoss aus dem das kroch ist fruchtbar noch*). In conditions of high unemployment, economic crisis and dislocation, the re-emergence of such movements as emerged with disastrous results in Italy and Germany in the inter-war period cannot be discounted. This is not to say that liberal-democratic systems are confronted today with a challenge from fascism in the same form as in the 1920s and 1930s, but the fascist 'style of politics' is not, unfortunately, absent from the politics of late twentieth-century Europe.

Analysing the original version of fascism thus seems a necessary condition for understanding and perhaps avoiding the success of similar movements and their coming to power. Such movements often harness ethnic and racial tensions and seek to create 'scapegoats' for the social and economic problems of liberal-democracy. Fascism is therefore a topic which seems still relevant – in some ways, perhaps, is an ever-present danger – to the politics of contemporary liberal-democracies. It also employs nationalism as one of its central themes, and the appeal and relevance of nationalism to the politics of liberal-democracy is the subject of Chapter 9.

There is a further reason for focusing on fascism and its relationship to other forms of authoritarianism. So far we have spoken of the fascist state as a rival to liberal-democracy. Fascist movements when they came to power installed a one-party system subject to the dictates of the ruler, the dictator, Duce or Führer. They also elevated the repressive elements of the state and destroyed the pluralistic structures of liberal-democracy. Nevertheless, in a certain sense and with important qualifications, fascism can be seen as an attempt to preserve the capitalist system, to defend the social context of liberal-democracy against what was perceived as a threat from the Left, whether revolutionary or reformist. In the inter-war period, fascist movements came to power at least in part because they were helped by those whose economic and social privileges were menaced by movements of the Left. This suggests something important about the limits of reform, or radical change, in liberal-democratic systems, in our time as well as more historically.

This is not to suggest that at any time, in a sort of automatic fashion, a radical challenge from the Left will bring with it a necessary response by dominant elites to support authoritarian movements of a fascist kind. In the present circumstances such a scenario looks rather remote, for a whole variety of reasons, including the lack of a strong challenge from the Left on anything like traditional Marxist or socialist lines, and historical memories of the evils of fascism. Nevertheless, reflection on the fascist experience, historically speaking, casts light on important questions concerning the state in liberal-democratic societies, and the relation between state and society. The historical record suggests that economically powerful groups, or sections of them, were prepared to abandon the parliamentary system when democratic rights and pressures seemed dangerously threatening to their social power. Such groups were willing to support, with greater or lesser degrees of reluctance, mass movements promising to install a 'strong state', what Poulantzas calls an 'exceptional state' (*état d'exception*).[3] Such a strong state manifested the features of strengthened executive power, bearing down heavily on society in a way similar to the Bonapartist state characterised by Marx in his text *The Eighteenth Brumaire of Louis Bonaparte*.

The historical experience of fascism thus raises certain important questions about the nature of liberal-democracy and the limits of its stability. Under what conditions economic elites would come to offer their support to authoritarian movements of the Right is a question still important for the politics of liberal-democratic societies, in the light of such experiences as Chile in 1973 or the coup of the Greek colonels in 1967, or possible authoritarian responses to the process of democratisation in South Africa. The topic of fascism and the question of how fascist-type movements came to power in the 1920s and 1930s raise issues that are still important for contemporary politics.

Reflection on the nature of the fascist state also involves the problem of the autonomy of the state, the idea of a strong state apparently subjecting all classes and groups in civil society to its will. Fascism is clearly fundamentally opposed to the pluralism and group activity of a liberal-democratic system. It represents the polar opposite, the imposition of a monolithic or totalitarian will on to the pluralistic conflicts of civil society typical of liberal-democratic systems. The deeper point, however, is that under certain circumstances such pluralism can give rise to tensions and demands which seek apparent resolution in a strong state. The political sociology of liberal-democracy thus leads to exploration of the subject of fascist and authoritarian movements and states.

What is fascism?

The fascist state developed out of tensions and problems within liberal-democracy. It is a rival to the liberal-democratic state, yet emerged historically in the context of liberal-democratic systems within a particular 'conjuncture' or situation. Fascism was in large part a response to antagonisms bound up with the essential nature of liberal-democracy and the class context within which that state form is situated.

The starting point has to be some definition of what fascism actually is, what the term means, and how fascist movements relate to other forms of authoritarian politics. There are indeed considerable problems with the definition of the term 'fascism'. Fascist movements can be seen as both revolutionary and anti- or counter-revolutionary; as basically anti-democratic yet appealing to the people; as anti-Marxist and anti-socialist yet claiming elements of 'socialism' (the Nazis called themselves the National Socialist German Workers Party). There is also an important distinction between fascism as *movement* and fascism as *regime*, or state. There are important differences between the two, which go beyond the obvious difference between a movement out of power and one in power and forming the state elite.

The term 'fascism' is employed throughout this chapter to refer to movements and forms of state whose classic exemplifications are the fascist regime of Italy, from 1922 to its overthrow in 1945, and the National Socialist dictatorship in Germany, which lasted from Hitler's accession to power in 1933 until 1945. However, it should be noted that there are differences between these two types of fascist regime. Italian fascism lacked the racialist, particularly the anti-Semitic and *völkisch* dimension characteristic of German National Socialism; it exalted the state rather than the nation, racially defined, as did the Nazis; and it is generally agreed that the Nazi regime came much nearer than did Italian fascism to fulfilling the criteria of a 'totalitarian' regime in its mobilising zeal and its ability to control all of society and destroy forms of opposition. There are thus significant differences that extend beyond the obvious one of the geographical area over which each of these forms of dictatorship extended its domain. Nevertheless, both regimes, and the movements out of which they grew, had certain features in common, which meet the criteria of 'fascism', and these criteria are explained below.

The crucial characteristic of fascism as movement can be said to be its mass base. Fascist movements arose in situations of dislocation and crisis in liberal-democratic systems after the First World War, and sought to rally the mass of the discontented and dislocated. The first explicitly fascist party, which gave its name to the whole phenomenon, was the Italian Fascist Party, founded by Mussolini in 1919. Some authorities argue that the ideological origins of fascism can be traced back to an earlier period. The Israeli scholar Zeev Sternhell talks of an 'incubation period' of fascism in the last quarter of the nineteenth century.[4] He convincingly traces out the development of a current of ideas and movements hostile to the tradition of the French Revolution, yet using themes of racist nationalism and populist socialism. Such movements appealed to the masses in a style of politics very different from traditional conservatism and from earlier movements of the Right that were much more elitist in their style. Traditional conservative movements sought to keep the masses out of politics. Movements of what we could call 'the radical Right', which arose towards the end of the nineteenth century, sought to harness mass support for authoritarian ends, and wished to sweep away the parliamentary republic. Sternhell gives clear examples of right-wing, mass-based authoritarianism in the Third French Republic in its pre-First World War phase, citing movements like Boulangism and *le parti national*, a broad-based movement formed after the Dreyfus case which mobilised support for the overthrow of the French Republic. Such movements, and the ideas underlying them, were undoubtedly examples of what we could call proto-fascism, which anticipated fascist movements properly so-called. These emerged in the crisis provoked by the First World War and the challenge of the Bolshevik Revolution, which led to fear of socialist or Marxist revolution sweeping through Europe.

Fascist states or regimes emerged on the basis of mass movements. Such movements exploited a crisis of confidence in the liberal-democratic state, a crisis of legitimacy of the existing order. At this stage we need to make a clear distinction between the terms of fascism (whether as movement or regime) and authoritarianism. 'Authoritarianism' can be used as a very general term to cover all non-democratic regimes, but it seems more useful to distinguish authoritarian regimes from fascist ones as representing different types of non-democratic or dictatorial regime. What characterises fascism as a phenomenon is the importance of the mass base of the movement, and the mobilising drive and attempted politicisation of all aspects of social life. In other words, fascism shared these totalitarian characteristics with communist regimes, although there are significant differences between communism and fascism. Fascist regimes attempted to impose one single ideology on the members of society, and were marked by the constant mobilising of mass support, using the rituals or façade of democracy to provide a pseudo-democratic endorsement for the leader. The fascist party was the instrument for this mass mobilisation and forced co-ordination (*Gleichschaltung*) of all aspects of social life.

By contrast, authoritarian regimes do not attempt what Neumann calls the total permeation of society by political power.[5] A totalitarian system, of which fascism is one example, operates on the principle that 'Who is not with us is against us'. Authoritarian regimes operate in different ways, at least in the sense that they are often satisfied with lack of opposition rather than the constant mobilising of the population to provide active endorsement of the ideology of the regime. What distinguishes a fascist regime from an authoritarian regime, such as a military dictatorship, is precisely the former's mass base, mobilised through the structure of a mass party which is led by a dictator. Fascist parties are parties of a 'Caesaristic' type, whose purpose is to drum up support for a dictatorial leader, build up popular support for that purpose, and serve as an instrument for the seizure of power and the inculcation of an openly proclaimed belief in the 'leader principle'. Military dictatorships, such as Chile under Pinochet, or Spain under Franco, would qualify as authoritarian but not fascist. This is because in these latter cases the 'pillars of the regime' were the traditional institutions of army and state bureaucracy, rather than a popular party with its mobilising and 'totalitarian' drives.

It was suggested in an earlier chapter that democracy was the prominant principle of legitimacy in modern politics. Fascist regimes paid a perverted homage to the democratic idea. They sought extensive support and they derived their legitimacy from the people, but this was done in a false and distorted way through the institution of the mass party. Fascist regimes, at least in their Nazi form, defined 'the people' in a racialist way: only the Aryans (in Germany) formed the political community – they constituted *das Volk* or the people, whose true expression was the will of the leader. *Das Volk* had to demonstrate, under the watchful eye of the party and its leadership, its unity, cohesion and support for the leader. For all their opposition to the principles of the French Revolution, fascist movements and states exploited the style of democratic politics and mass participation characteristic of modern democratic politics since 1789.[6] They employed explicitly and consciously certain practices and rituals of mass politics, rallies, demonstrations and open manifestations of popular support. In the case of fascism, however, they were stripped of genuine content, and used to bolster the power of the leader.

The mobilisation of the masses

The distinguishing and defining feature of fascism as a form of state is its emergence through a mass movement, in liberal-democratic systems facing a crisis situation. This was the case in Europe after the First World War. However, this leaves open the question of the precise nature of this mass base, the analysis of which groups constituted the bulk of fascist movements, and the reasons why they followed demagogic leaders who attacked the liberal-democratic state and the ideas underlying it. These issues are important for understanding the problems facing liberal-democratic states in that period, but they also have a contemporary relevance.

Support for fascist movements came from diverse and essentially incompatible sources. At an early stage in the history of fascism, with reference to the Italian experience, it was realised that fascism could not be understood simply as a reaction against the threat of socialism, although that was part of what brought fascism its recruits. As early as 1921 the Italian Marxist Gramsci referred to fascism as an 'anti-movement', harnessing a whole mass of resentments and bringing people together by exploiting their grievances and sense of dislocation. He described fascism as 'the anti-party' which 'has opened its gates to all applicants; has with its promise of impunity enabled a formless multitude to cover over the savage outpourings of passions, hatred and desires, with a varnish of vague and nebulous political ideas'.[7] This brings out well the idea of fascism as a politics of resentment, of dislocated groups swinging behind a vague rallying cry, a politics of the lowest common denominator. However, it is necessary to develop a more precise definition of the mass base of fascism.

Analysis of this kind can be taken to start with the Italian socialist Zibordi, in his book of 1922, contemporaneous with Mussolini's march on Rome.[8] In his study *Critica Socialista del Fascismo* Zibordi distinguished three elements in the mass base of fascism. The first element was a counter-revolution of the property-owning classes, alarmed by the prospect of socialist revolution, spreading in the wake of the Bolshevik Revolution. However, Zibordi argued, as did others in the same vein, that fascism was a much more dangerous enemy of both socialism and the democratic republic than a mere movement of what could be called straightforward reaction. It contained two further strands which made it a particularly menacing challenge. The second aspect of fascism was the military element, fascism as a military revolution, led by ex-officers, by those strata demobilised by the war, and unable to fit back into civilian life. They provided fascism with military discipline and organisation, making these movements such an effective opponent of the liberal-democratic state. Fascist movements also invoked a virulently militaristic ideology, exalting violence and combat, deeply imbued with nationalism of an extreme kind. Groups of ex-combatants filled with such ideas formed the original nucleus of fascism. The Italian groups were originally called the *fasci di combattimento*, and this gives an indication of the ideology of fascism. It was an ideology of vitalism, of activity for its own sake, an irrationalist doctrine scorning theory and rationalism. Fascist movements invoked an ideology of permanent conflict.

As Zibordi noted, however effective such groups of veterans or ex-combatants might be, on their own they would not be strong enough to threaten either the democratic republic or the working-class movement. As a third element he added what traditionally and correctly has been seen as the true mass base of fascist movements in their original shape, the intermediate classes or petty-bourgeoisie. They were in a state of panic because of conditions of economic crisis, the fear of socialist revolution, and social dislocation. It was Trotsky who described fascism as 'the petty-bourgeoisie run amok', and the analysis of fascism given by a variety of socialist and Marxist writers both at the time and since has pointed to these intermediary groups as providing the mass base of fascist-type movements.[9] Fearful of being economically ruined by big business and of sinking into the ranks of the working class, they expected no salvation from socialism, which seemed indifferent or even hostile to their concerns. Zibordi noted that the socialist movement had made no effort to win over these intermediary groups or to placate their fears. They therefore threw in their lot with movements which were explicitly anti-socialist and anti-collectivist.

Fascist movements claimed to offer a 'third way', which was to some degree anti-capitalist. Fascist movements in both Italy and Germany exhibited a strand of 'anti-capitalism': they declaimed against finance capital and big business, and sought to rally to their cause 'the small man', the petty producer in both town and country, infiltrating the pressure groups and associations which represented their interests. Thus these strata provided fascism with its 'shock troops' and with elements of its ideology before the seizure of power. The fascist party in Italy and the Nazi party in Germany professed an ideology and proclaimed a rhetoric of revolution, claiming to be against the established order. This rhetoric of revolution denounced the liberal-democratic system, international socialism or Marxism, and also capitalism. In theory the fascist movement promised a revolution appealing to the lower middle class, not only offering to avert the threat of left-wing revolution, but also opposing the power of large corporations or big business. However, the promise of social revolution was not fulfilled when these movements came to power.

This analysis therefore points to the heterogeneous character of fascism, the diverse nature of its mass base. Zibordi's analysis of 1922 was echoed in 1936 by the Austro-Marxist Otto Bauer, who applied a very similar threefold categorisation not just to Italian fascism but also to German Nazism, which had come to power in 1933.[10] Like Zibordi, Bauer analysed the mass basis of fascism in terms of three strata. He saw fascism as having its nucleus in violent and dislocated social groups, veterans of the war who could not readjust to civilian life after the war. In Germany gangs of demobilised soldiers had formed the Freikorps, which had repressed the socialist Spartacus revolution in 1919. Such bands of ex-soldiers were joined by disaffected nationalists and students to form groups vehemently opposed to both liberal-democracy and socialism. These groups gained support from other alienated and dislocated elements, including *déclassés* or drop-outs from the 'respectable' and established classes and professions of society, all of them at odds with democratic ideas and middle-class bourgeois society. In their place they exalted the values of exacerbated nationalism, activism and combat.

Bauer shared with Zibordi the view that such groups on their own could not have posed a threat to the liberal-democratic state. It was, for Bauer as for Zibordi, the panic of the intermediate strata (the petty-bourgeoisie) which drove them to support fascist groups and swelled their ranks. However, even these mass movements would not have succeeded in seizing power (according to this analysis) had it not been for the third group in Bauer's list, sections of the economically dominant and politically powerful ruling class, who opened the way to power for such a mass movement. They switched their support away from parties operating within the liberal-democratic framework to fascist or national socialist parties proclaiming their will for a strong state. The destruction of the parliamentary system was high on their agenda.

Bauer's analysis seems especially convincing on this point, and it raises certain crucial questions concerning the nature of the liberal-democratic state which merit further exploration. For Bauer, the fascist mass movement was invited into power by sections of the dominant class, the bourgeoisie. The property-owning classes and sections of their political representatives came to support fascist-type movements because they wanted to use them as a battering ram against the threat of the socialist movement.

There was thus a contradiction within fascism between its anti-capitalist slogans and its appeal as an instrument of capitalist reaction and defence. In conditions of crisis, the gains which working-class movements had made through their political parties, such as the German SPD, and the trade unions seemed, from the point of view of the dominant classes, dangerous erosions on the sphere of profit, threatening to impose limits on capitalist power. Fascism was therefore not merely a response to fear of socialist or Marxist revolution, as perhaps had been more clearly the case with Italian fascism. Italian fascism was a reaction to the aftermath of the Bolshevik Revolution which sparked off a wave of factory seizures in the north of the country, the *Biennio Rosso* or 'Red Two Years' of 1919–21. Even if in Germany in 1933 there existed no expectation of communist revolution, in both Germany and Italy under conditions of economic crisis the property-owning classes wished to do away with the institutions of working-class politics which imposed limits on capitalist power. Parties of the Left and trade unions were forces to be disposed of, and their power to be contained in a radical way. Therefore, despite elements of anti-capitalist rhetoric in its propaganda, fascism can be seen as a sort of 'capitalist counter-offensive', in which the capitalist class was willing, if not necessarily with total enthusiasm, to play the authoritarian card. This involved using the mass movement formed by the disaffected and dislocated strata (the military–nationalist nucleus plus the mass of the frightened petty-bourgeoisie) as a tool to smash working-class parties and unions. The aim was to install a strong executive-dominated state which would be the instrument for this bourgeois reaction, a counter-offensive against both reformist and revolutionary forms of socialism.

According to Bauer's analysis, fascist movements were helped to power by those who wanted to use them as a defence of capitalist interests. Bauer's argument followed the broad lines of argument which Marx had employed in *The Eighteenth Brumaire of Louis Bonaparte*. Marx's analysis of Bonapartism charted the transition in France from a liberal-democratic state to the authoritarian system of the Second Empire. His argument was that the property-owning classes came to support Louis Bonaparte and to abandon the parliamentary 'Party of Order' because they feared democracy as dangerous, giving advantages to the subordinate classes. The dominant classes were therefore willing to support the Bonapartist *coup d'état* which seemed to guarantee 'order'. They sacrificed their political interests so that their economic and social power would be preserved through a strong state.

Along similar lines, Bauer's analysis was that economically dominant groups were willing to hand power or give support to fascist movements because in that way their economic and social power could be protected, and the working-class movement kept at bay by a strong state. Thus they saw the fascist movement as an instrument, a tool, for the defence of bourgeois interests. Of course, following this line of analysis, it must not be assumed that dominant groups did this without any concern, especially since the anti-capitalist and revolutionary rhetoric of fascism suggested themes of social radicalism. Nevertheless, to return to Bauer's analysis, the support given to fascism by sections of the economic elite and by important politicians was based on the premise that the fascist mass movement could in fact be used as an implement to smash or repress the working-class movement.

However, once this mass movement came to power, assisted by the support of these groups, the instrument outgrew the user. A strong state was formed which was autonomous with respect to all groups and classes. Just as Marx had written of the Bonapartist state that 'all classes, mute and powerless, kneel beneath the rifle butt', so too the property-owning classes, sections of which had assisted fascist movements to power, found that a movement had come to power which threatened them as well. Fascist movements brought to power leaders who could not by any stretch of the imagination be called 'bourgeois politicians'. Fascist movements were led by demagogues who wished to gain support from all social classes, and a state was created which in its totalitarian drives seemed to be 'autonomous' from and to bear down on society. Those who thought that Hitler and his fellows could be made instruments for the defence of their privileges found that state power towered above all class interests. This raises the whole question of the relationship of the fascist state to the interests of capitalism, which is discussed further below. The fascist state should not be considered merely as an instrument of capitalist power, since this would be far too crude a view of what fascism is about.

So far then we have followed a line of analysis, exemplified by the Italian socialist Zibordi and by the Austrian Marxist Otto Bauer, that stressed the complexities of the fascist phenomenon. Fascism involved mass movements, which recruited support from different sections of the population. In this sense fascism was both opportunistic and contradictory. Fascist movements sought support wherever they could find it, building up a popular movement from different social groups all of whom were disaffected from the liberal-democratic state. To business groups, fascist leaders offered themselves as a defence against Bolshevism or communism; to the petty-bourgeoisie the theme was of the 'third way' between capitalism dominated by big business and an international socialism which spoke only for the working classes. German Nazis even sought to recruit sections of the working class, notably those unemployed workers who were disillusioned with social democracy and with communist parties.[11]

We should also note, in connection with the idea of fascism as a 'capitalist counter-offensive', that one condition for the victory of fascism, in both Italy and Germany, lay in divisions within the working-class movement, or its political formations. Divisions between Social Democrats and Communists resulted in the failure to prevent the rise of fascism, which was aided by a severe underestimation of its menace and by a misunderstanding of the nature of the whole fascist phenomenon. For a while (the famous 'Schlageter line') the German Communist Party (KPD) even made common cause with the Nazis against the Weimar Republic, seeing the Social Democrats as the chief enemy.[12] The Communists argued that the victory of fascism would soon be followed by a communist or socialist revolution ('*Nach Hitler kommen wir*').

It was this disastrously mistaken analysis of fascism that helped the fascist forces to victory. In the German case it was not so much a case of an underestimation of Nazism as a totally distorted grasp of its significance. The KPD thought that the coming to power of Hitler and the Nazis would be no different from other 'emergency governments' like those of Brüning, which strengthened executive power but did not do away with the structure of parliamentary government. Orthodox communist analysis also focused on the Social Democrats as the main target, and the absurd thesis of 'social fascism' propagated by Stalin saw the Social Democrats as the 'left wing of fascism'. Not that the Communists were the only ones to fail to grasp the significance of fascism: the social democratic analysis was equally at fault, in that many Social Democrats held that fascism was directed only against revolutionary, i.e. communist, challenges from the Left. Hence they thought that remaining within the bounds of legality and constitutionalism would disarm the fascist menace. However, as noted above, fascist movements derived support from those who wished to use fascism and Nazism as a means of destroying reformist as well as revolutionary socialism.

In sum, it was both the division between the forces of the Left and, linked with that, their mistaken analysis of the phenomenon that helped fascist movements with their mass base to come to power and to install a form of state very different from liberal-democracy. What that form of state was, and how it relates to the 'movement' stage of fascism, is discussed in the following section.

Party and state: the nature of the fascist regime

We have seen that fascist movements sought to recruit mass support from different sources, and that in this sense fascist movements could be seen as 'anti-movements', defined by the very different things which they were against. These included liberalism, democracy, socialism, clericalism, modernism, Marxism and internationalism, and the list can be extended further.[13] Fascist movements condemned the individualism of liberalism, seeking to annihilate the individual beneath the weight of the state, and, in the case of Nazism, under the weight of *das Volk*, the people, defined racially. Such movements also dismissed democracy, the idea of the people as sovereign, substituting instead the 'leader principle', the heroic leader manipulating the passive masses. And against socialism with its internationalist appeal to class struggle, fascist movements exalted the idea of a national community, in which all classes would co-operate in an organic whole and the evils of socialist revolution would be averted. In Italian fascism this took the form of appeals to the idea of the 'corporate state', which would override ideas of class conflict. In German Nazism the myth was one of the *Volksgemeinschaft*, the people's community, racially defined, a form of extreme 'social closure' based on ideas of 'friend and foe'. The Jew, and other categories of the enemy, were to be annihilated in the pursuit of ideas of racial exclusivity.

The reason why fascism was such a dangerous and virulent enemy of the ideas of the French Revolutionary tradition – liberalism, democracy and socialism – was that it employed a perverted version of those ideas which it opposed. Against democracy, fascism employed the façade of mass participation and involvement, through rallies and parades and the style of politics developed since the French Revolution.[14] Against socialism, with its ideas of class struggle and internationalism, fascist movements invoked a form of national socialism, substituting in some cases ideas of a struggle of 'proletarian nations' versus 'bourgeois nations' for a conflict between classes.[15] As for liberalism, the case here is less clear. Fascist movements sought to substitute for liberal individualism the idea that the individuals would find their true identity in some organic whole, in total submission to the race or (in the case of Italian fascism) to the overarching power of the state. In Mussolini's words, 'for the fascist, everything is in the State, and nothing human or spiritual exists, much less has value, outside the State'.[16]

As far as the nature of the fascist state is concerned, the central point is clear, that the fascist state involved the destruction of the institutions of liberal-democracy. Fascism led to the replacement of a system of checks and balances by one in which power was concentrated in the hands of the leader, supported by a mass party which ruthlessly smashed all forms and overt expression of opposition in a process known by the German word *Gleichschaltung*, which we translate here as 'forced co-ordination from above'. This brought all institutions into line through terror and coercion, sought to annihilate all sources of opposition in the state and in civil society, and thus revealed the totalitarian drive to control and politicise all aspects of society.

We noted earlier that fascist movements developed their mass base by proclaiming their 'revolutionary' nature. The fascist party was supposed to be the vehicle for this revolution, seizing power and destroying the hated institutions of the liberal-democratic state and of the working-class movement, but this was designed to be only the prelude to a 'second revolution'. This was envisaged as a continuing social revolution, directed not just against the socialists, but against the conservative and traditional strata of society. Fascism in its 'movement stage' thus proclaimed itself as a movement for which the seizure of state power was only the first part of a process of permanent revolution, of continuing mobilisation and combat, of a ceaseless desire for activism and vitality, an idea of creating something new. A recent study of fascism by Roger Griffin uses the term 'palingenetic' to define fascism, suggesting the idea of a new birth, a new type of society. Griffin defines what he calls 'generic fascism', distinguished from its particular variants, in the following terms: 'Fascism is a genus of political ideology whose mythic core in its various permutations is a palingenetic form of populist ultra-nationalism', 'palingenetic' here deriving from the Greek words *palin* (again, renew) and *genesis* (birth), referring to an idea of a new start or regeneration after a phase of crisis or decline.[17]

This definition highlights the idea of fascism as having a 'mythic core', an irrational centre which appeals to the emotions through a myth. An important figure here is the French syndicalist and social critic, Georges Sorel, who spoke of the myth as the central aspect of social movements. Sorel invoked what he called 'the myth of the General Strike', described by him as 'a body of images capable of evoking instinctively all the sentiments which correspond to the different manifestations of the war undertaken by Socialism against modern society'.[18] Mussolini claimed that from no-one had he learned as much as from Sorel.[19] The lesson he learned was that the political leader could use a myth to mobilise mass support.

Griffin's description of fascism as 'palingenetic' points to the belief that fascist movements were engaged in a task of revolutionary renewal. However, the problem in studying fascism is that of the tension between the revolutionary pretensions of fascism in its movement phase and what actually happened when these movements came to power. Those who wanted the 'second revolution' of which the mass party would be the vehicle, did not have their hopes realised, in the actual practice of either Italian fascism or German Nazism. To summarise complex developments, the reality was that the mass party was forced to co-exist as a 'pillar' of the regime with sections of the existing state apparatus. This went clearly against the temper of those who wanted the fascist revolution to sweep away the old state apparatus in its entirety. In the Italian Fascist Party there was a struggle between the so-called 'intransigents', led by Farinacci, General Secretary of the party, and the 'revisionists', who were willing to see some accommodation with the existing order. As one of the 'intransigents' wrote, 'A Fascist revolution which settled down quietly in the State would be a revolution that has finished . . . A revolution which may be fully victorious at home but is opposed and undermined abroad cannot be defended and sustained unless the revolutionary temperature is constantly kept high.'[20]

Furthermore, as far as the social context of these regimes was concerned, the social radicalism of those who saw in fascism an anti-bourgeois or anti-capitalist revolution was not realised in the actual practice of these regimes. The fascist or Nazi state maintained private ownership and control of the means of production, even if the state dictated what should be produced, especially in the circumstances of war.

Thus in the study of fascist regimes the 'before' and 'after' with respect to the seizure of power has particular significance. Fascist movements when they came to power abolished the institutions of the liberal-democratic state, subjecting them to the grip of the one-party system. This process of destruction of elements of pluralism in the liberal-democratic state structure was achieved much more rapidly and thoroughly in Nazi Germany than in fascist Italy. In the latter case the process took some four years, from the date of the march on Rome in 1922 to the outlawing of other political parties in 1926 after the failure of those parties to oppose fascism effectively. In Germany the smashing of the liberal-democratic state went far more quickly, especially after the passing of the Enabling Act of March 1933, which 'enabled' Hitler to rule by decree. The early months of the Hitler regime were marked by the banning of all parties, and the successive destruction first of parties of the Left, then of liberal and conservative parties. The symbolic culmination of this 'ending of the parties' was the passing of a law of 14 July 1933, 'The Law against the

Establishment of New Parties', which declared that the NSDAP (the Nazi Party) was the only legal party in Germany, and banned attempts to maintain any other party organisation or to form a new party.[21]

The coming to power of fascist parties thus clearly led to the formation of a type of state quite different from the liberal-democratic state. In this sense the diagnosis of the leadership of communist parties was entirely false. They had argued that the formation of a fascist government would not mark a significant change from previous conservative governments which had strengthened executive power and ruled by decree within the framework of parliamentary rule. Fascist systems destroyed the power of the representative elements of the state apparatus. The representative assembly ceased to play any effective role in the state, parties were banned, and the order-maintaining or repressive parts of the state apparatus (military and bureaucracy) were enormously inflated in power. Still, in one sense fascist regimes can be said to have been 'conservative', since they disappointed the hopes of those who wanted a 'second revolution' to sweep away the old order. In both Italy and Germany, the fascist party was not the only pillar of the state, since it had to co-exist with elements of the old state bureaucracy and conservative state apparatus. This led to a series of conflicts between the fascist party or movement on the one hand and the state on the other, conflicts which were resolved through the intervention of the leader, Hitler or Mussolini, and which therefore heightened the leader's arbitrary power.

Thus while destroying the liberal-democratic state, the fascist movement did not achieve the total and unchallenged supremacy which the activists in the movement wanted, nor did they achieve a social revolution and transformation of the social context. Fascist regimes certainly created a strong state in which 'all classes kneel beneath the rifle butt', as Marx wrote of the Bonapartist state, but nevertheless the role of private profit was not ended, and private ownership of the productive resources was maintained, even though capitalists were politically subordinate to the dictates of the party–state. Again, one could suggest that Marx's observation of Bonapartism has relevance to fascist regimes, when he noted that the property-owning classes were willing to sacrifice their political power so that their social and economic power could be maintained. The same could be said to hold true of fascist systems, where capitalist interests were politically subordinate to the fascist state, yet socially and economically fascism preserved a capitalist system.

Perhaps the best way of summing up these complexities is to suggest that the fascist state carried the autonomy, or rather the *relative* autonomy, of the state to its ultimate point. Political power was held by the demagogic leaders of a mass movement. Those leaders certainly were not 'ordinary' bourgeois politicians, and through their mass movement they eluded the political control of the capitalist class. They created a strong state in which power was exercised through a mass monopolistic state party. After this party gained power, the wish of its activist members for total state power and replacement of the old state apparatus was not satisfied, and the party co-existed as a pillar of the regime jointly with elements of the old state apparatus, purged of its liberal and representative elements. Nevertheless, even here the autonomy of the fascist state was not complete. The fascist state still existed in a context of class power, even though the economic and social power of the capitalist class was exercised within a framework of political domination by the fascist party. In this sense, fascist regimes can be seen to have been defenders of capitalism, since they smashed the institutions of working-class politics, both political and economic (trade unions), and maintained the private ownership of the means of production.

The idea of the totalitarian state

We have emphasised the distinction between fascism as a mass movement and fascism as regime. As a mass movement, fascism opportunistically exploited the grievances of a cross-class base, and offered at least to some of its followers the prospect of a revolution. This revolution would destroy the corrupt and divisive liberal-democratic state and stamp out the forces of the working-class movement. The tenor of fascism was revolutionary, promising a 'New Order' to achieve the rebirth (palingenesis) of the society.

One of the difficult questions concerning fascism is whether it is in any genuine sense revolutionary. These movements had mass support and promised a revolution, which in certain respects was anti-bourgeois and definitely anti-socialist and anti-Marxist. Once in power, however, the dynamic of the mass movement was contained, elements of the traditional bureaucracy were left in place, and those who wanted to proceed to the 'second revolution' were purged, as for example happened with Röhm on the 'Night of the Long Knives' in June 1934. Thus in the fascist state the party remained a crucial institution, but its chief role was to whip up the mass support in the parody of democracy that was characteristic of fascist regimes.

What, then, was the character of the fascist state, once it was installed, and how does it compare with liberal-democracy? The term 'totalitarian' has been used to describe in the same category both of the main rivals to the liberal-democratic state in the twentieth century, namely communism and fascism, and to distinguish those regimes, as we have seen, from authoritarian forms of dictatorship. Some defenders of the term suggest that despite some undoubted differences between communism and fascism, what these regimes have in common is more important than what divides them, and that the term 'totalitarian' singles out the crucial distinction between such regimes and those of liberal-democracy, as well as demarcating them from regimes of 'simple dictatorship' or authoritarianism, which lack the drive to total power and mass involvement. The distinction is that totalitarian regimes, it is claimed, leave no room for a private sphere. Everything is politicised, there is constant mobilisation of the masses and the private sphere ceases to exist. In Neumann's words, 'society ceases to be distinguished from the state; it is totally permeated by political power'.[22] Such regimes of a totalitarian sort have two basic characteristics which contrast with the limited style of politics held to typify liberal-democratic systems. First, there is a 'total' ideology to which all aspects of life are supposedly subjected, and this ideology is one to which all members of the society are expected to conform openly and into which they are 'socialised' from birth. Second, it is the existence of a single mass party which distinguishes totalitarian regimes both from liberal-democracy and from non-democratic authoritarian systems. The mass party strives for the continuing mobilisation of its members and of the whole society; it is the vehicle for the politicisation of society, its domination through political power, which is held to be typical of totalitarian societies. The party seeks to penetrate into all aspects of social life, and is controlled by a dictatorial leader. In short, in a totalitarian system, 'civil society' has no autonomy from 'the state', and all institutions of civil society are reduced, at least in theory, to 'transmission belts' of the party, or its leaders. There is no 'space' which is free from this ideology and control from above.

In communist systems, the ruling party controlled appointments to the top positions in civil society through the *nomenklatura* system. In fascist systems, the process of *Gleichschaltung* was intended to have the same effect, depriving all groups of their autonomy. In short, the aim of such systems is total control, through the means of what Hannah Arendt called the 'atomisation' of society, the destruction of any intermediary associations standing between the party–state and the individual.[23] This would entail the destruction of pluralism and the annihilation of the division between state and civil society. Even if the aim of total control was never totally achieved by communist or fascist systems, this drive for total domination of the individual and the creation of an onward mobilisation form the underlying rationale of such systems.

There are a number of problems with this 'totalitarian' model and its application. In terms of the model itself, some of the most widely known statements of the concept, like that of Friedrich and Brzezinski, operate with the idea of totalitarianism as a 'syndrome', with a list of many features.[24] Some of these features, such as government control of the economy and intervention in the means of communication, also apply in systems which are considered democratic. Furthermore, it is not clear whether all the various features have to be present together before a system can be called totalitarian. Alternatively, it could be that there are some vital features of this 'syndrome', such as the mass monopolistic party or the single all-embracing ideology, or the unrestricted use of terror and coercion, which are the crucial ones, whether or not they are accompanied by the other features. There is also the problem of whether it is the *means* of mass terror and the destruction of intermediary institutions which form the hallmarks of totalitarianism, or the *end* of all-pervasive power.

There are also problems with the application of the totalitarian model, notably to the two most favoured examples, German Nazism (rather than Italian fascism) and the Soviet system, above all under Stalin's leadership from 1928 to 1953. Most versions of totalitarian theory seek to place communist regimes and fascist ones in the same category, but this is problematic. It could be argued that, while they do share certain similarities, they were each regimes of a fundamentally different kind, marked by differences in their ideology, in their origins, and in their internal evolution, and that to apply to both the label of 'totalitarian' blurs these distinctions. Communist systems originated in movements of social revolution inspired by Marxism, albeit, as we have noted, taking place under conditions very different from those which Marx argued were necessary for socialist revolution. Their move towards total power was the result of a process which was by no means inevitable. Finally, such systems eventually collapsed as a result of a process of internal reform, which exposed the contradiction between the official philosophy of emancipation proclaimed by these regimes, and their actual undemocratic practice.

The situation with fascist systems was different. The ideas underlying them were ideas which emphasised violence and an anti-democratic principle, and which glorified irrationalism and activism. They exalted the leader principle and aimed consciously at the destruction of democracy and the principles of 1789. They did not achieve in practice the actual transformation of the socioeconomic structure of society, whereas communist revolutions were revolutions which restructured society. It is true that both communist systems and fascist systems did aim at the constant mobilisation of the masses, and at total control. Students of communist systems, however, suggest that the totalitarian model, whatever its possible application for the Stalin period, is distinctly misleading as a label for these systems in their post-Stalin development. Not only did the bureaucratic elite seek stability rather than the constant dynamic mobilising of the masses characteristic of the totalitarian model, but also that perspective, it is suggested, gives a very static portrayal of the power structure of communist systems.[25] It paints a picture of a totally monolithic society, and neglects the conflicts over policy and decision making that actually took place beneath the façade of the single party in such systems. On the other hand, there are those who use similar arguments with respect to fascism, pointing out that in reality these regimes were much less monolithic than their rhetoric proclaimed. For example, beneath the surface there were bitter conflicts between the party and state bureaucracies. Even in Hitler's Germany, the aim of total power and all-pervasive acceptance of the ideology of Nazism was not fully realised. As Kershaw's study of Bavaria under Nazi rule suggests, there were still islands of resistance, and areas of at least quiescent non-acceptance of Nazism.[26]

The totalitarian model does indeed suggest that the aim of such regimes was the total politicisation of all aspects of social life, an aim realised to a greater degree in Hitler's Germany than in Mussolini's Italy. This aim was shared with communist systems, but the label 'totalitarianism' overlooks the profound differences between these two types of non-democratic regime, and fails to acknowledge the elements of pluralism or conflict beneath the monolithic façade of the single-party system in each case. Nevertheless, used as an ideal type, the idea of totalitarianism does suggest an important distinction between the regimes studied in the previous two chapters and liberal-democratic systems. This distinction is precisely the tolerance or acceptance of a division between state and civil society, and the opposition through institutional diversity and organisational pluralism to attempts at forced incorporation or the destruction of difference. Totalitarian systems seek to impose a monolithic structure of thought on to the members of society, and wish to annihilate pluralism. In this sense, to revert briefly to the question of communist systems as opposed to fascist ones, the revolutions of 1989 which led to the collapse of communism can be seen in part as 'pluralist' revolutions. As Steven Lukes has noted, 'the revolutionary movements of 1989' were 'pluralist movements that demanded an end to the monopoly of power, to the *Nomenklatura* . . . and to the denial of expression, and institutional embodiment, to cultural, notably ethnic and religious, identities'.[27] However, our main subject in this chapter is fascism, not communism, and we close this chapter by some reflections on the contemporary relevance of the fascist phenomenon.

The fascist phenomenon today

We focused earlier on the socioeconomic roots of the phenomenon of fascism, rather than its ideological origins. Of course, both would have to be considered in any total evaluation of fascism. Ideologically, it can be said that fascism was born out of a protest against the liberal-democratic principles of 1789, and their socialist derivations. Fascism is the politics of myth, of irrationalism, building up mass support through emotional mobilisation of a discontented following. As Lyttelton notes in his study of Italian fascism,

> The closest bond between Hitler and Mussolini was their belief that the road to power lay through the mastery of collective psychology, the manipulation of mass passions; they were both disciples of Gustave Le Bon and his 'psychology of the crowd'.[28]

Fascism in its original phase developed out of the crisis in Europe following the First World War, when movements developed which gave political voice and mass backing to the critique of bourgeois democracy and the principles of 1789. The main component of these movements was the *Mittelstand* or middle class, what Marxists would call the petty-bourgeoisie, spurred into panic by conditions of economic and social crisis and fear of socialist revolution. Fascist movements used whatever myths came to hand to stir up this mass following, whether those were the Nazi myths of racial purity, or the Italian fascist rhetoric of restoring the glories of ancient Rome or other 'palingenetic' myths in different movements.

There are those who argue that fascism was a product of a particular crisis in European history, which led to the creation of the fascist state. Such states were defeated in the Second World War, and therefore the episode of fascism is closed. European societies no longer have a panic-struck petty-bourgeoisie to be mobilised by fascist demagogic leaders, and the legitimacy of liberal-democracy, which we noted in Chapter 1, is such that attempts to install a strong state in such systems would not receive any support. On this argument, the forms of politics of the extreme Right which have recently surfaced in Europe are manifestations of marginal movements which can pose little threat to the stability of contemporary liberal-democracy.

However, in opposition to this point of view it can be argued that such arguments rather miss the point. The essence of fascism, as a movement, is a form of mass politics which preys on economic and social upheaval and seeks scapegoats for such discontent. In this sense, then, fascism is a more open-ended term, and cannot be limited to a closed episode in European history. The use of nationalist rhetoric is something equally crucial to fascist movements. This seeks to operate as a form of 'social closure', creating a clear demarcation between 'insiders' and 'outsiders', the latter forming the scapegoats for social grievances. This target group is often that of immigrants or ethnic and racial minorities.[29]

In short, fascism can arise in situations where a number of conditions are fulfilled. Such new forms of fascism might differ from the old versions in terms of the strata they appeal to, and the precise content of the 'myth' or the slogans used to mobilise a discontented mass base. Yet this would not mean that they were not 'fascist', even with due precautions taken against extending the term unduly. The term 'fascist' could here be used for movements which arose in conditions of economic crisis, say high unemployment, or dislocatory political change, for example German unification and its unsettling effects.

Fascist movements typically seek to secure a mass base, although of course in this respect they are no different from other movements of modern politics. However, the mobilisation of the masses does distinguish fascism from traditional movements of a conservative type, which seek to maintain forms of traditional hierarchy and preserve existing institutions, and which are wary of bringing the masses into politics. Fascist movements aim at the replacement of the liberal-democratic state by an authoritarian structure of political power, criticising parliamentarism and democratic rights, seeking not to extend these but to destroy them through the creation of a 'New Order' which is homogeneous and nationally cohesive.

There seem to be no lack of such movements of the extreme Right in contemporary political life. The implication seems to be that fascist or neo-fascist movements can arise where capitalist or ex-communist systems are in crisis or deep difficulty. Very often it is nationalism, of the exacerbated and extreme kind that Griffin calls 'populist ultra-nationalism', which is used by such groups. It works as a symbol of the 'in group' and marks out the targets or scapegoats which are held responsible for the plight of the disoriented groups who rally to forms of extreme right-wing politics.

The conclusion must be that, while liberal-democratic systems seem to have acquired considerable legitimacy and to have survived the rivalry from those fascist states which were defeated in the Second World War, such systems of liberal-democracy are not immune from pressures towards authoritarianism and movements resembling fascism. While fear of a socialist revolution may not be the motivating factor behind such movements, or the main factor which rallies people to that cause, it may be economic crisis and fear of unemployment which builds up support for demagogic movements of the extreme Right. Fascism therefore may be regarded as a movement which came to power in the inter-war period, but similar movements continue to exist and pose a challenge to the contemporary liberal-democratic state. They also exist in ex-communist societies where the transition to liberal-democracy and market relations is being imposed 'from above', often with little regard for those who lose out in the process.

Movements of this neo-fascist kind harness nationalism, which has throughout the modern period been a powerful force in political life, whether as a force in opposition to the state or as one binding the state together. Our next chapter examines nationalism not just because of the contribution of nationalism to the politics of movements of the extreme Right. As we noted in Chapter 1, modern states are essentially nation-states, and we need to understand what the nation is before we can understand both the modern state and the force of nationalism in the modern world.

Notes

1. Hamilton, R., *The Appeal of Fascism: A study of intellectuals and fascism 1919–1945*, Anthony Blond, London, 1971.
2. On neo-fascism, see Cheles, L., Ferguson, R., and Vaughan, M. (eds), *Neo-Fascism in Europe*, Longman, London, 1991; and Griffin, R., *The Nature of Fascism*, Routledge, London and New York, 1993, Chapter 6.
3. Poulantzas, N., *Fascism and Dictatorship*, New Left Books, London, 1974.
4. Sternhell, Z., 'Fascist Ideology' in Laqueur, W. (ed.), *Fascism: A reader's guide*, Penguin, Harmondsworth, 1979.
5. Neumann, F., *The Democratic and the Authoritarian State: Essays in political and legal theory*, The Free Press, New York and London, 1957, p. 244.
6. Mosse, G.L., 'Fascism and the French Revolution', *Journal of Contemporary History*, vol. 24 no. 1, 1989, pp. 5–26.
7. Gramsci, A., 'On fascism', in Beetham, D. (ed.), *Marxists in Face of Fascism: Writings by Marxists on fascism from the inter-war period*, Manchester University Press, Manchester, 1983, p. 84.

8. Zibordi, G., 'Towards a definition of fascism', in Beetham, *Marxists in Face of Fascism*, p. 88.
9. For Trotsky's analysis, see Trotsky, L., *The Struggle against Fascism in Germany*, Penguin, Harmondsworth, 1975.
10. Bauer, O., 'Fascism', in Bottomore, T.B. and Goode, P. (eds), *Austro-Marxism*, Clarendon Press, Oxford, 1978, pp. 167–86.
11. See Kele, M.H., *Nazis and Workers: National Socialist appeals to German labor 1919–1933*, University of North Carolina Press, Chapel Hill, NC, 1972.
12. On the 'Schlageter line', see Carr, E.H., *The Interregnum 1923–1924*, Penguin, Harmondsworth, 1969, pp. 184ff.
13. Linz, J., 'Notes towards a comparative study of fascism', in Laqueur (ed.), *Fascism: A reader's guide*, p. 29.
14. Mosse, 'Fascism and the French Revolution'.
15. As, for example, proposed by the Italian nationalist, and later fascist, Enrico Corradini. See Corradini, E., 'The principles of nationalism', in Lyttelton, A. (ed.), *Italian Fascisms, from Pareto to Gentile*, Jonathan Cape, London, 1973, p. 148.
16. Mussolini, 'The doctrine of fascism', in Lyttelton (ed.), *Italian Fascisms, from Pareto to Gentile*, p. 42.
17. Griffin, *The Nature of Fascism*, p. 26.
18. Sorel, G., *Reflections on Violence*, trans. T.E. Hulme and J. Roth, Collier Books, New York, 1961, p. 127.
19. Roth, J.J., *The Cult of Violence: Sorel and the Sorelians*, University of California Press, Berkeley, CA, and London, 1980.
20. Quoted in Lyttelton, A., *The Seizure of Power: Fascism in Italy 1919–1929*, Weidenfeld & Nicolson, London, 1973, p. 293.
21. Broszat, M., *The Hitler State: The foundation and development of the internal structure of the Third Reich*, Longman, London, 1981, p. 90.
22. Neumann, *The Democratic and the Authoritarian State*, p. 244.
23. Arendt, H., *The Origins of Totalitarianism*, Meridian Books, Cleveland, OH, and New York, 1958.
24. Friedrich, C.J., and Brzezinksi, Z.K., *Totalitarian Dictatorship and Autocracy*, Praeger, New York, 1963, p. 9.
25. Brown, A.H., 'Political power and the Soviet state', in Harding, N. (ed.), *The State in Socialist Society*, Macmillan, London, 1984.
26. Kershaw, I., *Popular Opinion and Political Dissent in the Third Reich: Bavaria 1933–1945*, Clarendon Press, Oxford, 1983.
27. Lukes, S., 'The principles of 1989', in Lukes, S., *Moral Conflict and Politics*, Clarendon Press, Oxford, 1991, pp. 316–17.
28. Lyttelton, *The Seizure of Power*, p. 364.
29. See Hainsworth, P. (ed.), *The Extreme Right in Europe and America*, Pinter, London, 1992.

9 | Nationalism and the nation-state

Introduction

This chapter is concerned with an exceedingly powerful force in modern politics, the power of nationalism. It is necessary to start by explaining how this fits into the general argument of the book, and what place it has in its overall structure. There are a number of reasons why any study of the modern state, and in particular its liberal-democratic form, needs to include the phenomenon of nationalism.

In the first place, as noted in Chapter 1, the modern state claims to be a 'nation-state'; this is seen as the 'normal' form of the state in the modern world. This is, of course, a large generalisation, to which significant exceptions can be noted. Indeed, the American scholar Walker Connor points out that in reality only a minority of states meet the criteria of the nation-state strictly defined: that is, that there is a population which shares a common culture and has a state to itself.[1] However, the dominant form of the modern state is a unit which at least in theory brings together the cultural unit of 'the nation' with the political unit of 'the state'.[2] This model of the nation-state was developed initially in Western Europe, with France as the classic example. However, the idea of the link between state and nation, of the nation-state as the desirable model of a political unit, has long ago been taken up by societies beyond the European ambit. In such societies, as well as in Europe, the idea of 'nation building', of creating through state action a common national consciousness overriding what were claimed to be subsidiary divisions, has occupied a central place on the political agenda.

It is, of course, also true that the course of modern politics has witnessed a series of challenges to the nation-state. These challenges have stemmed both from international factors and from forces emerging within the nation-state.[3] Among the latter one can mention what has been called 'sub-state nationalism'. This finds expression in movements seeking to break up along ethnic lines apparently unified states like Spain and France. Examples of such sub-state nationalism would be movements of Basque, Catalan or Breton nationalism. While the nation-state may be experiencing difficulties for various reasons, it remains an important framework for political action in the modern world. In the words of a recent study, 'Those who herald the emerging postnational age are too hasty in condemning the nation-state to the dustbin of history. They underestimate the resilience, as well as the richness and complexity, of an institutional and normative tradition that, for better or worse, appears to have life in it yet.'[4]

However, if the nation-state has been and remains important, we need to explain why the state in the modern world has been or sought to be a *nation*-state, and the significance of this combination of the cultural unit (the nation) with the political unit of the state. It is this link between the two which is the goal sought by nationalism as a theory of politics, and its realisation is the aim of nationalist movements. There are thus two points of investigation: the nature of the nation-state, and the significance of nationalism, as an ideology or doctrine.

Nationalism as a theory asserts the desirability of maintaining the nation-state as the chief unit of political life. Nationalist movements strive to form a nation-state in a situation where a particular nation does not have its own state: in other words, where a nation is ruled by people from another nation, or where one nation is divided among several states. 'One nation, one state' is the goal of nationalism, even though, as has been pointed out by Gellner among others, this is an aim unrealisable in the modern world. Since there are many hundreds of nations, however those are defined, to call for each one to have its own state would lead to an infinite regress. Any existing nation-state will have minorities in it, different in culture from the majority. Habermas also observes that 'According to the form of national identity, each nation should be organised in one state, in order to be independent. However, in historical reality the state with a nationally homogeneous population has always remained a fiction.'[5]

The dominance of the nation-state as the 'normal' and apparently desirable form of the state in the modern world thus forms the first reason for investigation of this topic. The second justification is the power of nationalism in the modern world, as a force moulding political action. Any attempt at a theoretical understanding of modern politics and the modern state needs to come to grips with this powerful force, and to seek to explain it.

This chapter also involves consideration of what could be called the ethnic and nationalist challenge to liberal-democracy, and this requires some explanation. The problem here stems from what has been called the basic malleability of nationalism.[6] In its origins, nationalism went along with ideas of democracy and liberalism. The nation was defined in terms of the people, and the democratic idea of 'people power' was at one with the idea of national self-determination, the people as a national people ruling themselves, internally free and not subject to outside oppression by an alien power or nation. In the nineteenth century liberals, and indeed democrats and socialists too, generally supported movements struggling for national independence and freedom from foreign rule, such as in Poland, Greece and Italy. In this sense, movements of what has been called 'Risorgimento nationalism', modelled on the struggle for Italian unification and independence, were part and parcel of the liberal-democratic tradition, whose aim was to create a world of democratic nation-states.[7]

However, equally important is the fact that in some of its forms nationalism has been deeply opposed to liberal-democracy, and has stimulated movements of opposition to the liberal-democratic state, and indeed to other forms of state too. One example of this is movements of the sort studied in Chapter 8, movements of a fascist kind, which use as part of their appeal what has been called a form of 'populist ultra-nationalism'.[8] Nazi parties used a racial definition of the nation and used the myth of the nation in the form of a 'people's community' or *Volksgemeinschaft*. This was a means of rallying support to overthrow the liberal-democratic state. Other examples of nationalism in opposition to the state could be found in the contemporary situation in Eastern and Central Europe, where nationalism is presently leading to conflicts along ethnic lines and forms of politics hostile to the institutions and values of liberal-democracy. The example of former Yugoslavia is an obvious one here.

It is worth dwelling for a moment on the question of why nationalism, at least in some of its many and diverse forms, can lead to a form of politics opposed to the liberal-democratic state, and why the discussion of nationalism here situates it under the general heading 'rivals to the liberal-democratic state'. The idea of the liberal-democratic state rests on principles of tolerance, equality of citizens and a limited style of politics. Politics and the scope of state action are seen as limited in that the state should not infringe too far on the sphere of a diverse 'civil society'. The aim is to prevent the politicisation of all issues, since this would lead to the totalitarian model of an all-pervasive state power. There should be a basic consensus on political procedures and on what Bobbio calls 'rules of the game'. If this breaks down, as it did when certain groups responded to the appeal of fascism, then liberal-democracy is finished.

Nationalism in some of its manifestations opposes this liberal-democratic model of politics. Nationalism in general terms can be defined as the doctrine or belief that 'state' and 'nation' should coincide. In actual political life, the politics of nationalism often involves the idea that the nation is the supreme political unit to which all else must be subordinate. People should sacrifice themselves for the national cause, so that nationalism in the modern world often elevates 'the nation' to the position of absolute superiority, a characteristic of what Alter calls 'integral' nationalism, opposed to the emancipatory form of 'Risorgimento' nationalism.[9] This type of integral nationalism involves the abandonment of the principles of tolerance and relativisation of values necessary for liberal-democracy, since it elevates tight national cohesion and security to the rank of an absolute value on which there can be no compromise.

One further problem emerges with the definition of the term 'the nation'. If the nation is understood as an ethnic group whose interests are seen as overriding other interests and other groups, then nationalist politics in this sense destroys the idea of citizen equality, an equality of all who are citizens irrespective of their ethnic characteristics or national origins. If the nation is defined in ethnic, let alone racial terms, this restricts full or 'true' membership of the citizen body to those of a particular ethnic or national affiliation. This concept of the nation is employed by several groups of the extreme Right in contemporary Europe whose activities may remain marginal but who still pose a threat to liberal-democracy.

Similarly, if national identity is held to be the overriding source of personal or group identity and value, and if this is given absolute status, then the compromise necessary for democratic politics may well break down. This seems highly relevant to the present situation of democratic transition in Eastern and Central Europe.[10] In the countries of the former Communist bloc, nationalism is a very powerful force. People are 'mobilised' to rally round parties offering national or ethnic identity as a 'bonding' device. Yet this form of nationalism can all too easily fuel bitter conflicts of one national group against another. If several different national groups live together in the same territorial area, one of them in a majority position, then embittered national conflict makes democracy or liberal-democracy difficult, if not impossible, to achieve. The rights of members of the minority nation or ethnic group are not respected, and obviously this is at odds with any idea of citizenship equality and democratic consensus. One dramatic illustration of this is given by a recent account of events in former Yugoslavia, where it was noted how members of each national group came to describe people from different ethnic or national backgrounds as 'congenital monsters'.[11] In this way, where the idea of the nation is bound up with religious or ethnic exclusivity, nationalist politics can lead to intolerance and violent conflict.

More importantly, forms of nationalism can go against the democratic tendency which seeks to extend the bounds of citizenship by ignoring the distinctions of class, gender, wealth, age, ethnic and racial division which for many years restricted the citizen body and limited the category of those who could be described as constituting 'the people'. Democratic pressure has involved a process of extending the scope of 'the people'. Nationalist movements, at least in some of their forms, seem to reverse this trend, because 'the people' is defined as including only those of a particular ethnic stock, so that national minorities who live in the same territory may come to see themselves excluded from citizenship rights.

An example of this is the situation in the Baltic republics, in the period before and after their independence from the former Soviet Union, concerning the criteria of citizenship. The question was whether those Russian speakers who lived in the territory of Lithuania or Estonia or Latvia were to be given citizenship rights, or whether these were to be restricted to 'natives' of those areas who spoke the national language and who were of the relevant ethnic stock.[12] A strict nationalist response would restrict citizenship to those who satisfied the ethnic criteria, defined in this case primarily through language, and this is in contrast to the demands for widening the boundaries of the citizen body.

Nationalism and nationalist movements can thus pose a challenge to the liberal-democratic state. Certainly this was the case with the kind of nationalism exemplified in fascism, but the argument can be extended to other forms of nationalism based on a view of the nation as an ethnic community. Hence we are dealing here with those forms of nationalism which act as a force hostile to the liberal-democratic state – not exactly a rival in the same sense as communism or fascism, but setting up a style of politics which can threaten the stability of the liberal-democratic order.

Yet describing the modern state as a nation-state also involves understanding the ways in which nationalism can function as a force of cohesion and legitimation of the existing order. The paradox is that nationalism can work as both oppositional movement and conservative force, as a factor opposing the state and as one legitimating it. This raises the whole question of nationalism and the state, the relation between the idea of nationalism and the functioning of the modern state, notably in its liberal-democratic form.

In his book *Nationalism and the State*, the historian John Breuilly suggests that nationalism is essentially an anti-governmental or oppositional political movement, seeking to remould or reconstruct existing political structures, whether by breaking away from them or reforming the state to give greater expression to the national idea. He sees nationalism as essentially non-governmental nationalism, defining it as 'a form of politics, primarily opposition politics'. Such nationalist opposition can, he suggests, 'stand in one of three relationships to the existing state. It can seek to break away from it, to take it over and reform it, or to unite it with other states.'[13]

While there is no denying the importance of nationalism in these oppositional forms, nationalism can and does also exist as a force seeking to keep existing political structures intact. Nationalism can even be described as the most important legitimation for governmental power in the modern world. States nowadays not only seek democratic legitimation, in line with the fact that all states in the modern world claim to be democratic, reflecting the will of the people. By the same token, and linked historically with the idea of democracy or popular sovereignty, states often describe themselves as nation-states. They seek to portray their use of political power as maintaining the cohesion and interests of the nation. The state elite in liberal-democratic as in other systems sees itself as working in 'the national interest', with the state as the institution or set of institutions for defending the supreme interests of the nation, however 'nation' may be defined.

The implication is that states therefore seek to heighten national consciousness or national cohesion by a variety of devices, claiming that the basis of the state is the will of the nation, that the state derives its power from the nation, and that it speaks for the nation. Historically, an example of the attempt to develop and intensify national consciousness is provided by the Third French Republic. There, in conditions of defeat in the war of 1870–1 with Germany and the resultant attempt at national recovery and *revanche* (revenge) against this national enemy, the state elite set out to create a republican national consciousness. This was done through such state institutions as the school and the army. Both were seen as forging a new national awareness, which would form a solid basis for the democratic republic, and as opening up this new national community to the new social strata (*nouvelles couches sociales*) who had hitherto been excluded or marginalised.[14] Other examples are provided by the process of nation building in post-colonial states, where the post-colonial elite sought to gain legitimation by forging a new identity, cutting across tribal and ethnic divisions.[15]

Nationalism can thus function as reinforcing, rather than threatening, the liberal-democratic state. The task, then, is to explain this paradox of how nationalism can be both anti-governmental and pro-governmental. The broader issue is the significance of national identity in the politics of the modern world.[16]

The ambiguities of 'the nation'

Our task here is to explain in brief compass the appeal of nationalism and its implications for the politics of the liberal-democratic state. There are two questions to be explored, namely the nature of the modern state as a nation-state, and the different forms that nationalism takes in the politics of the modern world, or the political consequences of nationalism.

The modern state has been defined as a membership organisation, as well as a territorial organisation.[17] This means that the modern state not only rules a particular territory, but decides on the criteria of those who are to be admitted to the category of 'citizen', those who form the members of the state. If we are to understand the force of nationalism in the modern world, we need to understand the concept of 'the nation' and the contrasting ways in which the term has been presented. It has been argued above that nationalism has had widely different political implications. In its fascist form of what Griffin calls 'populist ultra-nationalism', it prompted movements seeking to overthrow or undermine the liberal-democratic state. However, this is not true of all forms of nationalism, since nationalism of a more moderate form has been and remains an integral element of cohesion in the modern liberal-democratic state.

The core idea of nationalism, as we have seen, is that 'state' and 'nation' should coincide. The nationalist aspiration is that each nation should have its own state, and that each state should be the state of only one nation. The classical nationalist vision was of a world of nation-states, in which the 'vertical' divisions between nations are the most significant demarcation lines in modern politics. But why has nationalism been such a central strand in the formation and development of the modern state, and with what results?

There are a number of problems here, the first of which relates to the question of definition of 'the nation'. Historically, we can point to a process through which the definition of the term 'the nation' changed, from the French Revolution definition of the nation as an association of citizens, to a much more exclusive concept of the nation as an ethnic community, closed to those who were not of the same descent or ethnicity.

The term 'nation' was in its origins bound up with a democratic idea, that all those within the same territory were members of the nation, sharing a common history and the same political rights, and that was the sense in which nation and state went together. A joint history of assertion and defence of those rights constituted the national community which was at one and the same time a political community with its own sovereign state.

This kind of nationalism emerged in the period of the French Revolution.[18] It furnished a criterion of membership of the political community, a means of legitimising the state, and a criterion of *exclusion*, or social closure, as well as *inclusion*. Membership of the nation, and hence of the political community, was seen as a quality of all those who lived in the national territory and who participated in the democratic process. The state power was legitimated or justified because it was the power necessary to defend and protect this association of citizens, and they were distinguished from other nations (associations of citizens) by their common history and traditions. A.D. Smith refers to this as 'the standard Western model of the nation', and summarises its components as 'Historic territory, legal–political community, legal–political equality of members, and common civic culture and ideology'.[19]

This became the traditional model of the liberal-democratic nation-state. It was a 'voluntarist' conception of the nation, since membership depended on consent, on voluntary participation in the national political community. At the time of the French Revolution it was held that 'peoples' everywhere should and would constitute such communities of self-determining citizens, sharing common democratic rights and a sense of history, and the world would be formed by a variety of such democratic nation-states, peacefully co-existing with each other. Nationalism thus furnished a principle of social solidarity, and each state was seen as the expression of a distinct national community.

This may seem a somewhat idealised description of nationalism and of the formation of the nation-state. Its formation was also related to profound economic transformations which accompanied the beginnings of modernity. The idea of nationalism provided a basis of legitimacy for the state, and helped bolster the position of the holders of state power. The nation-state also involved a common educational system and a shared language, spread among or enforced on the inhabitants of the nation. This was part of the transition to a modern industrial society. In such a society, as social mobility was a functional necessity, people could not remain in one local area, tied permanently to one job. For such a society, a shared common language and a common educational system were essential, and these were things which a nation-state could provide. Nationalism is thus linked to the transition from an agricultural, 'segmented' society to an industrial one.[20]

This section is headed 'the ambiguities of the nation' because 'the nation' can be defined in terms very different from the ones used so far. At the risk of simplifying unduly, it is possible to make a distinction between the kind of nationalism which maintains the cohesion of liberal-democratic societies, which has been described above, and a form of nationalism which is, at least potentially, more dangerous to liberal-democracy. This latter is best described using the label of ethnic nationalism, whose components are listed by A.D. Smith as follows:

> Genealogy and presumed descent ties, popular mobilization, vernacular languages, customs and traditions: these are the elements of an alternative, ethnic conception of the nation, one that mirrored the very different route of 'nation-formation' travelled by many communities in Eastern Europe and Asia and one that constituted a dynamic political challenge.[21]

It is this force which can be a threat to liberal-democratic societies, and which remains an important one in the politics of our time.

This type of nationalism defines the nation as an ethnic community, rather than as an association of citizens. The two different traditions of the nation have been exemplified by 'French' nationalism on the one hand and 'German' nationalism on the other. This distinction is not to be taken too literally, hence the inverted commas, since there are examples of a citizenship nationalism in the German case, and of an ethnic nationalism in the French case – well exemplified towards the end of the nineteenth century by writers such as Barrès and Maurras.[22] However, there is historically a difference between a French tradition of national citizenship, based on *jus soli*, and a German tradition of citizenship, based on *jus sanguinis*. The former attributes citizenship to all who inhabit the territory, irrespective of ethnic origin or character. The latter makes citizenship available only to those of common ethnic descent, and therefore functions in a more exclusive way.[23]

A conception of the nation therefore emerged which saw the nation as an ethnic community, and laid greater emphasis on language and culture as 'markers' of such an association. A deterministic concept of the nation made membership of the nation reflect characteristics whose acquisition did not depend on individual choice. One's national milieu in this sense was given by birth, and there was nothing one could do about it. Nationalists like the German philosopher Fichte exalted a unique language and the traditions of a particular people, the Germans, who had preserved their purity and character intact and without, as he saw it, 'contamination'. In this form of nationalism, an individual's real identity was given by his or her nation, seen as the supreme good or goal, and one for which individuals must be prepared to sacrifice their lives. The nation was defined mystically as a communion of *la terre et les morts*, the earth and the dead, anticipating later Nazi ideas of *Blut und Boden*, and not as a community which people could join voluntarily.

There are thus distinct concepts of the nation which have quite different political implications. It is possible to oppose a citizenship concept of the nation to one based on ethnicity. The latter is much more likely to find expression in movements which seek to make ethnic identification and affiliation the overriding criterion of political identity. Such movements express a form of nationalism which asserts the supremacy of the nation over all other associations. It involves a definition of the nation in terms of ethnic community and establishes a sharper sense of social bonding. This makes it more difficult for non-members of the nation to become members and hence citizens, and produces a sharper sense of the distinction between the two groupings. Such forms of nationalism tend to make the nation the only source of value, and they can lead to a sense of intolerance and denial of the value or worth of other nations.

This expression of nationalism is quite different from the 'citizenship nationalism' described earlier, and is likely to be at odds with some of the preconditions of liberal-democracy: particularly an attitude of tolerance and relativism, the belief that all creeds and perspectives are worthy of respect, and the view that there is no final truth in politics. Political movements that take a view akin to 'my nation right or wrong', or who see the nation as an ethnic community whose interests are supreme, fit uneasily with the pluralism which is claimed to underlie liberal-democracy. Hence the ambiguities of nationalism: the emergence of forms of nationalism that are both supportive of liberal-democracy and at the same time undermine it.

It should be mentioned that some students of contemporary nationalism and racism take a more sceptical view of the universalist pretensions of the 'citizenship' model (what has here been called the 'French' concept) of the nation. They suggest that it can function as masking a very particularist set of assumptions, no less ethnic or cultural than the overtly 'ethnic' model of the nation. The civic model of the nation offers a view of the nation or national community, supposedly rising above any particular group or culture, to which immigrants have to assimilate, sacrificing their own culture and identity to achieve citizenship rights and attain membership of the nation. Yet this supposedly universalist model of the nation contains a hidden agenda, a particular culture which claims to be universal, and which appears to welcome new members while always rejecting them. As is noted in a recent study of immigrants, racism and citizenship in France by Max Silverman, 'assimilation maintains that there is both an initial difference which must be obliterated ("you must be like us") and an initial difference which can never be obliterated ("you can never be like us")'.[24] In other words, in this attempt to 'deconstruct' the nation, the universalist pretensions of the civic model of the nation are viewed as less open and general than they appear.

Nationalism and democracy, democracy and the nation-state

In modern times, i.e. post-1789, the idea of democracy as 'people power' has found its chief realisation in the institution of the nation-state. The idea of democracy has been associated with the people constituting the nation as a self-determining democratic community. The aspiration has been to create a nation-state which was internally and externally democratic. Internally, the national community (the nation-state) is supposedly ruled through democratic procedures according to which the people are sovereign. There is supposed to be, according to traditional democratic theory, both *symmetry* and *congruence* in democratic practice.[25] By 'symmetry' is meant that political decision-makers and those subject to their decisions live in the same unit, that of the nation-state. The output of the decision-making process affects those, and only (or only significantly) those, who are citizens of the particular political unit, which again is the unit of the nation-state. Externally, the assumption has been that there must be limited external interference with the political decisions of a self-governing people. Democratic theory has condemned foreign rule as violating the principle of autonomy which is a basic principle of democracy. In the classic words of J.S. Mill's *Representative Government*, 'Where the sentiment of nationality exists in any force, there is a prima facie case for uniting all the members of the nationality under the same government, and a government to themselves apart. This is merely saying that the question of government ought to be decided by the governed.'[26]

Since the French Revolution, the democratic idea of 'the people' has been associated with the idea of a national community determining its own destiny. In practice this amounted to the creation and defence of a sovereign nation-state. Democratic theory invoked the sovereignty of 'the people', but traditionally 'the people' have been seen not as a random abstract collection of individuals, but as a nation, a national people. The assumption was that 'the people' constituted a nation – they shared a particular culture, language, history and traditions. 'The people' formed a national group which ought to be self-governing, autonomous and independent of rule by some foreign power, and thus the people or nation should have its own state. Hence the original connection of nationalism with democracy, or democracy with nationalism.

The nation-state has therefore been seen as the unit within which democracy was to be realised, internally and externally. In other words, nations were the building blocks for a democratic world, and the nation-state was justified in terms of democratic theory. Nation-states were also seen as providing economic advantages, since the nation formed a unified and large-scale internal market, and the state backed up the nation's overseas expansion and trade. The nation-state was further defended on cultural grounds, since the state would bring all its citizens into the single and shared national culture, and through a common education system spread national awareness and homogeneity. Politically, the nation-state was seen as guaranteeing security in an uncertain world, through its armies which defended the population of the nation. Democracy meant in practice a world of nation-states which formed the structure through which democracy would be realised.[27]

The question is to what extent this assumption of the congruence between a democratic society and a nation-state can be maintained in the contemporary world, and whether the nation-state can be seen as an adequate framework for the realisation of democracy. There are a number of problems in this connection, which throw some doubt on the easy and harmonious connection of nationalism and democracy.

First, the argument establishing a close connection between nationalism and democracy took over uncritically some of the rhetoric of nationalism, to the effect that each nation was a culturally homogeneous whole. Traditional national-democratic rhetoric assumed that 'the people' were a unified national whole, sharing a common culture, forming one nation, with their own state which they ruled democratically, through institutions of popular control such as elections and competing parties. The assumption of traditional democratic theory, as represented by Rousseau, for example, was that the people who constituted the nation should be culturally and nationally homogeneous.

The problem arises, evidently, of what happens if this somewhat unrealistic assumption is removed. What if 'the people' do not form one nation in the cultural sense, if there are several ethnic groupings within the citizen body? The danger then arises that national minorities may be excluded from citizenship or if they are formally citizens, they may become 'second-class citizens' and not full members of the democratic community. A 'tyranny of the majority' could then be practised in which nationalism and democracy would go separate ways. The nationalism of the dominant or majority culture might lead to a situation of denial of democratic rights to the minority. This is all the more likely if the nation is defined in ethnic terms, rather than as an association of citizens.

In the contemporary world these are very real problems. Questions of national oppression or inequality within one supposedly democratic polity are high on the agenda of contemporary politics, and the case of what used to be Yugoslavia is only an extreme example, resulting in the limiting case of 'ethnic cleansing'. The force of nationalism may turn against democracy, rather than be yoked to it, as is assumed in the traditional model of democratic nationalism. If there are ethnic minorities, nationalism and democracy can oppose each other.

In that case the minority group in a democratic polity, if it remains a permanent minority because of its ethnic or national composition, might have two possibilities. One would be assimilation to the dominant majority; the other would be secession, if its democratic rights continue to be violated.[28] Each has its own problems. For example, if one national group secedes, this may reflect 'the will of the people', in the sense of the will of that particular national group. But there may be new minorities within that seceding group or on the territory of its new nation-state who themselves become oppressed, and so the process can go on indefinitely, leading to the breakdown of the polity into ever smaller units, to the limits of what is practical. In a situation where different ethnic or national groups share the same territory, the connection between nationalism and democracy is not as evident as it seemed in the age of the French Revolution. The demand for the recognition of the cultural or national rights of one (majority) group may involve a denial of democratic rights to another (minority) group. The nation is often defined in terms of shared ethnicity or cultural community. However, if not all the people share the dominant culture or are members of the same ethnic group, then the democratic rights of some citizens, who are not members of the dominant ethnic group, may well be threatened.

The second problem with the straightforward connection between democracy and nationalism, and with the assumption that the nation-state is the real framework for a democratic system, emerges clearly from what was said above concerning the ambiguities of nationalism. We have seen that nationalism can take many forms, some of which are very much opposed to democracy, the obvious example being the fascist nationalism studied in Chapter 8. We have seen that nationalism can be highly divisive, leading to the exclusion of sections of the people from the citizen body. Thus the idea of 'one nation, one state' and the claim that nationalism is essentially connected with democracy is open to challenge from the historical and contemporary record, to the effect that nationalism in some of its forms is hostile to democracy. What has been called 'integral nationalism' would be the chief example of this.

'Integral nationalism' was the name given to the nationalism of the ultra-right or anti-republican and anti-democratic organisation Action Française in France at the end of the nineteenth century. This organisation denounced Jews, freemasons, foreigners and Protestants as the 'four estates' who might form part of the *pays légal*, the official nation, but were not part of the *pays réel*, the real nation; they could never be 'true Frenchmen'. Hence this organisation practised a form of nationalism which was highly exclusive. Moreover, such forms of nationalism were not only exclusionary and abrasive, but they also elevated the nation to the status of an absolute end and the sole focus of loyalty.

A recent survey of nationalism makes the distinction between two forms of nationalism, contrasting *integral nationalism* on the one hand and *Risorgimento nationalism* on the other.[29] The latter offers a prospect of emancipation and democracy, while the former often offers a racialist definition of those who form the 'real' nation along racialist lines, and pushes the nation to the role of an absolute value on which there can be no compromise. Thus the ambiguity and malleability of nationalism, as well as its emotional pull and mobilising power, result in the fact that nationalism has been used by groups and movements highly at variance with the democratic ideal. It should be noted that a movement like *Action Française* was the forerunner of groups of the radical Right and neo-fascist parties in contemporary politics.

The third problem stems from the question of the limits on the sovereignty of the nation-state in the contemporary world. The traditional view of the democratic nation-state rests on certain assumptions about the core value of sovereignty. The tradition of democratic nationalism assumed a world of nation-states, each of them sovereign, democratically self-determining and free from external constraint. In this way the nation-state remains, theoretically, the 'shell' for popular power. The key and obvious question here is whether the nation-state remains an effective framework within which citizens can in fact exercise their democratic rights. If there are constraints on democracy imposed by the international context of politics, then the idea that it is within the nation-state that democracy can be fully and effectively exercised begins to look increasingly unrealistic.

The question is thus posed of the extent to which the idea of the democratic nation-state as a sovereign body still holds true. The treatment given here is not meant to be an exercise in international relations, but raises the question of the importance of the international dimension for understanding power and democracy. The key issue is whether there is an *international* structure of power which may hinder the realisation of democracy in a national context. We must consider whether one can understand the prospects for democracy as 'people power' by concentrating exclusively, or even primarily, on the national context.

The nation-state was supposed in theory to provide political protection through the force of the state, in an insecure world. It was also the framework for economic development and progress, through its provision of a large internal market and through its role in securing overseas trade. Finally, it was supposed to secure cultural homogeneity, or reinforce it where it already existed, by developing the national culture and providing it with the resources of the state. Nations which had already formed their nation-state were to defend that unit, in the nationalist world-view. For those nations which were ruled by foreign rulers, or which did not have a state of their own, national independence was the goal to be fought for. The nineteenth and twentieth centuries both witnessed a series of struggles for national independence, generally supported by liberals and democrats.[30] They were supported by socialists too, notably in the case of 'Third World' movements of national liberation from colonial rule. Finally, this was all blessed in the name of democracy, since a group of people aware of itself as a nation was held to be a unit which ought to have a state of its own, and this formed the doctrine of national self-determination. The aspiration was to found an independent and democratic nation-state.

However, traditional democratic theory has uncritically taken over this assumption of the necessary framework of the nation-state. In an increasingly international world, it is necessary to pay attention to a further deep structure of power, whose implications need to be examined. Just as Marxism and feminism in their different ways brought out the idea of a 'deep structure' of class or gender power, here we need to focus on a similar context of international power and examine its implications for the achievement or attainment of democracy.[31] There are two points to be considered: first, whether the nation-state can realise the goals sketched out above; and second, whether the nation-state remains any longer, if it ever was, an adequate context for dealing with problems of power and the state in the modern world.

Beyond the nation-state?

The question is thus whether there is a further 'deep structure' which it is necessary to grasp before one can fully understand the power structure of the contemporary liberal-democratic state. Has the nation-state been transcended, or does it still provide the context for achieving democracy?

The argument here points to the need to grasp these issues in a wider context, since the forces of globalisation have changed the very framework within which political action and the exercise of power take place. The nation-state is no longer a self-sufficient and sovereign entity, if it ever was, or at least its degree of self-sufficiency and sovereign power have greatly diminished, and political theory needs to recognise this totally new context for the politics of our time. There exists an international context of power, which involves forces impeding or constraining democracy, although perhaps also offering some new possibilities for a genuine and effective democracy in the twentieth and twenty-first centuries.

The democratic nation-state operates within the framework of a world of states, and so each nation-state exists within a 'force field' of global political and economic interconnections which can constrain the role or power of a particular national state elite, and which need to be taken account of in any realistic theory of power and the state. This international context poses a challenge to the nation-state in each of the three areas of the nation-state listed above, the political, the economic and the cultural. Politically, a system of military alliances and superpowers can limit the ability of a particular state to defend itself. Economically, the power of national governments to decide for themselves is highly limited, because of the speedy and powerful impact of cross-national economic transactions or currency flows. The famous case in Britain of 'Black Wednesday' on 16 September 1992, when the British government was forced to devalue the currency and leave the European exchange rate mechanism, provides a graphic example of the way in which government policies are subject to international economic forces which they do not control. Another example would be the constraints on the initially reforming policies of the Mitterrand government in France after 1981, which also found its room for manoeuvre severely limited, and responded by a drastic change of direction. Finally, the idea of the nation-state as presiding over and developing a particular unique national culture also seems somewhat out of date in an age of satellite television and an international cultural community no less powerful than the international economic forces limiting government action.

Our purpose here is to suggest some implications for democracy and power in general of such a pattern of globalisation. We have seen that there are challenges to the idea of the sovereignty of the nation-state on three levels: economic, such as through the power of multinational corporations; political, through superpower hegemony or networks of alliances; and cultural, from different directions, sub-state and supra-state. The cultural challenges to the nation-state can come from particularist movements of ethnic nationalism, or sub-state nationalism, but equally from supra-state movements of an international common culture which span national boundaries. All of these elements however share one feature, which is that they undermine the nation-state's claim to be the sole or even the most important focus for democracy, or the chief locus of power.

Clearly, the existence of such an international context of power means that some of the assumptions of 'congruence' and 'symmetry' need to be recast. It is no longer, if it ever was, the case that the only decisions taken which affect the life of citizens are taken by their governments, supposedly accountable to their citizens. Decisions are taken by multinational corporations – for example, on questions of employment and investment – and these are no less important for the people of a particular area than the decisions of 'their' government. However, in this case there is no mechanism of control or accountability over the decision-takers (the company executives). Key decisions are thus taken which escape the control of the nation-state and its democratic structures.

By the same token, it is not only the case that decisions are taken which escape any serious degree of democratic control and accountability. The other side of the congruence/symmetry requirement is not met either. This means that decisions are taken which, because of the interconnectedness of the global system, affect a much wider constituency – they affect those who are not members of the particular nation-state. A change of interest rate in one country, say Germany, affects those who are not citizens of the German nation-state, and who may have limited means of control over that decision.

The best way of understanding these processes is to suggest that they are challenges to the autonomy or sovereign power of the nation-state, and that they pose a problem in connection with the feasibility of democracy in the modern world. One solution, offered by David Held, has been to propose a model of what he calls 'cosmopolitan democracy', with a range of international associations seeking to safeguard human rights and create the accountability of international institutions which so far have eluded any democratic control.[32]

There is a deeper problem, however, concerned with the sovereignty of the modern state. We noted in Chapter 1 that the modern state involved the idea of a sovereign power, regulating the affairs of the people in a particular territory, and deciding on criteria of membership. The problem of the international dimension of power is that there is a structure of power which eludes the grip of any one particular nation-state. The implications for the future of democracy seem problematic. A pessimistic view would be that, because of the scale and complexity of these global or international economic, political and cultural forces, popular control is quite difficult to achieve, even to envisage. We have already seen that democracy is difficult enough to achieve even in the context of the nation-state, because of class or economic power, gender power, the importance of elites, the 'distancing' effect of representation, and educational and social differences between elite and non-elite. Yet at least it can be said that within democratic nation-states there are some, however inadequate, structures of democracy, accountability and representation which provide the possibility of popular power, whatever the extent to which this is attained in practice.

Moving to the international level, however, it could be said that questions of scale and complexity make democratic control over this structure much more difficult to attain. Held's version of 'cosmopolitan democracy' could thus be labelled a heroic but somewhat Utopian attempt to create an international set of institutions or structures to perform the same tasks of control and accountability at the supra-national level. He writes of the need for the 'extension and deepening of mechanisms of democratic accountability across major regions and international structures', and for 'restrictions of the activities of powerful transnational interest groups to pursue their interests unchecked'.[33] It is not clear who would bring into being these mechanisms, or how they would be created to achieve the goal of helping to 'regulate resources and forces which are already beyond the reach of national democratic mechanisms and movements'.

In response to this, a more optimistic scenario would suggest that there are already signs of a growing international awareness of common human rights, which can be enforced even when particular national governments are not willing to guarantee them. The European Court of Human Rights is an example of an international organisation that is able to transcend the limits of the nation-state, which is no longer a self-sufficient sovereign entity. The basic problem, however, seems to be that there is a contradiction between ideas of state sovereignty and a growing international awareness of human rights and democratic procedures. This problem has emerged with particular significance in the field of human rights. As one student of international affairs has noted, the principle of sovereignty entails 'the requirement of non-interference in the domestic affairs of other states'.[34] However, a growing international emphasis on human rights would call for a modification of this principle of non-interference. The same author brings out the contradiction very clearly by observing that 'modern attempts to breach the non-interference principle in the interests of protecting fundamental human rights . . . invariably, and

inevitably, run up against the core doctrine of sovereignty'.[35] The situation in
Iraq with regard to violations of the rights of the Kurdish population there is
one topical example of this. Similarly, the debate about whether, and how,
there should be international involvement to protect the rights of Bosnian
Muslims against Serb and Croat aggression in former Yugoslavia provides a
graphic example of the difficulties of the issue, and suggests a rather pessimistic
conclusion, pointing to the failure of international censure and the difficulties
of imposing sanctions on those who violate human rights in a particular
national context.

The issue is hard to resolve. It suggests that the power structure of the
modern world has in certain respects developed beyond the traditional
categories used to analyse and discuss power. The fundamental theories of
modern politics took the nation-state as the framework of political action. They
saw the nation as the context within which democratic relations were supposed
to obtain. Pluralism, for example, looks at power relations within the context
of the nation-state. With Marxism the situation is rather different. Marxism
took the international dimension much more seriously, since Marxist theory
stressed the inevitable internationalisation of the economy as a result of the
development of capitalism. Marx stressed the importance of capitalism as a
world-system, spreading across national boundaries and creating a new
international community. This would mean that the nation-state, if it did not
disappear completely, would cease to be, in the foreseeable future, the most
important framework of action. Marxism obviously placed great importance
on the united action, cutting across national boundaries, of the working-class
movement – 'the workers have no fatherland', in the words of the *Communist
Manifesto*, and national affiliation was seen as relatively unimportant to them.

The implications of this for understanding modern politics are suggestive.
On the one hand, Marxism did show a prescient grasp of what we might now
call the force of multinational corporations, of economic forces cutting across
national boundaries, and the inability of the nation-state to cope with these
forces. On the other hand, the belief in proletarian internationalism, as we
noted in Chapter 5, does not seem to have been borne out, since the nation as
a source of identity seems historically to have been more effective than
international working-class identity. The paradox seems to be one which has
hit Marxism as well as other theories of politics. Marxism analysed well the
economic forces of what is now called globalisation, yet underestimated the
continuing impact of nationalism and certainly did not foresee the force and
power of ethnic nationalism in the modern world.

We started this chapter by noting the importance of nationalism as a
challenge to the liberal-democratic state, especially nationalism in its ethnic
form, yet the paradox is that nationalism also functions as a 'cement' or basis
for the modern liberal-democratic state. At the same time there is another
problem which is no less important for understanding modern politics and the
power of the state. While nationalism remains an exceedingly powerful force

in the modern world, there is a significant dimension of power to be considered, a further 'deep structure' stemming from the global or international context. In the modern world, both the power of nationalism and the significance of globalisation have increased. The former can be used in movements of opposition to liberal-democracy; the significance of globalisation, on the other hand, seems to be that there are organisations which take 'key decisions' and yet escape conscious control and evade any possibility of democracy. If politics is concerned with power, then the international dimensions of power need to be considered in any adequate theory of power. But what exactly are those 'international dimensions of power'? They can be listed, we have seen, as corresponding to the three headings of the political, the economic and the cultural which formed the basis for understanding the nation-state. The nation-state offered gains for its citizens under each of these headings, yet in the contemporary world it is being challenged by international structures of polity, economy and culture which make the doctrine of the sovereignty of the state seem outmoded.

An attempt to reconcile these paradoxes is left until Chapter 10, which deals with the question of the crisis of the nation-state, and challenges to the state at various levels. At the moment we can suggest that these problems can be resolved to the extent that nationalism and internationalism need not be incompatible. Both are effective in offering forms of *identity*. The power of nationalism stems from its ability to satisfy a demand for a sense of community. Nationalism offers an identity which nationalist movements seek to heighten, often in terms of hostility to other national groups, sometimes taking extreme and pathological forms. Yet in terms of power, as opposed to identity, the locus of power seems to have shifted away from the nation-state to be located in an international structure. This is a structure which eludes human control because of the absence of institutions which exercise any effective control at this level. Held seeks to sketch out a picture of 'cosmopolitan democracy' which would remedy this lack, but such institutions as he desires are as yet still conspicuous by their absence, or at least by their lack of power in contemporary politics.

Our conclusion thus has to be that power has to be understood as working at different levels, not all of which operate at the level of the nation-state. Power and the conditions for democracy need to be conceptualised at various levels, sub-national, national and now, in the modern world, increasingly at the international or supranational level. It is these international or global processes that are an integral part of the crisis of the state, or perhaps more precisely the crisis of the nation-state, which forms the subject of the concluding chapter. There we seek to answer the question of which, if any, of the various theories discussed in the book furnishes an adequate theory of power. We also seek to answer the question of the nature of the crisis of the state. In what does the crisis of the state consist? What challenges does it pose for the theory and practice of modern politics?

Notes

1. Connor, W., 'A nation is a nation, is a state, is an ethnic group is a . . .', *Ethnic and Racial Studies*, vol. 1, no. 4, 1978, pp. 377–400.
2. Gellner, E., *Nations and Nationalism*, Blackwell, Oxford, 1983.
3. On international forces, see *Journal of Democracy*, vol. 4, no. 3, 1993, special issue on 'International Organisations and Democracy'.
4. Brubaker, R., *Citizenship and Nationhood in France and Germany*, Harvard University Press, Cambridge, MA, and London, 1992, p. 189.
5. Habermas, J., *Eine Art Schadensabwicklung: Kleine politische Schriften VI*, Suhrkamp, Frankfurt, 1987, p. 166.
6. Smith, A.D., *Nationalism in the Modern World*, Martin Robertson, Oxford, 1979, p. 4.
7. Teich, M., and Porter, R. (eds), *The National Question in Europe in Historical Context*, Cambridge University Press, Cambridge, 1993.
8. Griffin, R., *The Nature of Fascism*, Routledge, London and New York, 1993, p. 36.
9. Alter, P., *Nationalism*, Edward Arnold, London, 1989.
10. Bugajski, J., 'The fate of minorities in Eastern Europe', *Journal of Democracy*, vol. 4, no. 4, 1993, pp. 85–99.
11. Glenny, M., *The Fall of Yugoslavia: The Third Balkan War*, Penguin, London, 1992, p. 85.
12. Drobizheva, L.M., 'The role of the intelligentsia in developing national consciousness among the peoples of the USSR under *perestroika*', *Ethnic and Racial Studies*, vol. 14, no. 1, 1991, pp. 87–99.
13. Breuilly, J., *Nationalism and the State*, Manchester University Press, Manchester, 1985, p. 11.
14. Girardet, R. (ed.), *Le Nationalisme français 1871–1914*, Armand Colin, Paris, 1966.
15. Chatterjee, P., *Nationalism and the Colonial World: A derivative discourse*, Zed Books, London, 1986.
16. Smith, A.D., *National Identity*, Penguin, London, 1991.
17. Brubaker, *Citizenship and Nationhood in France and Germany*.
18. Hobsbawm, E.J., *Nations and Nationalism since 1780: Programme, myth, reality*, Cambridge University Press, Cambridge, 1990, p. 18.
19. Smith, *National Identity*, p. 11.
20. Gellner, *Nations and Nationalism*.
21. Smith, *National Identity*, p. 13.
22. On Barrès, see Sternhell, Z., *Maurice Barrès et le Nationalisme français*, Armand Colin, Paris, 1972.
23. Brubaker, *Citizenship and Nationhood in France and Germany*.
24. Silverman, M., *Deconstructing the Nation: Immigration, racism and citizenship in modern France*, Routledge, London and New York, 1992, p. 32.
25. Held, D., 'From city-states to a cosmopolitan order?', in Held, D. (ed.), *Prospects for Democracy: North, South, East, West*, Polity, Cambridge, 1993, p. 25.
26. Mill, J.S., *Three Essays*, Oxford University Press, Oxford, 1975, p. 381.
27. See Beetham, D., 'The future of the nation state', in McLennan, G., Held, D., and Hall, S. (eds), *The Idea of the Modern State*, Open University Press, Milton Keynes, 1984, pp. 208–22, for this division into political, economic and cultural factors.

28. For an examination of the arguments justifying secession, see Buchanan, A., *Secession: The morality of political divorce from Fort Sumter to Lithuania and Quebec*, Westview Press, Boulder, CO, and Oxford, 1991.

29. Alter, *Nationalism*.

30. Teich and Porter (eds), *The National Question in Europe in Historical Context*.

31. See Held, 'Democracy: from city-states to a cosmopolitan order?', and *Journal of Democracy*, vol. 4, no. 3, 1993, special issue on 'International Organisations and Democracy'.

32. Held, 'From city-states to a cosmopolitan order?'.

33. Held, 'From city-states to a cosmopolitan order?', p. 42.

34. Mayall, J., *Nationalism and International Society*, Cambridge University Press, Cambridge, 1990, p. 20.

35. *Ibid*.

Conclusion

10 | Which theory, which reality? Challenges to the state in the contemporary world

Challenges to the state

This concluding chapter seeks to draw together the themes of the earlier chapters, and to present some general conclusions concerning the nature of the state in the modern world, and the challenges which it faces, especially in its liberal-democratic form.

The aim of the book has all along been to understand the nature of the modern state and the power it wields, and to review a number of theories which contribute to answering this question. The purpose of this final chapter is to compare the different theories which were examined earlier, and see which one offers the most adequate concepts for understanding the nature of the contemporary state and for understanding power in the modern world. We need to consider also whether these theories (pluralism, elitism, Marxism, feminism) are mutually exclusive, or whether the insights each offers can to some extent be combined. In that way a fuller and more adequate theory of the state and its role might be reached through a perspective which draws on elements from different theoretical traditions. Obviously it is a question not of adding pluralism to elitism to Marxism to feminism to make some 'super theory', but of seeing what the relationship between the different theories is, and whether and to what extent they are compatible rather than mutually exclusive. That is the first theme of this concluding chapter – a review of the various theories and a comparative assessment of their contribution to the goal of understanding the role of the state in the modern world.

There is, however, a second theme which relates to the object of investigation, the modern state, rather than the theories describing it and analysing it. There are two questions here to structure the ensuing discussion:

1. To what extent is it right to speak of the triumph of liberal-democracy? Is it realistic to envisage alternatives to this state form in the modern world, especially in the light of the collapse, explained in earlier chapters, of its main rivals in twentieth-century politics?

2.   What is the nature of the challenges, internal and external, to the state in
     its liberal-democratic form, and are these challenges specific to liberal-
     democracy or problems which confront all modern states?

First comes the question of the liberal-democratic state. At various points
in the earlier chapters, it was stated that in the conditions of late twentieth-
century politics this form of state has conquered the field by maintaining itself
while its two main rivals, fascism and communism, have collapsed. Beyond
that, it seems that in the areas dominated until recently by communist systems,
the overwhelming demand, at least as articulated by influential elite groups,
is for a transition to the model of a liberal-democratic state, and for a market
society, a 'free economy', as the appropriate context for such a political system.
Thus, it seems not only that the liberal-democratic form of state has held the
field against its contenders, but that it apparently possesses a power of
attraction for those who have recently emerged from alternative forms of state
in Eastern and Central Europe. The same may be true in a wider geographical
area, since there are some one-party regimes in Africa which are now
undergoing the challenge of multi-party elections, as in Kenya, and embracing
some other aspects of liberal-democratic politics.

Questions of transition to democracy seem to mean the achievement of one
kind of democracy, namely liberal-democracy, marked by the political forms
and institutions of political pluralism, electoral competition and an economy
whose main resources are privately owned and controlled. This seems to
suggest that aspirations to a different kind of system from that of liberal-
democracy are rather marginal in the modern world. Not only have the main
historical challengers to liberal-democracy been 'seen off', but even the wish
to realise aims of more direct and participatory democracy has become less
significant and been condemned as unrealistic.

In line with this argument, the Italian political philosopher Norberto Bobbio
suggests that representative democracy is 'the only form of democracy which
exists and is operative', and that any alternatives in terms of a form of direct
democracy are not feasible in the complex conditions of modern politics.[1] This
would suggest that Rousseau-like ideas of the direct involvement of 'the
people' in the affairs of state are Utopian in the modern world. Bobbio
interestingly observes that 'the project of political democracy was conceived
for a society much less complex than the one that exists today', and this gives
rise to what he calls the 'broken promises of democracy', which we shall come
back to below.[2] These 'broken promises', the gap between the normative
aspirations to popular power held out by democratic theory, and the much less
inspiring actuality of 'real existing democracy' are, so Bobbio thinks, up to a
certain point inevitable. They stem from the necessary adaptation of ideas of
direct democracy and citizen rule, of 'transparency' and public knowledge of
the affairs of the community, to a much more complex society whose power
relations are necessarily less open and capable of public control. This does not

mean, for Bobbio, that democracy is impossible, or that there is no difference between a democratic society and an autocratic one. However, he seems to be suggesting that democratic sights have to be lowered: the most that one can hope for is control of elites and scrutiny of specialists taking technical decisions, with guarantees of basic citizen rights and civil liberties through the rule of law.[3]

The implications of this argument are twofold: liberal-democracy seems to have won out over alternative forms of state, and in terms of the meaning of 'democracy' itself, the Schumpeter-type revision of democratic theory has been accepted so that democracy in the 'real world' is seen as being a form of competition between elites in which popular input is restricted and the people as a whole play a rather passive role.

This judgement of the apparent 'victory' of liberal-democracy should itself be challenged as parochial or 'Eurocentric'. There are large parts of the world where this supposed desirability or popularity of liberal-democracy does not exist at all, such as countries where the dominant view is one of religious fundamentalism, or where questions of economic survival are so pressing as to obliterate the supposed desirability of liberal-democracy. Then again, where questions of ethnic nationalism loom large, the chances of transition to liberal-democracy seem diminished, and liberal-democracy seems subordinate to aims of ethnic and national 'purity'.

Nevertheless, over large parts of the globe, with the collapse of the Soviet model and the earlier military defeat of fascism, 'democracy' is held to be the desirable political system. This is understood as a system of liberal-democracy, marked by the characteristics and institutions noted above. With all due qualifications as to the statement of the supposedly universal victory of liberal-democracy, the liberal-democratic state remains one of the central state forms in the modern world, aspired to by many people in place of other systems which have recently collapsed. However, this does not mean that there are no alternatives possible to this set of political arrangements. Furthermore, the term 'liberal-democracy' can cover a very wide variety of institutional and political arrangements, involving greater or lesser degrees of popular participation, greater or lesser degrees of state intervention in the economy, and a wider or more narrow range of alternative possibilities canvassed for popular consideration. Much depends, therefore, on the precise shape of liberal-democracy, which can assume a spectrum of different forms, ranging, for example, from a 'New Right' vision of a minimal state to a social democratic interventionist state securing a greater degree of social equality and political involvement.

If there is agreement on the central place that liberal-democracy occupies in the present world, even though its nature is far from being unquestioned, the issue remains of whether the liberal-democratic state in its present form does indeed realise those twin, and to some extent conflicting, goals of liberalism and democracy analysed in Chapter 2. The problem is whether liberal-democracy is successful in meeting the criteria it sets for itself. The analyses provided by the various theories of liberal-democracy (pluralism, elitism, Marxism, feminism) will need to be drawn on, to suggest obstacles in the way of liberal-democracy realising its promises, and the degree of imperfection of present-day 'real existing democracy'. These theories pose the question of whether liberal-democracy is everything it is claimed to be, and of the reasons why it is held to be, at least by some, such a desirable political system, set in a context which supposedly guarantees freedom.

This leads on to consideration of the second question raised above, the problem of challenges to the state, especially in its liberal-democratic form, and the problem of whether these challenges constitute a 'crisis of the state'. The sociologist Gianfranco Poggi proposes a number of arguments 'to the effect that in the contemporary situation the state is undergoing a serious crisis'.[4] He suggests that the challenges which the contemporary state faces include nuclear war and all those processes which can be considered under the heading of globalisation. Finally, he considers the danger that the state apparatus itself expands in size and complexity so that it loses any rational unity. Sections of the state apparatus can become 'colonised' by special interests, resulting in corruption: 'Many administrative units . . . establish close, privileged relationships with organised social interests . . . these, in turn, seek to use administrative units as their own bridgeheads within the state apparatus.'[5] The Italian political system seems until recently to have provided many examples of this, with its system of *Tangentopoli* embracing large parts of the political class.[6]

There are many challenges to the state in contemporary politics, which may amount to a 'crisis of the state' in its liberal-democratic form, even though this does not necessarily imply that it is a crisis that the state is unable to surmount. However, we can list a number of difficulties for the contemporary state which create problems for the idea of state sovereignty, the capacity of the state to exercise its monopoly of power over a particular territory. These, it should be added, are not problems that confront the liberal-democratic state alone, although they assume forms specific to that particular state. Speaking now of the modern state in general, liberal-democratic or not, we have seen that the state in the modern world is for the most part a nation-state, or at least that modern states usually claim to be nation-states, even though this may be more myth than reality. Walker Connor points out that, if one takes the idea of the 'nation-state' seriously, as one state presiding over one nation, then only about 10 per cent of states in the modern world are actually nation-states strictly speaking, where most of the population share a single ethnic identity.[7]

The modern state claims a monopoly of power over a unified national territory, and seeks to gain legitimation for this power. In other words, the modern state aspires to regulate the affairs of a particular national territory, securing the safety, the economic well-being and the cultural cohesion of its citizens. It involves the creation and development of a differentiated apparatus, a specialised and complex machine, for the attainment of these ends.

The liberal-democratic state, in particular, claims to have two specific characteristics which differentiate it from other forms of state. These link it with the core concepts of liberalism and democracy. The liberal-democratic state claims to realise, first, the idea of freedom *from* the state, in the sense of a limited state which offers civil society its own 'space', an area of social life free from the grip of the state. This civil society is also itself pluralistic, in the sense that within it a number of distinct interests and groups express themselves and seek to influence the holders of political power.

The other forms of state considered in this book (communism and fascism) sought with varying degrees of success the politicisation of this civil society, through the device of the monopolistic state party. Some authors suggest that in Soviet-type systems this led to a situation of the 'absence of politics'. Poggi puts it like this:

> In fact, if by politics we understand a process whereby within the public sphere multiple, autonomous collective actors openly and legitimately compete with one another, each on behalf of special interests, to limit, influence and determine policy, we might go as far as saying that *there is no politics in the Soviet-type state*.[8]

However, we argue that the reverse was the case in Soviet-type systems. In an important sense it was not the case that there was 'no politics', but 'everything was politics': all of civil society was politicised and controlled by the party-state apparatus, and civil society had no space of its own. By contrast, liberal-democratic societies offer, at least in theory, a limited state and a space for a pluralistic and diversified civil society free in some sense from the interference of the state.

Second, the particular characteristics of the liberal-democratic state include, on the democratic side, the institutions or processes which supposedly achieve citizenship: that is, input from the citizens into the making of the laws, or rules governing society. This is achieved through a structure of representation, and the corollary of representative government is that there is a system of accountability and control over the representatives.

What, then, are the challenges facing all modern states, but which assume a particular form for the liberal-democratic state in the light of the two features (freedom from the state, citizen input into the laws) singled out above? We can divide the challenges facing the liberal-democratic state into two broad types, calling the one external and the other internal. By external challenges are meant those stemming from forces of globalisation or internationalisation, from pressures which tend to escape the control of the state, at least at the national level. We refer here to what was mentioned at the end of Chapter 9 as a 'deep structure' of international power which acts as an obstacle to democratic sovereignty at the level of the nation-state, and which remains relatively uncontrollable in the present order of things by the popular will. This international structure poses a challenge both to the sovereignty of the state in general and to the democratic claims of the liberal-democratic state in particular.

Internal challenges refer to demands on the state both from socially 'subordinate' groups and 'dominant' groups. The crucial problem is that the state, in its liberal-democratic or any other form, is not removed from social pressures – it exists in a particular social framework or context. Subordinate groups, by which is meant those who are disadvantaged in the market situation, and dominant groups, those who own and control the productive resources of society, both make demands on the state in the conditions of liberal-democracy. As Poggi points out, from the 'demand' side 'those in a position of economic inferiority used the quantum of *political* power acquired through electoral participation to widen the scope and increase the penetration of state action, in order to restrict and moderate the impact of that economic inferiority on their total life circumstances'.[9]

Yet such demands on the state are the preserve not only of those in a situation of economic inferiority. The liberal-democratic state is 'pressurised' also by economically stronger or superior groups, since (Poggi's words are worth quoting once more) 'the dependency of private economic forces on positive state action . . . became a systemic feature of industrial capitalism, associated with the most advanced and important, not the weakest or most backward-looking units of the system'.[10]

The implications of this situation, of demands on the liberal-democratic state, need some more probing. Professor Galbraith in his recent book *The Culture of Contentment* brings out well a paradox of state action in the contemporary liberal-democratic state. As he points out, state action of an interventionist sort is generally decried and rejected by the 'contented' majority in contemporary democracy, especially when such state action is directed towards the economic underclass or subordinate groups in general. The reason for this is that such state action involves expenditure, which in turn involves taxation, higher taxes on the 'contented' majority, who themselves may well derive little immediate or even long-term benefit from such government expenditure. As Galbraith notes, in this case those who pay do not benefit.[11]

Galbraith notes a further paradox in the contemporary liberal-democratic state. Where some degree of state action is required to safeguard the interests of the economically 'contented', who to varying degrees form a majority in today's society, then the previously mentioned antagonism to state action fades away to be replaced by demands for state intervention and expenditure to preserve the economic and social interests of the 'contented' majority. There are two paradoxes here. The first is that state action is generally abhorred by the majority especially if it involves higher taxes, but it is not rejected for certain tasks seen as necessary to defend the existing structure of society. The second is that those who would be liable for higher taxes do not, on the whole, benefit from more state expenditure. Since they may form the majority of voters, especially where the less privileged are also those who are likely to be less participatory in the political process, then a democracy has emerged which systematically neglects a section of its population.

The situation is therefore that demands on the liberal-democratic state are made both by economically disadvantaged groups, and by economically privileged ones. In one sense, each group wants the state to take action, to satisfy their interests, by state policies in the interest of each group. However, in conditions of economic difficulty state expenditures might not suffice to meet both sets of interest which are pressurising the state for expenditure and action. There is also an asymmetry, in that the majority may want to cut state expenditure, except for the category of special exceptions noted above, and the minority may want an increase in state expenditure to redress the inequalities stemming inevitably from the market. In that sense there are demands on the state both from 'above' and 'below', and the resources to meet these conflicting demands are limited. Hence the dominant voice is, if Galbraith is right, that of the 'contented majority' who want limited government or state action. For them, extending government action means raising taxes and having to pay money now for uncertain benefits, benefits which might never come.

These, then, are some of the challenges to which the contemporary liberal-democratic state is exposed, and they raise the question of whether this constitutes a 'crisis of the state'. Any answer to this question must rest on an examination of the theories considered in the first part of this book, theories which seek to explain the working of the liberal-democratic state. The next section discusses which theory offers the best insight into the power structure of liberal-democracy, what the relationship is between each of the theories, and whether they are mutually exclusive or can be reconciled.

Review of the theories

We start with the pluralist theory, linking this to the claim by Bobbio of the 'broken promises' of democracy. The argument proposed here is that pluralism does point out some of the features of liberal-democracy, but that it is too limited in the perspective it offers on power.

Pluralism is evidently a theory of party competition and group conflict in modern complex Western societies. The problem for democracy or for liberal-democracy in particular is that the supposed free and relatively equal competition between the groups may not be realised. We can take a hint from Bobbio again, who notes that classical democratic theory envisaged the sovereignty of individuals, rather than of groups, as constituting the sovereignty of the people. For Rousseau, in the *Social Contract*, intermediary organised groups were dangerous: they could substitute themselves as factions for the people as a whole. Traditional democratic theory envisaged individuals themselves constituting the sovereign people, as one bloc.

However, Bobbio puts it well when he notes that modern reality differs from this perspective of the sovereign people as a collective body composed of different individuals:

> Groups and not individuals are the protagonists of political life in a democracy; there is no longer one sovereign power, namely the people or nation, composed of individuals who have acquired the right to participate directly or indirectly in government, the people conceived as an ideal (or mystical) unit. Instead the people are divided into opposing and conflicting groups, all relatively autonomous, in relation to central government.[12]

The conclusion which Bobbio draws is that 'the real society underlying democratic government is pluralist'.

This would seem to suggest that the pluralist perspective, in a general way, gives both a realistic picture of modern liberal-democracy and a criterion for distinguishing this kind of system from the other 'failed' rivals to it. These were would-be totalitarian systems of monolithic unity which denied group conflict, seeking to smother it or annihilate its conditions through the device of the monopolistic state party. It would also suggest that pluralist perspectives are satisfying in normative terms: they suggest a model which is both desirable and feasible in relation to the complexities of modern politics.

However, it is argued here that this would be too facile a conclusion. There are a number of problems with the pluralist model, which other views of power have identified, and which cast doubt both on the accuracy of its analysis of liberal-democracy, and also on the desirability of the normative picture it presents of 'the good society'. The first problem is that the pluralist analysis sees human beings as group-forming animals, as D.B. Truman put it. Power rests in groups, and this leads those who wish for political power to form organised groups and to push for political influence. Such groups, of course, include political parties. Yet there may be some interests which are not strongly organised, or indeed not organised at all, for various reasons, and which lose out to powerful vested interests, which have considerable resources and organisational ability. There are in any society some interests that are not organised in effective groups, and the danger arises that they do not get any effective representation in the political process. For example, unemployed workers are not represented by trade unions in any direct sense, so it is questionable if there is there any effective influence for this group of people.

Even for those interests that are represented or at least organised in groups, there is the danger that some organised groups are more powerful than others, and have greater access to the centres of power, through inside contact or privileged connections. It has often been noted that groups which make most 'noise' or seek most loudly to draw attention to their cause are not necessarily the most powerful, but on the contrary may be the weaker groups. Strength may mean not having to take any overt action. Those who refer to 'neo- pluralism' suggest that more sophisticated variations of pluralism do take the power of different interests into account, and that pluralist thought has long ago rejected naive ideas of an equilibrium of power between all the various groups in the political process. However, this would seem to suggest that pluralism in its revised 'neo-pluralist' form has taken a leaf out of the Marxist critique, and that it has recognised inequalities in power stemming from the economic context within which pluralist competition or group conflict is situated. Thus pluralism would purchase more credibility, but only at the expense of taking on insights from a very different school of social analysis, namely the Marxist view.

A more general and theoretical point of criticism raises the question of whether any sense of 'common good' can emerge from a theory which stresses the virtue and necessity of partial or special interests. Perhaps this critique suggests that there is a reverse side to the pluralist praise of diversity and variety of interest representation. Pluralist thought certainly recognises the necessary complexity of a modern society, which has gone far beyond Rousseau's idea of a simple city-state. The problem which faces all analyses of power is how to combine this recognition of diversity with some idea of consensus, and a common good. The pluralistic perspective seems to reduce politics to a process of bargaining, in which no concept of a common good emerges; or if it does, it is just a by-product of the group conflict of assorted interest groups and producer groups of a complex economy.

Bobbio again touches on this issue when he suggests that one of the many dangers of contemporary democracy is that, if representation is exercised on the model of the 'delegate' rather than the 'representative', then this may lead to what he calls 'the victory of the representation of interests over impartial political representation'. In other words, the problem is that politics is seen merely as interest representation and bargaining, and this neglects consideration of the forces that hold society together. Pluralism emphasises diversity over unity, and this neglects the need for some framework and idea of consensus as a metaphorical 'glue' to hold society together. There is no space here to enter into the issue of 'community' as opposed to individualism, but perhaps the pluralist analysis of group conflict can be criticised, like liberal thought in general, for not paying enough attention to issues of community and social solidarity.

This defect or gap in pluralist-type analysis has led some commentators and political theorists to take a view more sympathetic to ideals of 'civic republicanism'.[13] This view of politics takes a rather lofty distance from the idea of politics as interest representation. It calls up images of the good citizen as someone animated by a sense of common good, or civic virtue, rather than the citizen as someone who is nothing but a bundle of interests, and who participates in a number of groups to articulate and express those interests. This view of civic republicanism has its problems too, and seems to be rather abstract and idealistic. It is not clear where the sense of civic virtue is going to come from, or how it could be sustained. Perhaps this is why nationalism has been prominent in pluralist societies, as a modern 'civic religion' which easily provides, at quite basic levels, a sense of identity and cohesion that is not provided for by the 'normal' process of politics as group competition. Yet as was explained in Chapter 9, nationalism too has its dangers, because it can be exclusive as well as inclusive, depending on how the nation is defined.

To sum up this critique of pluralism, then, we have seen that at the surface level pluralist perspectives do point to an important aspect of the politics of liberal-democratic systems. Yet such perspectives are defective in failing to take account of interests that are not organised, in failing, except perhaps in the form of neo-pluralism, to take account of structural imbalances in group competition and conflict. Finally, there is the problem of the lack of any concept of a common interest, or an idea of politics as concerned with something more than partial group interest and the process of reconciling diverse interests through the state as a neutral arbiter.

We can also add some problems concerning the pluralist view of the state. Pluralism has often been criticised for underestimating the power and influence of the state, and for failing to see either that the state has interests of its own, or that its role might be less neutral than has been claimed by at least some versions of pluralism. Poggi's previously cited reference to the way in which sections of the state apparatus are colonised by particular interest groups would furnish an empirical example of this process, in which the state is far from neutral. Thus pluralism has further problems in its analysis of the state and its underestimation of the grip or weight of the state apparatus.

The question then must be raised of whether the other theories do any better in their analysis of the liberal-democratic state, and what their relation to pluralism is. We noted in Chapter 4 that one element in the elitist critique of democracy was the argument that the internal structure of groups was elitist or oligarchical. Therefore the pluralist claim that democracy was realised in a society marked by pluralist competition was held by elitists to be false. It was elitism, not popular power, that characterised such societies. The reason for this was that the groups which dominated the pluralist process, the interest groups of a large society, were themselves ruled by elites.

Our argument here is similar to that levelled against pluralism. Both pluralism and elitism make valid points, but in some sense they present a distorted or rather incomplete view of the power structure of liberal-democracy. Against the elitist view it could be said that, first, it is too deterministic, at least in some of its forms, with respect to the inevitability of elite rule. One can question the extent to which tendencies towards oligarchy are 'iron', and the degree to which the masses are as ignorant and passive as proclaimed in elite theory.

In this regard, Bobbio's analysis of 'the uneducated citizen' as another of the 'broken promises' of democracy is worth pondering. Bobbio writes that the most well-established democracies are impotent before the phenomenon of increasing political apathy, which has overtaken about half of those with the right to vote . . . there are good reasons to believe that the use of the vote as an expression of opinion is declining, while what is increasing is the use of the vote as a means of exchange.[14]

This could be linked with theories of classical elitism, which dismissed as impossible the democratic vision of an educated and participatory citizenry. Democratic theorists like John Stuart Mill thought and hoped that extending democratic participation would develop the capacities of the citizens, and in that sense strengthen the forces of democracy and knowledge. The participatory citizen would increasingly come to be a knowledgeable citizen, and in this way the power of 'sinister interests' or self-interested power blocs would be overcome. Yet it seems, according to Bobbio, that this has not been the case, and that the extension of the suffrage has not led to the fulfilment of the Enlightenment dream of an informed and active citizenry.

How is this relevant to elite theory and to its criticism of democracy? At first glance it seems that the reality of contemporary democracy supports the view of elite theory of a rather uneducated or apathetic citizenry confronting, or perhaps subordinate to, a creative elite group of leaders. But here again several points of criticism can be levelled against elite perspectives. Elitism is too deterministic and pessimistic, about what it sees as the *inherent* limitations of the masses. Mass passivity or lack of knowledge and interest could be viewed not as elite theory sees it, the inevitable result of the nature of the mass, but as a result of particular social factors which are capable of change. For example, the influence and nature of the mass media are an important factor affecting the nature of people's political consciousness, and to some extent are responsible for the phenomenon of 'the uneducated citizen'. This is not some inherent and unalterable fact of human nature, but the result of a particular structure of power, of the nature of the means of intellectual production in a particular society. Thus elite theory may be correct in analysing oligarchical tendencies, but not in suggesting that such tendencies could never under any circumstances be overcome. Elite theory thus points out problems but sees these problems as inherent in the human condition or human nature, rather than capable of being changed through political action.

Elite theory in its classical form established the oligarchical tendencies of large-scale organisations. Yet in many of their pronouncements, theorists like Mosca, Pareto and Michels never envisaged the possibility of any counter-tendencies to these oligarchical pressures. More recent elite theorists such as Schumpeter accepted the idea of the plurality of elites, and thus sought to reconcile elitism with pluralism in the so-called 'competitive theory of democracy'. We can raise here two basic problems concerning elitism in this more pluralistic form. First, the theory of competitive democracy tends to neglect the structural conditions, the context within which there takes place the pluralist competition between elite groups seeking the support of the people. It is this structural context of class and gender power which is highlighted by theories of Marxism and feminism, different though each of these theories may be. Second, the elite theory of democracy, or the elite theory in general, is open to a two-pronged critique: In its classical form, elite theory is too deterministic and too 'monistic', i.e. it speaks in terms of one elite (the political class) which seemingly controls everything. This appears to be an inaccurate picture of the power structure of liberal-democratic societies. It seems more accurate to speak of a variety of different groups, or different elites, which express a plurality of distinct interests. Yet in its pluralist form, too, the elite theory seems to paint too simple a picture. It neglects the idea of 'elite consensus', an agreement on fundamentals which limits the degree of competition and restricts the issues which are raised for discussion in the pluralist system. The line of argument which has been expressed by such theorists as Bachrach and Baratz, Schattschneider and Lukes, among others, is relevant here – that power involves the exclusion of certain issues from the agenda of politics, and that therefore the concentration of elitism and pluralism on the overt issues of politics gives an inadequate picture of the power structure of liberal-democratic systems.[15]

We are thus led to our final question in this section, which is to ask whether Marxism and feminism do any better as theories of power, and whether their insights can be reconciled with those of pluralism and elitism to offer a more rounded theory of the power structure of liberal-democracy. The problem with this kind of assessment is that all these terms are generalities and abstractions: 'Marxism', for example, as we noted earlier, is a very broad theory which has taken many different forms, even though there are core concepts common to the 'family' of Marxist thought, and the same is true of feminism.

The strength of the Marxist approach is that it sets the political struggle between parties and groups within the wider context of a structure of economic and social power, i.e. class power. Marxist theories recognise the constraints on political action stemming from socioeconomic power, which we earlier labelled a 'deep structure' of class power. Marxist theories, of whatever kind, point to the accumulation of economic and social power which still exists in liberal-democratic societies, and their implications for political action. Indeed, it is essential to keep these insights in mind all the more in this period of 'celebration' of liberal-democracy, which is presented as the 'realm of freedom'.

Perspectives on power stemming from Marx point to the contradiction (noted in Chapter 5) between the political rights of the supposedly equal citizens of liberal-democracy and the deeper economic structure which is one of inequality and subordination. The 'freedom' of the citizen, the political rights which were eventually, after a series of democratic struggles, extended universally, are crucial characteristics of liberal-democratic societies. Nevertheless, we should note the words of Marx in his *Grundrisse* that the equality of exchange relations in capitalist society appears only on the surface, 'beneath which, however, in the depths, entirely different processes go on in which this apparent individual equality and liberty disappear'.[16] This does not mean that the individual political rights and liberties afforded in this type of society are without significance; nor, indeed, are group rights of meeting, organisation and group formation in 'civil society' unimportant. The argument maintained here is that Marxism as an analysis of power remains essential for understanding the full structure of power of liberal-democratic societies. The analytical power of the Marxist view as a critique of liberal-democracy remains, focusing on the contradiction between political equality on the one hand and social and economic inequality on the other.

Of course, there is more to the Marxist critique than the mere statement of the tension between the two dimensions of social existence, political and economic. We noted above that Marxist perspectives presented the idea of a system which in many respects escapes human control. In the economic sphere, for example, contemporary society is marked by economic exchanges across national boundaries which are free from the control of the supposedly sovereign nation-state.

This is not meant to suggest that Marxist perspectives, any more than the pluralist and elitist ones, are immune from criticism, or that there are not problems in their analysis of power. The problems rather lie with how Marx and his followers thought the power structure of capitalist society could be transformed, and their emphasis on working-class action. It could be said that Marx's view of the capitalist system remains broadly true in its analysis of its structure and dynamics, but the revolutionary challenge which he saw as coming from the working class, a working class unified and disciplined, has not materialised. In addition, the way in which revolution took place in the Soviet Union and the way in which what passed for 'Marxism' was implemented there reinforced the attachment of the working class and other citizens of liberal-democracy to that form of state, imperfect though it was.

With regard to feminism, all that can be said at this point is that feminist theories suggest an essential dimension of power which the other theories ignore. The 'rethinking' stimulated by feminist perspectives, as noted in Chapter 6, has compelled a re-evaluation of key figures of political thought and of the whole canon of traditional political theory. Moreover, the feminist analysis of questions of the public and the private, and its critique of the sexual division of labour, really sheds new light on the fundamental categories of democratic theory and liberal-democratic practice, such as participation, equality and the concept of 'the political' itself.

Nevertheless, with due regard for the variety of feminist theorising, the difficult question remains of how the 'gender dimension' of power is related to other, no less important, dimensions of power, such as class, ethnicity and elite power. There also remains the problem of by what means the sexual divisions which limit and distort liberal-democratic societies, not to mention others, are to be removed, and what this involves for deep-rooted conceptions of human nature – whether men and women have innately different characteristics, and to what extent sexual differences are social creations which can, somehow, be altered. Here too, it seems, the problem may be one of reconciling the insights and perspectives of feminism, in its broadest sense, with other theories, rather than seeing feminism on its own as providing a 'total theory' of politics, the state and the structure of power in the modern world.

The future of the state

The last section of this book seeks to offer a concluding overview of the problems of contemporary politics as they have been presented in the previous chapters. We started from the idea of the modern state as the sovereign and central political association, and from the statement of the apparent triumph of liberal-democracy. We have seen that the state today is subjected to a variety of challenges which throw that sovereignty into doubt. There are challenges from the external context, from forces of what are called globalisation, which seem to evade or elude the supposedly sovereign grip of the state. There are challenges internally to the liberal-democratic state, of two kinds. Where it is relatively well established, the liberal-democratic state faces challenges from groups that demand different types of state action. On the one hand, there are those whom Galbraith calls the contented majority, who are happy to acquiesce in the narrowing down of the range of state action. On the other, there are those who wish the state to redress or at least minimise the inequalities stemming inevitably from the unrestrained system of the market.

However, in those parts of the world where the so-called transition to democracy (by which is to be understood liberal-democracy) is on the agenda, there are different internal challenges to the state. In particular, we have noted the force of nationalism, which in at least some of its manifestations can press the state power into the service of an intolerant and exclusive nationalism. A recent study of fascism expresses the view that 'It may well be that the history of the next few decades will be substantially shaped by the conflicts between centrifugal liberal nationalisms with a pacifistic and universalistic orientation on the one hand and centripetal illiberal nationalisms of a violent and separatist impetus on the other'.[17] This is a bit of a mouthful, but one can endorse the analysis that nationalism remains a potential challenge to the liberal-democratic state, as well as to those states that are making the transition from a one-party system to something approaching the multi-party pluralistic system of liberal-democracy. The contemporary situation seems to be rather paradoxical, since at the same time there are moves towards a much more global structure of internationalism and possibly supra-nationalism. This may mark a further shift away from the apparently sovereign nation-state, to one in which the nation-state would have to reduce its pretensions to be the sole holder of power; it would have to share its power with regional associations, with sub-state units, and also with supra- or international associations, in a different kind of political order.

This is a pluralistic picture of the future of the state, in which the state is not so much the first among equals but one focus of loyalty among others, and among 'the others' are international and regional associations. It contrasts with other tendencies in the politics of the modern world. There are tendencies for the state, captured by one national group, to be a strong or 'exceptional' state, intolerant of pluralism and diversity. In this nationalist perspective the state becomes an instrument for the defence of one national group. The 'ethnic cleansing' taking place in former Yugoslavia seem to be an extreme example of this scenario.

The challenges which face the state in the modern world thus stem both from the international context and from the national one. In the latter, there are challenges concerning the exact limits to the sphere of state activity, and at least in some contexts there are challenges stemming from a form of 'integral nationalism', which wants to make the state the instrument of one particular nation and annihilate forms of pluralism. Such a state of exacerbated nationalism would not only destroy the liberal idea of the limited state, but also end any idea of democracy based on the equal participation of all citizens irrespective of national or ethnic origin, and deal a death-blow to the idea of democratic citizenship.

It is hard to predict 'the future of the state', even in its liberal-democratic form, because this is a highly general question, the answer to which depends on a host of factors, many of them unpredictable. Perhaps all that can be said is to offer a fresh paradox, that the liberal-democratic state seems to have reached a pinnacle of prestige just at the time when it is facing new and severe problems that may undermine its ability to satisfy the demands that are being placed on it.

We noted in Chapter 1 the importance of legitimacy for the study of politics. Power does not rest on force alone, and power-holders strive ceaselessly for the justification of their power, because without such legitimation there is no alternative but to use force to secure obedience. This dependence of power on force opens the way to contingency, risk and the difficulty of securing obedience on this basis alone. We also noted that in the modern world legitimacy had increasingly, possibly exclusively, come to depend on invocation of the popular will, and the values of democracy. Popular sovereignty, or at least some version of it, is the dominant form of legitimacy in the modern world. Our concluding question is concerned with how successfully the contemporary liberal-democratic state can justify its claim to be a state that satisfies both requirements of liberalism and democracy. Do the challenges that face the state make it more or less likely that this form of state will be able to justify itself in these terms?

The classical democratic perspective started off, as we saw in Chapter 2, from premises of citizen equality and (for Rousseau, at any rate) direct participation. Partly as a result of the challenges of elite theory, democracy later came to be redefined as the competition between leadership teams, one of which would be invested with state power as a result of victory in electoral competition. This Schumpeterian view of contemporary democracy takes a fairly minimal view of the role of the citizens. Their task is to produce a government, and that is all. In one sense, this view of democracy preserves the aims of pluralism, since there are competing teams of leaders, and there is clearly no unified power elite. However, this view of 'competitive democracy' has been criticised as ruling out any creative initiative from a public which is presented as mainly passive in its role. While this theory might offer a realistic view of the process of choosing a government, it neglects various factors which could be considered necessary for 'democratic deepening'. In turn, such 'deepening' might be thought necessary for a more adequate realisation of democracy in the contemporary world.

Democracy in contemporary liberal-democratic systems might indeed be accurately described in terms of the Schumpeterian model, as a system in which elites compete for popular support. However, this model is open to a number of objections.

In the first place, we return to Bobbio's point about the 'uneducated citizen'. To fulfil adequately the task of choosing between competing teams of leaders, let alone achieve any higher degree of popular involvement, those who choose between the competing teams of leaders – that is, the electorate, the people, the voters – need information and the capacity to use that information. Yet in the modern world the range of political debate and the scope of political education are limited, and there do not seem to be the agencies for the creation of an effective and informed public will. It is such a public will, or set of wills, that makes the choice, in a democracy, between the competing leaders. Yet if this 'public' is not well enough informed, the choice is a false one, or at least is one which is open to manipulation at the hands of those elites who are to be chosen by the people themselves.

In other words, the view of democracy proposed by theorists of 'competitive democracy' does not pay enough attention to the conditions necessary for its own realisation, let alone for any greater degree of 'democratic deepening'. The theory of democratic elitism neglects any real discussion of the way in which political education is achieved, yet this political education is needed if the democratic process is to have any effect. The American sociologist C. Wright Mills referred to the mass media as the 'means of mass distraction', suggesting that they do not seem to contribute adequately to the necessary process of education and citizen development which is required for liberal-democracy in the modern world to live up to its promise.[18]

Second, this process of choosing between competing elites does not take enough account of any further degrees of what can now be called democratic deepening, extending the range of areas within which democratic control takes place. No less important, in those areas of social life which are already open to democratic control, the task is one of extending or deepening the effectiveness of that control.

Our final section thus ends with some reflections on the nature of democracy in the modern world. To return to the oft-repeated antithesis between the liberal-democratic state and the regimes which challenged it in the twentieth century, we could say that as far as the communist system was concerned, it collapsed because it failed to realise the promise it held out in its origins of a form of democracy superior to the liberal-democracy of Western-type systems. Lenin denounced such systems as ones of 'bourgeois parliamentarism', claiming that the Soviet system would be able to create a higher form of democracy and then, ultimately, the state would wither away. Our historical analysis in Chapter 7 showed how this promise was not fulfilled.

For a variety of reasons, some contingent, some perhaps related to Marxism's underestimation of the importance of political rights, especially in a projected society where scarcity had been overcome,[19] the Soviet system created a highly powerful state dominated by the elite of a monopolistic state party. Lenin's text *What is to be Done?* with its emphasis on the party remained a better guide to the nature of that system than did the much more 'libertarian' views espoused in *The State and Revolution*. Once Gorbachev tried to reform the system through *perestroika*, this unleashed democratic pressures which could not be contained within the framework of the old-style communist system. These pressures, it should be noticed, were not purely democratic, since they included the forces of nationalism, often of an ethnic kind. Such forms of nationalism are impossible to reconcile with democracy.

The historic achievements of the Soviet system should not be forgotten, despite the disastrous experience of Stalinism. Nevertheless, even in its reformed version the system could not allow 'civil society' a space of its own, free from party interference. Despite considerable economic achievements, and the proclamation of values of participatory democracy, the system remained one in which the party was an elite dominating the society through the *nomenklatura* system, both in the USSR and in those systems whose political structure was constructed in imitation of the Soviet Union. The liberal-democratic state, despite the limitations on its democracy stemming from its socioeconomic context, was able to point to more adequate institutions and processes for realising the popular will than its communist rivals.

There has been in these liberal-democratic systems a long process of struggles for the extension of citizenship rights, bound up with the idea of the democratic nation as the framework within which people would exercise their collective sovereignty. In the words of a recent study of the history of universal suffrage in France by Pierre Rosanvallon, 'the notion of nationality ended up as identical with that of citizenship'. He notes 'the imperative of inclusion', the expectation at the time of the French Revolution that 'the progress of civilisation [would] allow the voting age to be lowered, and put an end to the exclusion of the poor and of those who had no home of their own. Thus the aspiration was to universalise the figure of the active citizen'.[20]

In the nineteenth century it was the French liberal aristocrat Alexis de Tocqueville who wrote, in a somewhat apprehensive way, about the current of democracy. He saw this as an irresistible and inevitable current which had to be accommodated. Without wishing to suggest that in the conditions of contemporary politics there is a similar situation, it seems clear that it was demands for a greater degree of democracy which undermined the communist regimes. The forms of direct democracy, those invoked by Lenin in *The State and Revolution*, had in practice quickly degenerated into forms of authoritarianism. The implications of this process have been well drawn out by Ralph Miliband, who notes with respect to the fall of communist regimes that one should pay 'attention to some quite ancient propositions. Of these, none is more important than the proposition that only power can check power.' He further observes that 'Such checking power has to occur both within the state and from the outside. Within the state, it involves mechanisms which Communist regimes, to their immense detriment, have spurned . . .'[21] The conclusion can be drawn that the liberal-democratic state 'won out', to the extent that it did, because the communist system did not achieve anything like a genuine socialist democracy, which would have given more voice to the popular will, or the different facets of that will.

We can quote once more from Miliband to suggest that this should not be taken to suggest that liberal-democracy is the perfect fully achieved democracy which alone can form a model in the modern and post-communist world. As Miliband notes,

> The notion that the battle for democracy has already been won in capitalist-democratic systems, save for some electoral and constitutional reforms at the edges, simply by virtue of the achievement of universal suffrage, open political competition and regular elections is a profoundly limiting and debilitating notion which has served conservative forces extremely well, and which has to be exposed and countered.[22]

This really leads to two conclusions. The first is that democratic striving remains strong in the modern world. This was and is true not only for societies of the Soviet type, which claimed that true democracy was realised in a one-party system. It is also important for contemporary liberal-democratic systems, where there remains an important agenda for extending and deepening democracy, and removing obstacles to its exercise. There is, possibly for the first time in human history, a widespread invocation and celebration of 'democracy'. This is now seen in large parts of the world as the only legitimate political system. Yet this leads to the second conclusion, which is that at the same time as this apparent unanimous praise for democracy, there remain serious obstacles to its full achievement, both in societies moving towards liberal-democracy, and in those which are already established liberal-democracies. Those obstacles have been listed above, some of them under the heading of challenges to the liberal-democratic state. These problems can be cited here once again as stemming from an international structure which eludes popular control, as well as from the forces of unbridled and exclusive ethnic nationalism, and arguments about the role of the state, the distinct pressures to which the state is subjected by those who want to extend and those who want to restrict its intervention.

Without descending to Utopianism, it may be possible to sketch out not a solution to these problems, but a diagnosis of how the state could respond to these challenges, and move further down the road to an adequate democracy, in which liberal-democracy would realise more fully its theoretical promises. The promises are those of democracy and 'people power' on the one hand, and the liberal agenda of an independent civil society on the other, in which the different interests of a complex and interdependent modern society find expression. Obviously this is a different picture from Rousseau's direct democracy in the context of a city-state. It is a democracy which has accomplished what Dahl calls the second 'great transformation', from the limits of a small-scale city-state to 'a new vision of a vaster democracy extended now to the giant compass of the nation-state', and indeed beyond the by now outmoded framework of the nation-state.[23]

Our argument has been that the rival state forms of fascism and communism were weak in legitimacy because of their inadequate realisation, not to say total denial, of democracy or 'people power'. Fascist regimes totally denied democracy, or at least perverted it by claiming that the masses formed *das Volk* and the leader alone intuited its wishes. In practice, of course, this led to the brutal suppression of all genuine forms of democracy and pluralism. By contrast, the communist system did not deny the value of popular power, but claimed to have achieved a higher realisation of that popular power, initially through the Commune state, and then through the vanguard role of the single party. In contrast, liberal-democratic systems base themselves on the twin values of liberalism and democracy, the limited state and the power of the people.

However, our argument here is that there remain severe obstacles to the attainment of these liberal and democratic ends. The first obstacle is that which the Marxist view, in its different manifestations, highlights: that which stems from continuing economic and social inequalities in liberal-democratic societies, which limit the capacities of 'the good citizen' to those people of superior economic resources and class position. *How* such inequalities are to be overcome and transformed is one of the challenges which remains for contemporary democracy, because it can be safely asserted that, if such a challenge is not met, there will be dangers for the stability, legitimacy and hence survival of liberal-democracy in the modern world. The dangers asserted by Professor Galbraith are real enough, that democratic societies may ignore the interests of a substantial section, if possibly still a minority, of its citizens. This might lead to authoritarian or fascist-type movements picking up support from those disillusioned with the failure of liberal-democracy, from those who feel excluded from its promise not just of political participation, but also of some degree of economic security and state assistance. It was partly from such groups of frightened, unemployed and desperate people in a situation of severe economic and social dislocation that fascism in the 1920s and 1930s drew its support. Recent events in Europe suggest the danger that desperate groups seek scapegoats, finding them in immigrant workers or people of different ethnic origin, and undermining democracy by responding to racist and other irrational appeals. While Roger Griffin's recent study *The Nature of Fascism* suggests that fascism succeeded only in highly unusual circumstances which are not likely to be repeated, one should not underestimate the degree to which failure to create a culture of common citizenship and some degree of economic equality can open up the opportunity for fascist-type groups to win support and threaten the workings of liberal-democracy.

The first obstacle to 'democratic deepening' thus remains the existence of the sharp economic and social divisions noted by the English socialist R.H. Tawney in his book *Equality*. Tawney suggested that such divisions constituted the framework within which the political structure of liberal-democracy existed and developed.[24] Despite much that has been written on the 'crisis of Marxism', it remains true that Marxist perspectives remain the chief theoretical framework for analysing these problems of liberal-democracy, and the economic and social obstacles to a democratic deepening in such societies.

Similarly, feminist theories have as one of their central strands the analysis of a further obstacle to the achievement of a genuine democracy. Such a democracy would involve a degree of involvement or participation encompassing all citizens as equal members of the citizen body. The limitations on the participation of women because of inequalities in the home and in the private sphere generally may be less than they were in the past, but in an important sense they remain as an impediment to the achievement of democratic participation and involvement. Feminist theories, as was noted in Chapter 6, have broadened the basic concept of politics and the analysis of power.

Our final conclusion can thus be that understanding the role of the state in contemporary politics does require a new theory of politics and the state, which draws on elements of all the different theories covered in this book. In that sense, the theories may almost be complementary rather than exclusive, with pluralism and elitism revealing some of the surface manifestations of politics in liberal-democratic systems, and Marxism and feminism showing certain deep structures which function as obstacles to the attainment of the values of liberalism and democracy. To this can be added a necessary understanding of nationalism. Nationalism can be said to be a highly powerful force in the modern world, as a sort of 'civic religion' which ties societies together, and justifies the role of the state as presiding over what is claimed (often falsely) to be a national community. Yet nationalism is also significant, we have seen, as a destructive and fragmentary force, which can be added to the list of problems for democracy and its continued survival. Ethnic nationalism can destroy any idea of a shared community based on common citizen rights.

The conclusion remains that the state in the contemporary world can be understood only through theories which grapple with some central paradoxes of the present situation, such as the celebration of democratic values co-existing with the survival, perhaps intensification, of obstacles to their full attainment and realisation. This is so despite the collapse of rival forms of state which failed in part because of their contempt for, as in the case of fascism, or failure to realise, as in the case of communism, the goals of people power, democracy. The paradoxes with which any adequate political theory must come to terms are those of the deepening crisis of the state, which emerges out of renewed or intensified demands for democracy on the one hand, and the persistence of obstacles to its achievement on the other.

We have stated what these obstacles are, and it is not the task of this book to sketch out means by which they might be removed. The task of a renewed political theory of the modern state must be to use the tools from a variety of political theories and concepts to come to an understanding of what remains the awesome power of the modern state. Perhaps in our more complex world, the nation-state has inevitably come to share its power with other institutions, both supra-national and sub-national. The task for the liberal-democratic state must surely be to maintain some degree of consensus and unity among its citizens, which entails a more interventionist role than 'New Right' or Hayekian theories would allow. However, this is to move into the sphere of normative analysis and value judgement, whereas the thrust of this book has been to review a range of theories which seek to explain the realities of the power structure of the modern state.

To understand the complexity of politics in a rapidly changing world, we need theories that are sensitive to that complexity and which help to unmask the different dimensions of power, laying them open to the understanding of those subject to the modern state and its demands. Only in that way, through a greatly expanded knowledge and understanding of the social and political world which surrounds us, can the first conditions be achieved which are necessary for any transformation of the state and society. The liberal-democratic state has a long way to go before it fully lives up to its promises, and before it can satisfactorily justify its apparent victory over the other forms of state dealt with in this book. The politics of our time suggests that there is a very large agenda here which remains as unfinished business, and which calls for imaginative and bold work, not just in the sphere of theory, but also, and perhaps more importantly, in the arena of political leadership and practice.

Notes

1. Bobbio, N., 'What alternatives are there to representative democracy?', in Bobbio, N., *Which Socialism?*, Polity, Cambridge, 1986.

2. Bobbio, N., *The Future of Democracy*, Polity, Cambridge, 1987, p. 37.
3. Bobbio, *The Future of Democracy*, p. 37.
4. Poggi, G., *The State: Its nature, development and prospects*, Polity, Cambridge, 1990, p. 189.
5. Poggi, *The State*, p. 184.
6. On recent developments in Italy, see Abse, T., 'The triumph of the leopard', *New Left Review*, vol. 199, 1993, pp. 3–28.
7. Connor, W., 'A nation is a nation, is a state, is an ethnic group, is a . . .', *Ethnic and Racial Studies*, vol 1, no. 4, 1978, pp. 377–400.
8. Poggi, *The State*, p. 151.
9. Poggi, *The State*, p. 113.
10. Poggi, *The State*, p. 116.
11. Galbraith, J.K., *The Culture of Contentment*, Penguin, Harmondsworth, 1993, p. 49.
12. Bobbio, *The Future of Democracy*, p. 28.
13. Oldfield, A., *Citizenship and Community: Civic republicanism and the modern world*, Routledge, London, 1990.
14. Bobbio, *The Future of Democracy*, p. 36.
15. Lukes, S., *Power: A radical view*, Macmillan, London, 1974.
16. Marx, K., *Grundrisse: Foundations of the critique of political economy (rough draft)*, trans. Martin Nicolaus, Penguin, Harmondsworth, 1973, p. 247.
17. Griffin, R., *The Nature of Fascism*, Routledge, London and New York, 1993, p. 36.
18. Mills, C.W., *Power, Politics and People: The collected essays of C. Wright Mills*, ed. I.L. Horowitz, Oxford University Press, New York, 1963, p. 227.
19. Lukes, S., *Marxism and Morality*, Clarendon Press, Oxford, 1985, pp. 98–9.
20. Rosanvallon, P., *Le sacre du citoyen: Histoire du suffrage universel en France*, Gallimard, Paris, 1992, pp. 73 and 89.
21. Miliband, R., 'Reflections on the crisis of communist regimes', in Blackburn, R. (ed.), *After the Fall: The failure of communism and the future of socialism*, Verso, London, 1991, p. 14.
22. Miliband, 'Reflections on the crisis of communist regimes', p. 13.
23. Dahl, R., *Democracy and Its Critics*, Yale University Press, New Haven, CT, and London, 1989, p. 23.
24. Tawney, R.H., *Equality*, Allen & Unwin, London, 1964, p. 78.

| Bibliography

Abse, T., 'The triumph of the leopard', *New Left Review*, vol. 199, 1993, pp. 3–28.

Ackerman, B., *The Future of Liberal Revolution*, Yale University Press, New Haven, CT, and London, 1992.

Alter, P., *Nationalism*, Edward Arnold, London, 1989.

Anderson, P., *Considerations on Western Marxism*, New Left Books, London, 1976.

Anderson, P., *A Zone of Engagement*, Verso, London, 1992.

Arblaster, A., *Democracy*, Open University Press, Milton Keynes, 1987.

Arendt, H., *The Origins of Totalitarianism*, Meridian Books, Cleveland, OH, and New York, 1958.

Aron, R., *Progress and Disillusion: The dialectics of modern society*, Penguin, Harmondsworth, 1972.

Bachrach, P., and Baratz, M., 'Two faces of power', *American Political Science Review*, vol. 56, 1962, pp. 947–52.

Bahro, R., *The Alternative in Eastern Europe*, New Left Books, London, 1978.

Bakunin, M., *Selected Writings*, ed. A. Lehning, Jonathan Cape, London, 1973.

Beetham, D., 'From socialism to fascism: the relation between theory and practice in the work of Robert Michels', *Political Studies*, vol. XXV, 1977, pp. 3–24, 161–81.

Beetham, D., *Marxists in Face of Fascism: Writings by Marxists on fascism from the inter-war period*, Manchester University Press, Manchester, 1983.

Beetham, D., *Max Weber and the Theory of Modern Politics*, 2nd edition, Polity, Cambridge, 1985.

Beetham, D., *The Legitimation of Power*, Macmillan, London, 1991.

Bernstein, E., *The Preconditions of Socialism*, ed. H. Tudor, Cambridge University Press, Cambridge, 1993.

Bialer, S. (ed.), *Politics, Society and Nationality inside Gorbachev's Russia*, Westview Press, Boulder, CO, and London, 1989.

Birch, A.H., *The Concepts and Theories of Modern Democracy*, Routledge, London, 1993.

Blackburn, R., *After the Fall: The failure of communism and the future of socialism*, Verso, London and New York, 1991.

Bobbio, N., *Which Socialism? Marxism, socialism and democracy*, Polity, Cambridge, 1986.

Bobbio, N., *The Future of Democracy*, Polity, Cambridge, 1987.

Bottomore, T.B., *Elites and Society*, Penguin, Harmondsworth, 1966.

Bottomore, T.B., and Goode, P. (eds), *Austro-Marxism*, Clarendon Press, Oxford, 1978.

Breuilly, J., *Nationalism and the State*, Manchester University Press, Manchester, 1985.

Broszat, M., *The Hitler State: The foundation and development of the internal structure of the Third Reich*, Longman, London, 1981.

Brubaker, R., *Citizenship and Nationhood in France and Germany*, Harvard University Press, Cambridge, MA, and London, 1992.

Bryson, V., *Feminist Political Theory*, Macmillan, London, 1993.

Buchanan, A., *Secession: The morality of political divorce from Fort Sumter to Lithuania and Quebec*, Westview Press, Boulder, CO, and Oxford, 1991.

Bugajski, J., 'The fate of minorities in Eastern Europe', *Journal of Democracy*, vol. 4, no. 4, 1993, pp. 85–99.

Burke, E., *Edmund Burke on Government, Politics and Society*, ed. B.W. Hill, Fontana/Harvester Press, Glasgow, 1975.

Burke, E., *Pre-Revolutionary Writings*, ed. I. Harris, Cambridge University Press, Cambridge, 1993.

Burstyn, V., 'Masculine dominance and the state', in *The Socialist Register 1983*, ed. by R. Miliband and J. Saville, Merlin, London, 1983, pp. 45–89.

Callinicos, A., *Against Postmodernism: a Marxist critique*, Polity, Cambridge, 1989.

Callinicos, A., *The Revenge of History: Marxism and the East European revolutions*, Polity, Cambridge, 1991.

Carr, E.H., *The Bolshevik Revolution 1917–1923*, vol. I, Macmillan, London, 1950.

Carr, E.H., *The Interregnum 1923–1924*, Penguin, Harmondsworth, 1969.

Chapman, J., *Politics, Feminism and the Reformation of Gender*, Routledge, London and New York, 1993.

Chatterjee, P., *Nationalism and the Colonial World: A derivative discourse*, Zed Books, London, 1986.

Cheles, L., Ferguson, R., and Vaughan, M. (eds), *Neo-Fascism in Europe*, Longman, London, 1991.

Connor, W., 'A nation is a nation, is a state, is an ethnic group is a . . .', *Ethnic and Racial Studies*, vol. 1, no. 4, 1978, pp. 377–400.

Coole, D., *Women in Political Theory*, 2nd edition, Harvester Wheatsheaf, Hemel Hempstead, 1993.

Crick, B., *The Reform of Parliament*, Weidenfeld & Nicolson, London, 1970.

Crosland, C.A.R., *The Future of Socialism*, Jonathan Cape, London, 1976.

Current Digest of the Soviet Press, Vols. XLI and XLII.

Dahl, R.A., *Dilemmas of Pluralist Democracy: Autonomy vs control*, Yale University Press, New Haven, CT, and London, 1982.

Dahl, R.A., *Democracy and Its Critics*, Yale University Press, New Haven, CT, and London, 1989.

Deutscher, I., *The Prophet Armed: Trotsky, 1879–1921*, Oxford University Press, Oxford, 1970.

Dogan, M., and Rose, R. (eds), *European Politics: A reader*, Macmillan, London, 1971.

Drobizheva, L.M., 'The role of the intelligentsia in developing national consciousness among the peoples of the USSR under *perestroika*', *Ethnic and Racial Studies*, vol. 14, no. 1, 1991, pp. 87–99.

Dunleavy, P., and O'Leary, B., *Theories of the State: The politics of liberal democracy*, Macmillan, London, 1987.

Dunn, J. (ed.), *Democracy: The unfinished journey, 508 BC to AD 1993*, Oxford University Press, Oxford, 1992.

Duverger, M., *Political Parties*, Methuen, London, 1954.

Elshtain, J.B., *Public Man, Private Woman: Women in social and political thought*, 2nd edition, Princeton University Press, Princeton, NJ, 1993.

Friedrich, C.J., and Brzezinski, Z.K., *Totalitarian Dictatorship and Autocracy*, Praeger, New York, 1963.

Friedrich, C.J., Curtis, M., and Barber, B.R., *Totalitarianism in Perspective: Three views*, Pall Mall Press, London, 1969.

Fukuyama, F., *The End of History and the Last Man*, Hamish Hamilton, London, 1992.

Galbraith, J.K., *The Culture of Contentment*, Penguin, Harmondsworth, 1993.

Gellner, E., *Nations and Nationalism*, Blackwell, Oxford, 1983.

Gerth, H.H., and Mills, C.W., *From Max Weber: Essays in sociology*, Routledge & Kegan Paul, London, 1948.

Girardet, R. (ed.), *Le Nationalisme français 1871–1914*, Armand Colin, Paris, 1966.

Glenny, M., *The Fall of Yugoslavia: The Third Balkan War*, Penguin, Harmondsworth, 1992.

Gobetti, D., *Private and Public: Individuals, households and body politic in Locke and Hutcheson*, Routledge, London and New York, 1992.

Gorz, A., *Farewell to the Working Class: An essay on post-industrial society*, Pluto, London, 1982.

Graham, B.D., *Representation and Party Politics: A comparative perspective*, Blackwell, Oxford, 1993.

Griffin, R., *The Nature of Fascism*, Routledge, London and New York, 1993.

Habermas, J., *Eine Art Schadensabwicklung: Kleine politische Schriften VI*, Suhrkamp, Frankfurt, 1987, p. 166.

Hainsworth, P. (ed.), *The Extreme Right in Europe and America*, Pinter, London, 1992.

Hajda, L., and Beissinger, M. (eds), *The Nationalities Factor in Soviet Politics and Society*, Westview Press, Boulder, CO, and London, 1990.

Hamilton, R., *The Appeal of Fascism: A study of intellectuals and fascism 1919–1945*, Anthony Blond, London, 1971.

Harding, N., *Lenin's Political Thought*, Macmillan, London, 1983.

Harding, N. (ed.), *The State in Socialist Society*, Macmillan, London, 1984.

Hart, H.L.A., *The Concept of Law*, Clarendon Press, Oxford, 1961.

Hayek, F., *New Studies in Philosophy, Politics, Economics and the History of Ideas*, Routledge & Kegan Paul, London, 1978.

Held, D., *Models of Democracy*, Polity, Cambridge, 1987.

Held, D. (ed.), *Prospects for Democracy: North, South, East, West*, Polity, Cambridge, 1993.

Hirst, P.Q. (ed.), *The Pluralist Theory of the State: Selected writings of G.D.H. Cole, J.N. Figgis and H.J. Laski*, Routledge, London and New York, 1989.

Hobsbawm, E.J., *The Age of Empire*, Weidenfeld & Nicolson, London, 1987.

Hobsbawm, E.J., *Nations and Nationalism since 1780: Programme, myth, reality*, Cambridge University Press, Cambridge, 1990.

Hosking, G., *A History of the Soviet Union*, Fontana/Collins, London, 1985.

Hunt, R.N., *The Political Ideas of Marx and Engels*, 2 vols., Macmillan, London, 1975 and 1984.

Journal of Democracy, vol. 3, no. 3, 1992, special issue on 'Capitalism, Socialism and Democracy'.

Journal of Democracy, vol. 4, no. 3, 1993, special issue on 'International Organisations and Democracy'.

Kariel, H.S., 'Pluralism', *International Encyclopedia of the Social Sciences*, Macmillan, New York, 1968.

Kautsky, K., *Selected Political Writings*, ed. and trans. P. Goode, Macmillan, London, 1983.

Keane, J. (ed.), *Civil Society and the State: New European perspectives*, Verso, London, 1988.

Kele, M.H., *Nazis and Workers. National Socialist appeals to German labor 1919–1933*, University of North Carolina Press, Chapel Hill, NC, 1972.

Kershaw, I., *Popular Opinion and Political Dissent in the Third Reich: Bavaria 1933–1945*, Clarendon Press, Oxford, 1983.

Kettle, M., 'Paying the price for party politics', *Guardian*, 19 June 1993.

King, D.S., *The New Right: Politics, markets, citizenship*, Macmillan, London, 1987.

Kolakowski, L., *Main Currents of Marxism*, 3 vols., Clarendon Press, Oxford, 1978.

Kukuthas, C., *Hayek and Modern Liberalism*, Clarendon Press, Oxford, 1990.

Laqueur, W. (ed.), *Fascism: A reader's guide*, Penguin, Harmondsworth, 1979.

Lenin, V.I., *Collected Works*, Vol. 5, Foreign Languages Publishing House, Moscow, 1961.

Lenin, V.I., *Selected Works in One Volume*, Lawrence & Wishart, London, 1969.

Lenin, V.I., *The State and Revolution*, ed. R. Service, Penguin, Harmondsworth, 1992.

Levin, M., *Marx, Engels and Liberal Democracy*, Macmillan, London, 1989.

Lewin, M., *Lenin's Last Struggle*, Pantheon, New York, 1968.

Lindblom, C.E., *Politics and Markets: The world's political-economic systems*, Basic Books, New York, 1977.

Lovenduski, J., *Women and European Politics: Contemporary feminism and public policy*, Wheatsheaf, Brighton, 1986.

Lovenduski, J., and Randall, V., *Contemporary Feminist Politics: Women and power in Britain*, Oxford University Press, Oxford, 1993.

Lukacs, G., *Lenin: A study in the unity of his thought*, New Left Books, London, 1970.

Lukacs, G., *History and Class Consciousness*, Merlin, London, 1971.

Lukes, S., *Power: A radical view*, Macmillan, London, 1974.

Lukes, S., *Marxism and Morality*, Clarendon Press, Oxford, 1985.

Lukes, S., *Moral Conflict and Politics*, Clarendon Press, Oxford, 1991.

Luxemburg, R., *The Russian Revolution* and *Leninism or Marxism?*, ed. B.D. Wolfe, University of Michigan Press, Ann Arbor, MI, 1961.

Lyttelton, A. (ed.), *Italian Fascisms, from Pareto to Gentile*, Jonathan Cape, London, 1973.

Lyttelton, A., *The Seizure of Power: Fascism in Italy 1919–1929*, Weidenfeld & Nicolson, London, 1973.

McLennan, G., Held, D., and Hall, S. (eds), *The Idea of the Modern State*, Open University Press, Milton Keynes, 1984.

Macpherson, C.B., *The Real World of Democracy*, Clarendon Press, Oxford, 1966.

Macpherson, C.B., *The Life and Times of Liberal Democracy*, Oxford University Press, Oxford, 1977.

Madison, J., Hamilton, A., and Jay, J., *The Federalist Papers*, ed. I. Kramnick, Penguin, Harmondsworth, 1987.

Mann, M., *States, War and Capitalism: Studies in political sociology*, Blackwell, Oxford, 1988.

Marshall, T.H., *Sociology at the Crossroads and Other Essays*, Heinemann, London, 1963.

Marx, K., *Capital*, Vol. I, Lawrence & Wishart, London, 1954.

Marx, K., *Capital*, Vol. III, Lawrence & Wishart, London, 1974.

Marx, K., *Grundrisse: Foundations of the critique of political economy (rough draft)*, trans. Martin Nicolaus, Penguin, Harmondsworth, 1973.

Marx, K., *The Revolutions of 1848*, ed. D. Fernbach, Penguin, Harmondsworth, 1973.

Marx, K., *Surveys from Exile: Political writings*, Vol. 2, ed. D. Fernbach, Penguin, Harmondsworth, 1973.

Marx, K., *The First International and After*, ed. D. Fernbach, Penguin, Harmondsworth, 1974.

Marx, K., and Engels, F., *The German Ideology*, Lawrence & Wishart, London, 1965.

Marx, K., and Engels, F., *Selected Works in Three Volumes*, Progress Publishers, Moscow, 1969.

Marx, K., and Engels, F., *Werke*, Vol. 2, Dietz Verlag, Berlin, 1970.

Mayall, J., *Nationalism and International Society*, Cambridge University Press, Cambridge, 1990

Medvedev, R., *On Socialist Democracy*, Macmillan, London, 1975.

Meisel, J., *The Myth of the Ruling Class*, University of Michigan Press, Ann Arbor, MI, 1962.

Michels, R., *Political Parties: A sociological study of the oligarchical consequences of modern democracy*, trans. E. and C. Paul, Dover Publications, New York, 1959.

Miliband, R., *The State in Capitalist Society*, Weidenfeld & Nicolson, London, 1969.

Miliband, R., *Capitalist Democracy in Britain*, Oxford University Press, Oxford, 1982.

Miliband, R., *Divided Societies: Class struggle in contemporary capitalism*, Clarendon Press, Oxford, 1989.

Mill, J., *Political Writings*, ed. T. Ball, Cambridge University Press, Cambridge, 1992.

Mill, J.S., *Three Essays* ('On Liberty'; 'Representative Government'; 'The Subjection of Women'), Oxford University Press, Oxford, 1975.

Mill, J.S., *The Subjection of Women*, in Mill, J.S., *On Liberty*, ed. S. Collini, Cambridge University Press, Cambridge, 1989.

Mills, C.W., *Power, Politics and People: The collected essays of C. Wright Mills*, ed. I.L. Horowitz, Oxford University Press, New York, 1963.

Mills, C.W., *The Power Elite*, Oxford University Press, New York, 1966.

Mosca, G., *The Ruling Class (Elementi di Scienza Politica)*, trans. Hannah D. Kahn, McGraw-Hill, New York, Toronto and London, 1939.

Mosse, G.L, 'Fascism and the French Revolution', *Journal of Contemporary History*, vol. 24, no. 1, 1989, pp. 5–26.

Neumann, F., *The Democratic and the Authoritarian State: Essays in political and legal theory*, The Free Press, New York and London, 1957.

Okin, S.M., *Women in Western Political Thought*, Princeton University Press, Princeton, NJ, 1979.

Okin, S.M., *Justice, Gender and the Family*, Basic Books, New York, 1989.

Oldfield, A., *Citizenship and Community: Civic republicanism and the modern world*, Routledge, London, 1990.

Panebianco, A., *Political Parties, Organization and Power*, Cambridge University Press, Cambridge, 1988.

Parekh, B. (ed.), *Bentham's Political Thought*, Croom Helm, London, 1973.

Pareto, V., *Sociological Writings*, ed. S.E. Finer, Pall Mall Press, London, 1966.

Pateman, C., *The Disorder of Women: Democracy, feminism and political theory*, Polity, Cambridge, 1989.

Phillips, A., *Engendering Democracy*, Polity, Cambridge, 1991.

Pierson, C., *Beyond the Welfare State?*, Polity, Cambridge, 1991.

Pitkin, H.F., *The Concept of Representation*, University of California Press, Berkeley, CA, 1967.

Pitkin, H.F. (ed.), *Representation*, Atherton Press, New York, 1969.

Poggi, G., *The State: Its nature, development and prospects*, Polity, Cambridge, 1990.

Polan, A.J., *Lenin and the End of Politics*, Methuen, London, 1984.

Poulantzas, N., *Fascism and Dictatorship*, New Left Books, London, 1974.

Proudhon, P.-J., *General Idea of the Revolution in the Nineteenth Century*, trans. J.B. Robinson, Pluto, London, 1989.

Przeworski, A., *Capitalism and Social Democracy*, Cambridge University Press, Cambridge, 1985.

Randall, V., *Women and Politics: An international perspective*, Macmillan, Basingstoke, 1987.

Rosanvallon, P., *L'État en France de 1789 à nos jours*, Seuil, Paris, 1990.

Rosanvallon, P., *Le sacre du citoyen: Histoire du suffrage universel en France*, Gallimard, Paris, 1992.

Ross, G., Hoffman, S., and Malzacher, S. (eds), *The Mitterrand Experiment: Continuity and change in modern France*, Polity, Cambridge, 1987.

Roth, J.J., *The Cult of Violence: Sorel and the Sorelians*, University of California Press, Berkeley, CA, and London, 1980.

Rousseau, J.-J., *The Social Contract and Discourses*, ed. G.D.H. Cole, Dent, London, 1968.

Salvadori, M., *Karl Kautsky and the Socialist Revolution 1880–1938*, New Left Books, London, 1979.

Sartori, G., 'Anti-elitism revisited', *Government and Opposition*, vol. 13, 1978, pp. 58–80.

Sassoon, A.S. (ed.), *Women and the State: The shifting boundaries of public and private*, Routledge, London, 1992.

Schapiro, L., *Totalitarianism*, Macmillan, London, 1972.

Schattschneider, E., *The Semi-Sovereign People*, Holt, Rinehart & Winston, New York, 1960.

Schorske, C.E., *German Social Democracy 1905–1917: The development of the great schism*, Harvard University Press, Cambridge, MA, 1955.

Schumpeter, J.A., *Capitalism, Socialism and Democracy*, Unwin University Books, London, 1965.

Schwarzmantel, J., *Socialism and the Idea of the Nation*, Harvester Wheatsheaf, Hemel Hempstead, 1991.

Shonfield, A., *Modern Capitalism: The changing balance of public and private power*, Oxford University Press, Oxford, 1965.

Silverman, M., *Deconstructing the Nation: Immigration, racism and citizenship in modern France*, Routledge, London and New York, 1992.

Singer, D., *Is Socialism Doomed? The meaning of Mitterrand*, Oxford University Press, New York, 1988.

Skinner, Q., 'The state', in Ball, T., Farr, J., and Hanson, R.L. (eds), *Political Innovation and Conceptual Change*, Cambridge University Press, Cambridge, 1989.

Smith, A.D., *Nationalism in the Modern World*, Martin Robertson, Oxford, 1979.

Smith, A.D., *National Identity*, Penguin, London, 1991.

Smith. G., *Politics in Western Europe*, Heinemann, London, 1972.

Smith, G. (ed.), *The Nationalities Question in the Soviet Union*, Longman, London and New York, 1990.

Sorel, G., *Reflections on Violence*, trans. T.E. Hulme and J. Roth, Collier Books, New York, 1961.

Sternhell, Z., *Maurice Barrès et le Nationalisme français*, Armand Colin, Paris, 1972.

Stuart, R., *Marxism at Work: Ideology, class and French socialism during the Third Republic*, Cambridge University Press, Cambridge, 1992.

Tawney, R.H., *Equality*, Allen & Unwin, London, 1964.

Teich, M., and Porter, R. (eds), *The National Question in Europe in Historical Context*, Cambridge University Press, Cambridge, 1993.

Therborn, G., 'The rule of capital and the rise of democracy', *New Left Review*, vol. 103, 1977, pp. 3–41.

Trotsky, L.D., *The Revolution Betrayed: What is the Soviet Union and where is it going?*, Pathfinder Press, New York, 1970.

Trotsky, L.D., *The Struggle against Fascism in Germany*, Penguin, Harmondsworth, 1975.

Truman, D.B., *The Governmental Process*, Alfred A. Knopf, New York, 1958.

Tucker, R.C. (ed.), *Stalinism: Essays in historical interpretation*, Norton, New York, 1977.

Unger, A.L., *Constitutional Development in the USSR: A guide to the Soviet Constitution*, Methuen, London, 1981.

van den Linden, M., 'The national integration of European working classes (1871–1914): Exploring the causal configuration', *International Review of Social History*, vol. XXXIII, 1988, pp. 285–311.

Vile, M.J.C., *Constitutionalism and the Separation of Powers*, Clarendon Press, Oxford, 1967.

Walby, S., *Theorizing Patriarchy*, Blackwell, Oxford, 1990.

Weber, M., *Gesammelte Politische Schriften*, 3rd edition, J.C.B. Mohr (Paul Siebeck), Tübingen, 1971.

Weber, M., *Selections in Translation*, ed. W.G. Runciman, Cambridge University Press, Cambridge, 1978.

West European Politics, vol. 16, no. 1, 1993, special issue on 'Rethinking Social Democracy in W. Europe'.

White, R.J. (ed.), *The Conservative Tradition*, A. & C. Black, London, 1964.

White, S., '"Democratization" in the USSR', *Soviet Studies*, vol. 42, no. 1, 1990, pp. 3–25.

White, S., *Gorbachev and After*, 3rd edition, Cambridge University Press, Cambridge, 1992.

White, S., Gardner, J., Schöpflin, G., and Saich, T., *Communist and Postcommunist Political Systems: An introduction*, 3rd edition, St Martin's Press, New York, 1990.
Wright, E.O., *Classes*, Verso, London, 1985.

| Name index

| Subject index